Freudians and Schadenfreudians

Also by Jeffrey Berman

Joseph Conrad: Writing as Rescue
The Talking Cure: Literary Representations of Psychoanalysis
Narcissism and the Novel
Diaries to an English Professor: Pain and Growth in the Classroom
Surviving Literary Suicide
Risky Writing: Self-Disclosure and Self-Transformation in the Classroom
Empathic Teaching: Education for Life
Dying to Teach: A Memoir of Love, Loss, and Learning
Cutting and the Pedagogy of Self-Disclosure (with Patricia Hatch Wallace)
Death in the Classroom: Writing about Love and Loss
Companionship in Grief: Love and Loss in the Memoirs of C.S. Lewis, John Bayley, Donald Hall, Joan Didion, and Calvin Trillin
Death Education in the Writing Classroom
Dying in Character: Memoirs on the End of Life
Confidentiality and Its Discontents: Dilemmas of Privacy in Psychotherapy (with Paul W. Mosher)
Writing Widowhood: The Landscapes of Bereavement
Writing the Talking Cure: Irvin D. Yalom and the Literature of Psychotherapy
Off the Tracks: Cautionary Tales about the Derailing of Mental Health Care (with Paul W. Mosher).
Mad Muse: The Mental Illness Memoir in a Writer's Life and Work
The Art of Caregiving in Fiction, Film, and Memoir
Norman N. Holland: The Dean of American Psychoanalytic Literary Critics
Psychoanalytic Memoirs
Psychoanalysis: An Interdisciplinary Retrospective

Freudians and Schadenfreudians

Also by Jeffrey Berman

Joseph Conrad: Writing as Rescue
The Talking Cure: Literary Representations of Psychoanalysis
Narcissism and the Novel
Diaries to an English Professor: Pain and Growth in the Classroom
Surviving Literary Suicide
Risky Writing: Self-Disclosure and Self-Transformation in the Classroom
Empathic Teaching: Education for Life
Dying to Teach: A Memoir of Love, Loss, and Learning
Cutting and the Pedagogy of Self-Disclosure (with Patricia Hatch Wallace)
Death in the Classroom: Writing about Love and Loss
Companionship in Grief: Love and Loss in the Memoirs of C.S. Lewis, John Bayley, Donald Hall, Joan Didion, and Calvin Trillin
Death Education in the Writing Classroom
Dying in Character: Memoirs on the End of Life
Confidentiality and Its Discontents: Dilemmas of Privacy in Psychotherapy (with Paul W. Mosher)
Writing Widowhood: The Landscapes of Bereavement
Writing the Talking Cure: Irvin D. Yalom and the Literature of Psychotherapy
Off the Tracks: Cautionary Tales about the Derailing of Mental Health Care (with Paul W. Mosher).
Mad Muse: The Mental Illness Memoir in a Writer's Life and Work
The Art of Caregiving in Fiction, Film, and Memoir
Norman N. Holland: The Dean of American Psychoanalytic Literary Critics
Psychoanalytic Memoirs
Psychoanalysis: An Interdisciplinary Retrospective

Freudians and Schadenfreudians

Loving and Hating Psychoanalysis

Jeffrey Berman

BLOOMSBURY ACADEMIC
LONDON • NEW YORK • OXFORD • NEW DELHI • SYDNEY

BLOOMSBURY ACADEMIC
Bloomsbury Publishing Plc
50 Bedford Square, London, WC1B 3DP, UK
1385 Broadway, New York, NY 10018, USA
29 Earlsfort Terrace, Dublin 2, Ireland

BLOOMSBURY, BLOOMSBURY ACADEMIC and the Diana logo are trademarks of Bloomsbury Publishing Plc

First published in Great Britain 2024

Cover design and illustration by Rebecca Heselton

A catalogue record for this book is available from the British Library.

Library of Congress Cataloging-in-Publication Data

Names: Berman, Jeffrey, 1945- author.
Title: Freudians and schadenfreudians : loving and hating psychoanalysis / Jeffrey Berman.
Description: London; New York: Bloomsbury Academic, 2024. | Includes bibliographical references and index. | Summary: "Focusing on ten key writers and scholars who either passionately loved or gleefully loathed Freud, this book represents Freud's wide legacy, the reach of his ideas, their controversies, and their ability still to provoke, inspire, confound, outrage, and compel. Writers examined include D.H. Lawrence, Vladimir Nabokov, Harold Bloom and Deborah P. Britzman"– Provided by publisher.
Identifiers: LCCN 2024005667 (print) | LCCN 2024005668 (ebook) | ISBN 9781350471832 (hardback) | ISBN 9781350471870 (paperback) | ISBN 9781350471849 (pdf) | ISBN 9781350471856 (ebook)
Subjects: LCSH: Freud, Sigmund, 1856-1939–Influence. | Psychoanalysis and literature. | Psychoanalysis and culture.
Classification: LCC BF109.F74 B465 2024 (print) | LCC BF109.F74 (ebook) | DDC 150.19/52092–dc23/eng/20240328
LC record available at https://lccn.loc.gov/2024005667
LC ebook record available at https://lccn.loc.gov/2024005668

ISBN: HB: 978-1-3504-7183-2
ePDF: 978-1-3504-7184-9
eBook: 978-1-3504-7185-6

Typeset by Deanta Global Publishing Services, Chennai, India

To find out more about our authors and books visit www.bloomsbury.com and sign up for our newsletters.

For Sander L. Gilman,
Whose Pioneering Work Has Enriched Psychoanalytic Scholarship

Contents

Acknowledgments

Most of my discussion of Vladimir Nabokov's writings first appeared in the chapter "Nabokov and the Viennese Witch Doctor" in my book *The Talking Cure: Literary Representations of Psychoanalysis* (New York University Press, 1985), 211–238. Part of my discussion of *Psychoanalytic Credos* appeared as a review published in the *Journal of the American Psychoanalytic Association* 71 (2023): 333–340.

I learned much about Frederick Crews from the online "Crews" discussion moderated by the late Paul Mosher, and attended by Paula Mosher, Ralph Fishkin, Gregory Lavigne, and Warren Procci.

As with my other books, I would not have been able to conduct my research without the invaluable help of the Interlibrary Loan staff at the University at Albany. Thanks to Timothy Jackson, Angela Persico, and Glen Benedict for fulfilling scores of Interlibrary Loan requests. Thanks to Robert Boyers, Professor of English at Skidmore College and the editor of *Salmagundi*, for reading the chapter on Lionel Trilling (about whom he has written an excellent book) and sharing his impressions with me.

I am grateful to my wife, Julie, for her love, assistance, and support. Without her technological help and magical touch, I never would have been able to teach during the Covid-19 pandemic.

I am beholden to Bloomsbury Academic's two anonymous reviewers who read an early draft of the manuscript and suggested several revisions that have strengthened the book. I was especially impressed with the following observation: "Lawrence's dogmatisms are usually signs of anxiety, or appeals to a reader to disagree." Exactly! I alone am responsible for whatever lingering weaknesses appear in the book. Thanks, as always, to my sterling editor at Bloomsbury, Ben Doyle, Publisher for Literature, Digital Cultures, and Medical/Health Humanities, who guided this book—and four earlier ones—to completion. I will always be grateful for Ben's support.

Finally, I dedicate this book to Sander L. Gilman, the world's greatest living psychoanalytic cultural historian. I have been reading his books on Freud's construction of psychoanalysis for decades, and he has served as a role model to me of the exemplary teacher/scholar. My discussion of his prodigious work, along with my interview of him, appears in my 2023 book *Psychoanalysis: An Interdisciplinary Retrospective*. The felicitous neologism Walter Kaufmann uses to describe Freud, *humbition,* the fusion of humility and ambition, is no less true of Sander Gilman.

Introduction

Sigmund Freud's Schadenfreude

The title of my book is surely odd: few people are familiar with the word *Schadenfreude*, let alone with my neologism, *Schadenfreudians*. The German compound noun *Schadenfreude* is composed of two words, *Schaden*, meaning "pain," "suffering," "damage," "harm," or "misfortune," and *Freude*, "joy" or "pleasure." (All nouns are capitalized in German, as Schadenfreude usually is in English.) Schadenfreude means the joy or pleasure in another person's distress or misfortune. The word originated in German in the mid-eighteenth century and entered our language, according to the *Oxford English Dictionary*, in 1852 when it was used for the first time by the English archbishop R. C. Trench. As John Portmann, the author of *When Bad Things Happen to Other People* (2000), argues, Trench was so disturbed by the idea—which is also an emotion—that he feared users of the word would be contaminated by it. "It was as though all German speakers carried an infection, just by virtue of their linguistic resources. Trench worried that the infection might spread to English speakers" (3).

Trench did not need to worry, for as Portmann remarks, unlike other German words that have become common in our language, such as "kindergarten," "sauerkraut," and "kitsch," Schadenfreude remains nearly as unfamiliar to most Americans now as it was a century and half ago. No English equivalent to the German word exists. There is growing interest in Schadenfreude, especially among psychologists and philosophers, who conclude that it is an "outlaw" emotion, one that most people feel uncomfortable acknowledging. Confessing that we feel pleasure or satisfaction in another person's pain or misfortune seems to go against our moral, ethical, or religious upbringing. "Rejoice not when thine enemy falleth," the *Book of Proverbs* warns us, "and let not thine heart be glad when he stumbleth" (*King James Bible* 24:17). Schadenfreude is thus a guilty pleasure.

And yet two authors of cultural studies of Schadenfreude, Portmann and Tiffany Watt Smith, offer qualified if ambivalent endorsements of the demonized emotion. Portmann views Schadenfreude as a "morally acceptable kind of pleasure in the setbacks of others" if it serves as an "emotional corollary of justice" (197), that is, if the pleasure is associated with a person who deserves comeuppance. Tiffany Watt Smith concurs. If a person does not cause another person's misfortune or suffering, she writes in *Schadenfreude: The Joy of Another's Misfortune* (2018), and if the suffering is relatively minor, not catastrophic, then we may feel "entitled" to the pleasure, though she readily concedes that it is the "most ethically ambiguous of emotions" (138). Schadenfreude tells us things about ourselves that we don't want to know, Smith affirms cheerfully in the afterword, advising us to own up to our own Schadenfreude—sometimes. We may not agree that the early twenty-first century is the "Golden Age of Schadenfreude," as a person lamented in the *New York Times* in 2008 (T. Smith, 11), but the more people demonize those with whom they disagree, or who are simply different from them, the more likely they are to enjoy their adversaries' failures, defects, or absurdities. Smith is a cultural historian, not a psychologist, but she seems to be accurate when she observes that the "smiles of Schadenfreude and joy are indistinguishable except in one crucial respect: we smile more with the failures of our enemies than at our own success" (3).

The opposite of Schadenfreude is another neologism, "freudenfreude." In a 2022 article in the *New York Times*, Juli Fraga summarizes the new research on freudenfreude, finding joy in another person's good fortune. Freudenfreude closely resembles empathy. Fraga cites a program developed by Catherine Chambliss, a professor of psychology at Ursinus College, called "Freudenfreude Enhancement Training." Chambliss and her colleagues found that depressed college students who used the practices for two weeks "had an easier time expressing freudenfreude, which enhanced their relationships and improved their mood" (Fraga). In their 2016 edited book *Empathy Rules: Depression, Schadenfreude and Freudenfreude Research on Depression Risk Factors and Treatment*, Chambliss and Amy C. Hartl argue that freudenfreude is the social glue that makes relationships enjoyable.

Psychological research suggests that Schadenfreude is a multifaceted concept. In a brief article appearing in the journal *Emotion* in 2011, four Dutch researchers report a negative relationship between Schadenfreude and self-esteem. The negative relationship is contingent on the opportunity to affirm the self. "When no self-affirmation opportunity is available, low self-esteem participants experience a stronger self-threat when confronted with a high-achiever, and this self-threat increases their schadenfreude. This response is attenuated when they are given an opportunity to self-affirm" (van Dijk et al., 1448). The consensus of the contributors to *Schadenfreude: Understanding Pleasure at the Misfortune of Others*, edited by van Dijk and Ouwerkerk (2014), is that membership in a low-status group or having low self-esteem heightens one's tendency toward Schadenfreude. In a 2019 article published in *New Ideas in Psychology*, Wang, Lilienfeld, and Rochat argue that Schadenfreude is based on three motives: concerns for social justice, self-evaluation, and social identity. Their tripartite motivational model posits that dehumanization plays a major role in eliciting Schadenfreude and integrating its various facets, which include justice, rivalry, and aggression.

Notwithstanding the vast commentary surrounding Sigmund Freud's life and work—"Among historical figures," Frederick Crews writes in *Freud: The Making of an Illusion* (2017), one of the biographer's few comments with which I agree, "Sigmund Freud ranks with Shakespeare and Jesus of Nazareth for the amount of attention bestowed upon him by scholars and commentators" (1)—little has been written about his relationship to Schadenfreude. Despite his name, the founder of psychoanalysis was not the most joyful of people. Given his tragic vision of life, his emphasis on the destructive consequences of repressed sexual and aggressive drives, and his conjecture of a death instinct, Freud may have been struck by the irony of his surname. Nor is psychoanalysis an ode to joy, especially because of Freud's wry self-fulfilling observation that psychoanalysis brings out the worst in people. Moreover, as Adam Phillips and Barbara Taylor point out in *On Kindness* (2009), "the pleasures of cruelty and the cruelty of pleasures are famously Freud's touchstones of modern life" (64). Like any master theory, psychoanalysis has its defenders and critics. No one has used the word *Schadenfreudian* to characterize a person who does not simply disagree with Sigmund Freud's creation but who hates it passionately, intensely, gleefully. (The word Schadenfroh is used to characterize a person who feels Schadenfreude, but the pun on Freud's name is then lost.) Schadenfreudians, I argue, reveal a paradoxical attitude of "loving hate" toward Freud, a situation where a person preserves a relationship by maintaining a passionate negative feeling—or as Christopher Bollas suggests in *The Shadow of the Object* (1987), a relationship in which "hate is not the opposite of, but a substitute for love" (118). I do not wish to imply, however, that anyone who disagrees with Freud is a Schadenfreudian. Rather, I suggest that those who delight in demonizing Freud, seeing him as the embodiment of evil, rendering him into a cruel caricature, are Schadenfreudians. But before examining in detail some of Freud's most influential supporters and detractors, I want to look at how the creator of psychoanalysis was himself a Schadenfreudian and what this might mean according to his own theory.

Jokes and Their Relation to the Unconscious

Surprisingly, Freud wrote only once about Schadenfreude,[1] a passing reference in *Jokes and Their Relation to the Unconscious* (1905). If someone falls down, Freud observes, a child might laugh from a "feeling of superiority or from *Schadenfreude*: 'You've fallen down, I haven't,'" adding that "Certain motives for pleasure in children seem to be lost to us adults" (*SE*, vol. 8, 224). That's all Freud says about Schadenfreude, a glaring omission in light of his willingness to theorize the darkest subjects. Ironically, it's questionable whether children experience Schadenfreude. According to the developmental psychologist Caspar Addyman, the founder of the Baby Laughter Project, children may laugh at themselves falling down but not when someone else tumbles. "Historically, everyone thought babies were amoral, and you had to teach them right from wrong, but they do have a sense of fairness and a strong sense of empathy—if someone has hurt themselves, babies can see that and are concerned" (T. Smith 26). The jury is not yet out, however, on the question of whether young children experience Schadenfreude. In a 2014 study at the University of Haifa in Israel, S. G. Shamay-Tsoory and her fellow psychologists claim to have observed Schadenfreude in children as young as a year old. As early as 1920 Lou Andreas-Salomé speculated in a letter to Freud that the sadistic pleasure girls experienced while beating their favorite dolls revealed "pure *Schadenfreude* and satisfaction" (102).

Freud may have been mistaken about the meaning of children's laughter, but *Jokes and Their Relation to the Unconscious*, one of his most famous and popular works, abounds in examples of Schadenfreude, though he never uses the word when relating Jewish jokes about a "schnorrer" (a Jewish beggar) and a "schadchen" (a Jewish marriage-broker). These jokes reveal not only pleasure in mocking the stereotypical foibles and deficiencies of Jews but also the satisfaction of deriding Christian attitudes toward Jews. In offering one Jewish joke after another, as if he were a stand-up comic, Freud betrays a deep ambivalence over being Jewish, an ambivalence that was a central aspect of his identity. Perhaps most important of all, Freud's Schadenfreude may be seen in the construction of psychoanalytic theory, in which he projects, albeit unconsciously, his patriarchal gender beliefs onto women, who, in his judgment, have an inferior moral conscience.

[1] The word *Schadenfreude* appears only once in the *Standard Edition*, but in his 1919 essay "The 'Uncanny'" Freud offers, as one definition of "canny" (*heimlich* in German), looking on "with pleasure at someone's discomfiture" (*SE*, vol. 17, 223).

Nowhere does Freud consider the possibility that Schadenfreude is characteristic of laughter in general. This is F. H. Buckley's unsettling conclusion in his study of Schadenfreude and laughter. "Schadenfreude is not some nasty outlier, but more like the epitome of laughter. When we laugh, we do take pleasure in the butt of the joke's discomfiture. We just don't want to admit it" (219). Buckley does not mention Freud, but he would find many examples of his thesis in *Jokes and Their Relation to the Unconscious*, in which Freud insists that there is "no laughter without a victim, and no victim without a message of a risible inferiority" (219).

Throughout *Jokes and Their Relation to the Unconscious*, Freud writes as a psychoanalyst, humorist, and moralist—and as a Jew. These roles are in sharp conflict with each other, and Freud must have felt wary in exposing these contradictions to public scrutiny. He knew that many of his tendentious jokes ("non-innocent") depended upon linguistic complexities, including puns and double entendres that could not be translated into other languages. "*Traduttore—Traditore!*" he exclaims: "Translator—Traitor!" But another problem in joke-telling is acknowledging the *pleasure* of the concealed sexual and aggressive content of jokes. "Other people's misery," Freud asserts, in one of his most startling assertions, "makes it impossible to enjoy one's own happiness" (*SE*, vol. 8, 113). This statement, made by Freud the moralist, would seem to deny the existence of Schadenfreude, which depends on the ability to feel pleasure or satisfaction over another person's misery. It's true that Freud places "Other people's misery" in quotation marks, suggesting that he is citing conventional wisdom, not the truth; but in light of his later statement implying that only children, not adults, feel Schadenfreude, we can conclude that he was reluctant to offend the reader's moral sensibility.

Nietzsche, by contrast, had no fear of offending his readers. Indeed, he wrote as a provocateur, a writer who thrived on controversy. "To see others suffer does one good," he proclaims in *On the Genealogy of Morals*: "This is a hard saying but an ancient, mighty, human, all-too-human principle to which even the apes might subscribe" (503). Nietzsche was reacting against Schopenhauer's condemnation of Schadenfreude in *On the Basis of Morality* as an "infallible sign of a thoroughly bad heart and profound moral worthlessness" (135). Nietzsche viewed Schadenfreude as the revenge of the impotent, an example of *ressentiment*, when a slave morality becomes creative. An early theorist of Schadenfreude, Nietzsche prefigures Freud in recognizing the aggressive nature of jokes, as can be seen in his observation in *The Gay Science*: "Laughter means: to rejoice at another's expense, but with a good conscience" (422).

One more Nietzschean insight is worth quoting, one of his most profound: "Gradually it has become clear to me what every great philosophy so far has been: namely, the personal confession of its author and a kind of involuntary and unconscious memoir" (203)—a statement that is also true of Freud's joke book.

Freud was no Nietzsche, and he is careful to assert in *Jokes and Their Relation to the Unconscious* that the people about whom he writes are admirable. Jews might be regarded by foreigners as comic figures but, Freud is quick to point out, their ability to make fun of themselves bespeaks strength, not weakness. Moreover, Freud asserts, making an extreme generalization, Jews portray a "democratic mode of thinking," making no distinction between lords and serfs, a gift that "also, alas, upsets discipline and co-operation" (*SE*. vol. 8, 112). In his late essay "A Comment on Anti-Semitism" (1938), he cites an unknown source, probably himself, who extols the Jews.

> They do not need so much alcohol as we do in order to make life tolerable; crimes of brutality, murder, robbery and sexual violence are great rarities among them; they have always set a high value on intellectual achievement and interests; their family life is more intimate; they take better care of the poor; charity is a sacred duty to them. (*SE*, vol. 23, 292)

Nevertheless, despite or because of these obligatory disclaimers, Freud was ashamed of his parents' humble Eastern European origins. Jacob and Amalia Freud came from an Orthodox and Hasidic background in Galicia, a province in modern-day west Ukraine and southeastern Poland. As *Ostjuden*, Eastern Jews, they were looked down upon in cosmopolitan Vienna. "Once a group of Jews became established and assimilated in Vienna," Emanuel Rice avows in *Freud and Moses* (1990), "they began to resent the newly-arrived immigrants, whom they deemed to be primitive, uncultured and uneducated" (10). Although Freud admired Galician Jews' survival instincts, he sought to dissociate himself from them through assimilation and academic success. Rice demonstrates that Freud's adolescence, when he was most rebellious against his parents' religious and cultural values, was marked by an "ethnic self-hatred that would make an anti-Semite proud" (21). Freud identified with non-Jewish heroes, such as Hannibal, Alexander, Oliver Cromwell (after whom he named one of his sons), and Napoleon; denied that he understood Yiddish despite the fact that it was the language his parents spoke at home; and forbade his wife, who came from a prominent Jewish family, to observe any religious rituals at home. To narrate Jewish jokes, then, to gentile readers about Jewish beggars and unscrupulous marriage-brokers implicated Freud in a risky activity, for he was writing about his own religious background and culture.

Many psychoanalytic scholars have written about Freud's Jewish jokes, including Norman N. Holland, who argued in "Tickled Rats and Human Laughter" (2007) that "*Schadenfreude* laughter seems to be a subspecies of Freud's comic, and, so too, in-group against out-group gibes as in the jokes one ethnic group tell against another" (52). In *Difference and Pathology* (1985), Sander L. Gilman points out that Freud was highly conflicted about his identity as an Eastern European Jew. "Jews assumed the status of the proverbial leper during the Middle Ages" (151), an association that continued through Freud's age. Freud's Jewish jokes rely on mauscheln, broken German, a macaronic language that conjures up laughter if not ridicule. Mauscheln is the language of failed cultural assimilation, spoken with the accent of Eastern European Yiddish along with a hint of Hebrew, the language of liturgy. A Jew's use of mauscheln, Gilman contends, was an obstacle in being accepted into German society. Gilman identifies mauscheln, with its fantastic intonation, vocabulary, and grammar, as the hidden language of the Jews. Freud's Jewish jokes, Gilman demonstrates in *Difference and Pathology*, belie his efforts, largely unconscious, to distance himself from his humble religious and racial roots and ally himself with modern "scientific" discourse, the language of the cultural elite. Peter Gay, Freud's biographer, acknowledges that the "cruelty of Freud's jokes goes beyond casual indifference to the lot of some miserable, unmarriageable women" (*Reading Freud* 148), but he explains this as a reflection of Viennese culture. Nor does Gay invoke Jewish self-hatred to explain Freud's fondness for malicious Jewish jokes.

Freud was a compulsive teller of Jewish jokes, just as Freud himself, along with his iconic cigar and analytic couch, became the object of countless jokes. Jewish humor has become a staple of literature, film, and television, but the Jews were "not a notably 'humorous' people" before the beginning of the Emancipation in Germany in the second half of the eighteenth century, as Sig Altman remarks (135). Jewish humor was "suffused with the tensions of a multiple ambiguity concerning one's own ultimate worth and situation in life" (140). These tensions may be seen in Freud's jokes.

Freud's contribution to the psychology of humor involves his recognition that tendentious jokes involve three people: the joke-teller, the object of the joke's hostile or sexual aggression, and the one in whom the joke's aim of producing pleasure is fulfilled—the reader. Freud did not anticipate affective or reader-response criticism that began to develop in the 1960s and 1970s. Consequently,

Freud assumed that his readers would share his own interpretation of the jokes he narrated. Interpretations change over time, however, and what is funny to one person may not be funny to another. Reading these jokes today, more than a century after the publication of Freud's comic book, raises a problem that the founder of psychoanalysis could not have predicted: our heightened sensitivity to jokes about the disabled. The rise of disability studies in the last three decades has sensitized us to the challenges of people who are physically or psychologically impaired. How can we laugh at people who suffer from a disability for which they are not responsible? How can we delight in another's pain? But this is precisely the nature of Schadenfreude, taking pleasure in others' misfortunes. The challenge of writing about Freud's Schadenfreude in his Jewish jokes is to avoid coming across as humorless or hypocritical—especially if one enjoys the jokes. Nothing ruins a joke more quickly than analyzing it. Or as E. B. White quipped, "Analyzing humor is like dissecting a frog. Few people are interested, and the frog dies of it."

The most problematic of Freud's jokes involves a marriage-broker trying to convince a young man to marry a woman with a "hunchback":

> The *Schadchen* was defending the girl he had proposed against the young man's protests. "I don't care for the mother-in-law," said the latter. "She's a disagreeable, stupid person."—"But after all you're not marrying the mother-in-law. What you want is her daughter."—"Yes, but she's not young any longer, and she's not precisely a beauty."—"No matter. If she's neither young nor beautiful she'll be all the more faithful to you."—"And she hasn't much money."—"Who's talking about money? Are you marrying money then? After all it's a wife that you want."—But she's got a hunchback too."—"Well, what *do* you want? Isn't she to have a single fault?" (*SE*, vol. 8, 61)

Freud intends for us to laugh at the hunchback woman's single fault, but it's no laughing matter that he saw *all* women as, if not deformed, then nevertheless suffering from a lack—the absence of a penis and, therefore, suffering from "penis envy," a central aspect of classical Freudian psychoanalysis. Freud regarded the sexual life of adult women as psychology's "dark continent," an image he expressed in *The Question of Lay Analysis* (1926):

> We know less about the sexual life of little girls than of boys. But we need not feel ashamed of this distinction; after all, the sexual life of adult women is a "dark continent" for psychology. But we have learnt that girls feel deeply their lack of a sexual organ that is equal in value to the male one; they regard themselves on that account as inferior, and this "envy for the penis"

> is the origin of a whole number of characteristic feminine reactions. (*SE*, vol. 20, 212)

Freud writes here as a psychoanalyst, not as a joke-teller, but his pleasure is that of a man unlocking one of the secrets of female psychology. Unlike the schadchen's duplicitous, mendacious logic, Freud claims to use the scientist's objective logic, and he is not "ashamed" of his conclusion because it is based on observation. But his observations, of course, are highly selective—and, in this case, antifeminist. Tellingly, Portmann observes that because Schadenfreude exposes a system of moral domination, where one person seeks to dominate another, women are more often than not its victims. This can be seen in Freud's Jewish jokes, where the female hunchback becomes the object of male derision.

One of the many ironies of Freud's Jewish jokes was that he viewed himself as "something of a schnorrer," as Elliott Oring asserts in his 1984 study *The Jokes of Sigmund Freud* (17). Oring cites abundant biographical evidence to support this claim. "Freud's economic position was for many years a tenuous one in which he, like the schnorrer, was repeatedly forced to accept gifts and loans from his friends" (18). Oring points out, additionally, that like the bride in Freud's Jewish jokes, his wife was "indelibly flawed," not because she was a hunchback but because she came from a long line of highly distinguished Jews. "This was a flaw as debilitating as a hunched back or a lame leg, as it severely reduced her stature in Freud's eyes. It was the linkage to this princess of her tribe that Freud's unconscious rejected" (41).

Jonathan Swift, arguably the greatest English satirist, specifically ruled out using corrosive humor to mock physical defects that were not correctable, as his 1739 poem "Verses on the Death of Dr. Swift" reveals:

> Perhaps I may allow, the Dean
> Had too much Satyr in his Vein;
> And he seem'd determin'd not to starve it,
> Because no Age could more deserve it.
> Yet, Malice never was his Aim;
> He lash'd the Vice but spar'd the Name.
> No Individual could resent,
> Where Thousands equally were meant.
> His Satyr points at no Defect,
> But what all Mortals may correct;
> For he abhorr'd that senseless Tribe
> Who call it Humour when they jibe:
> He spar'd a Hump or crooked Nose,

> Whose Owners set not up for Beaux.
> True genuine Dulness mov'd his Pity,
> Unless it offer'd to be witty. (571–2)

Freud was acquainted with Swift's writings—he cites *Gulliver's Travels* in both volumes of *The Interpretation of Dreams* (1900) and *Civilization and Its Discontents* (1930)—but he didn't agree that humor should spare non-reparable flaws. Freud was also familiar with Heinrich Heine's writings, and a footnote to *Civilization and Its Discontents* reveals Freud's belief that imaginative writers like Heine—and, we may add, like himself—express dark truths that are otherwise forbidden. He then cites Heine's confession that if God grants him complete happiness, he will have the joy of seeing six or seven of his enemies hanged from trees. "Before their death I shall, moved in my heart, forgive them all the wrong they did me in their lifetime. One must, it is true, forgive one's enemies—but not before they have been hanged" (*SE*, vol. 21, 110, n.1).

To see Freud's Jewish jokes as containing an element of Schadenfreude is to recognize how vexing these jokes are in their conscious and unconscious meanings. Schnorrer humor reflects, as Eliezer Diamond recognizes, a "rueful acceptance of the claims that the poor have upon religiously conscientious Jews at the same time as they express annoyance with the burden created by this obligation" (49). But schnorrer and schadchen jokes also confirm the pleasure in not being part of this crazy world—Freud's pleasure at the expense of the misfortune of these stock caricatures, pleasure that his social identity was not that of Eastern Jews. Laughter may be the best medicine, as we have come to believe, but Freud's Jewish jokes combine pleasure and pain that continue to be unsettling, disturbing, destabilizing—a prescription fraught with untoward side effects.

Apart from characterizing his Jewish jokes, Schadenfreude appears in one of Freud's most autobiographical books, *The Psychopathology of Everyday Life* (1901), where he discusses his encounter while on a holiday trip with a young man of "academic background" who is familiar with Freud's publications. The young man struggles to remember a quote from Virgil's *Aeneid* that involves the forgetting of the indefinite pronoun *aliquis*, which means "someone"—a curious word not to recall. "Please don't look so scornful," the traveling-companion irritably exclaims to Freud, "you seem as if you were gloating over my embarrassment" (*SE*, vol. 6, 9). In other words, Freud's interlocutor says, do not respond to my confession with Schadenfreude. What makes this moment so remarkable and ironic is that the young man who cannot remember "aliquis" is none other than Freud himself. The aliquis incident, a seemingly trivial incident about the forgetting of a non-substantive word, has long fascinated Freudian sleuths. Had Freud known that scholars would unmask the identity of the interlocutor, it's doubtful that he would have written about the incident—especially in light of the fact that his detractors have experienced Schadenfreude when writing about it.

Another example of misremembering, this time involving his own last name, appears in *The Psychopathology of Everyday Life*. During the time he was working on *The Interpretation of Dreams*, he frequently walked in Paris, feeling lonely and filled with longing. Writing a passage on daydreams, he thought about the poor bookkeeper in Alphonse Daudet's novel *Le Nabab*, whose name he mistakenly refers to as "Monsieur Jocelyn." Only later, to his "very great shame and consternation," did he realize that the correct name was "Monsieur Joyeuse" (*SE*, vol. 6, 149)—the French translation of his own name. It's likely that Freud mused over the fact that his own surname forms an essential part of *Schadenfreude*, but if so, he never admitted this.

Does experiencing Schadenfreude make one a bad person? "Concerning this moral verdict," van Dijk and Ouwerkerk conclude in the introduction to their coedited volume, "the jury is still out" (5). Peter Gay never doubts the moral justification of feeling Schadenfreude in his 1998 memoir *My German Question: Growing Up in Nazi Berlin*. Acknowledging that he had "sweet moments of *Schadenfreude*" in 1936 when some of the early Nazis, not yet firmly in power, were disgraced, Gay asks bitterly, and rhetorically, "Is there any significance to the fact that this word for pleasure in the discomfiture of others exists only in German?" (72–3). Witnessing in person the highly favored German women lose the 4 × 100-meter relay race because of a dropped baton during the 1936 summer Olympics, which was touted by Hitler as a show of Nazi superiority, Gay observes, without qualification, "Schadenfreude can be one of the greatest joys in life" (83). It took Gay decades before he stopped believing that the only good German was a dead German.

A hint of Schadenfreude appears in *Fragment of an Analysis of a Case of Hysteria* (1905), in which Freud, writing about Dora's "craving for revenge," reveals his own anger and vexation. Freud interprets Dora's sudden termination of analysis as an "unmistakable act of vengeance" on her part, a form of self-injury, he believed, as a result of his insights into her hysterical illness. In hurting herself, Freud suggests, she was trying to hurt him too, as he implies in the following rationalization. "No one who, like me, conjures up the most evil of those half-tamed demons that inhabit the human breast, and seeks to wrestle with them, can expect to come through the struggle unscathed" (*SE*, vol. 7, 109). After abruptly breaking off analysis, Dora visited Freud one more time, still suffering from hysterical symptoms, such as her "alleged facial neuralgia." Freud cannot resist making what surely ranks as the most spiteful remark in any of his case studies. "I do not know what kind of help she wanted from me, but I promised to forgive her for having deprived me of the satisfaction of affording her a far more radical cure for her troubles" (*SE*, vol. 7, 122). Freud may not be taking pleasure in her continued suffering, but he does not appear overly troubled by it. His wounded narcissism is evident, and contrary to his own words, he has not forgiven her; he appears to take stark satisfaction in her distress. Empathy is the opposite of Schadenfreude, Richard H. Smith suggests in *The Joy of Pain* (2013), a word that is strikingly absent from Freud's most problematic case study. Nor does the word "compassion" appear. "Sympathetic" appears three times, but in an unusual context: Dora's "sympathetic imitation" of her father's sexual fixation (*SE*, vol. 7, 83). By contrast, nearly one-quarter of the 100 references to "revenge" in Freud's writings appear in *Fragment of an Analysis of a Case of Hysteria*. As Hannah S. Decker remarks in her 1992 book on the case study, Freud paid "scant attention to countertransference" (192): the term appears only twice in his writings.

Freud's refusal to analyze the hidden dynamics of Schadenfreude was uncharacteristic of the man who rarely missed the opportunity to deliver unpalatable truths. Schadenfreude did not awaken his interest, at least on a conscious level, but the subject fascinated him on an unconscious level, and his Jewish jokes reveal that he was indeed both a Freudian and a Schadenfreudian. In retrospect, Schadenfreude would have been a perfect subject for Freud to explore, for it conveys unsettling truths about human nature that awaken the greatest resistance to acknowledge. Psychoanalysis, which can be called simply the study of ambivalence, or the study of what we don't want to know about ourselves, is supremely equipped to analyze Schadenfreude, which involves the connection between pleasure and pain.

* * *

In the following chapters, I discuss eight eminent scholars and novelists who passionately loved or gleefully loathed Freud, four Freud idolaters and four Schadenfreudians, or Freud bashers, twin sides of the same coin. I have selected the Freud idolaters based on the depth of their knowledge of Freud and psychoanalysis along with their influence in the intellectual community. I have chosen the Schadenfreudians based on the virulence of their criticisms: they do not wish merely to reform Freudian thinking but to annihilate it from existence. Part I, Freud idolaters, focuses on highly prolific scholars whose admiration for Freud is boundless. Indeed, one will scarcely find a word of criticism of the founder of psychoanalysis, although there may be objections to Freud's theory of art. Lionel Trilling and Harold Bloom were two of the century's most influential literary critics—and two of the country's greatest supporters of Freud. Both had personal reasons for their attraction to psychoanalysis, including their struggles with depression, though their experience with the talking cure as therapy was not entirely successful. Trilling's most anthologized short story, "Of This Time, of That Place," curiously suggests that the brilliant young student in love with poetry, Ferdinand R. Tertan, cannot be helped by therapy, a judgment that calls into question the clinical value of psychoanalysis. Why does Trilling believe in Freud's greatness as a literary value if his creation, psychoanalysis, has little therapeutic value? The same question may be asked about Harold Bloom. Trilling and Bloom were preoccupied with the literary Freud, not with psychoanalysis, but the latter appropriated Freudian theory, using it in his most celebrated book, *The Anxiety of Influence* (1973), to advance an Oedipal interpretation of creativity. Bloom lived nearly twenty years longer than Trilling, and in his late writings we see what Freud called the *work of mourning*. Scholars have not yet appreciated how late Bloom is different from his early blossoming more than half a century earlier—and how bereavement affected his final writings.

The Viennese-born Kurt R. Eissler, the creator of the Freud Archives, was Freud's most loyal American disciple, doing everything he could to preserve and protect his master's reputation, often to the dismay of other Freud scholars who were unable to access all of the papers in the collection. Eissler regarded changes to Freudian theory as the "poison of eclecticism," and he denounced all revisions regardless of their merits. Eissler wrote two books defending Freud against the controversial accusation that he was complicit in the suicide of one of his most talented disciples, Victor Tausk, though the books only called further attention to the controversy.

Peter Gay, the author of many books on psychoanalysis, including a magisterial biography, acknowledged minor criticisms of Freud but never doubted that he was the culmination of Enlightenment thought, thoroughly rational and scientific. Gay, a historian who went through psychoanalytic training, wrote an extended clinical vignette that may have been a disguised autobiography. If so, the vignette, when read along with one of his wife's books, shows how Gay used his psychoanalytic education to understand the value of reason in grasping thorny inner conflicts.

Part II, Schadenfreudians, explores another four writers whose aim was not simply to debunk Freud and destroy his monstrous creation but to cast both into hell. D. H. Lawrence and Vladimir Nabokov were two of the twentieth century's greatest novelists, and although they had little in common with each other, they both regarded Freud as the embodiment of evil. Accusing Freud of destroying the beauty and mystery of sexuality, Lawrence wrote two books attacking psychoanalysis, yet ironically, he anticipated many psychological insights that Freud missed. Lawrence warned of the danger of mother–son incest, an Oedipal situation with which Freud would certainly agree, but the novelist also dramatized the problems associated with the "smother-mother" and the "Magna Mater," a psychological dilemma that Freud was slow to theorize. Despite Lawrence's shrill anti-psychoanalytic outbursts, he was *almost* a Freudian. I first wrote about Nabokov's anti-Freudianism in my 1985 book *The Talking Cure: Literary Representations of Psychoanalysis.* I reprint my original discussion and then update it with contemporary views of the novelist's obsessive efforts to slay the "Viennese witch doctor." The idea of Freud filled Nabokov with Schadenfreude, yet like Lawrence, some of Nabokov's insights parallel Freud's, especially the existence of rescue fantasies and the family romance.

Thomas Szasz, a professor of psychiatry and a trained psychoanalyst, was the leader of the antipsychiatry movement. In his most consequential book, *The Myth of Mental Illness*, Szasz denied the existence of mental illness, and he never wavered despite clinical and medical evidence to the contrary. Early in his career, Szasz spoke positively about Freud, but praise soon gave way to unequivocal condemnation. Szasz's writings have been closely scrutinized, but no one has commented on the extent to which his former wife's suicide, immediately after the end of their eighteen-year marriage, may have shaped his insistence that psychiatrists, along with spouses, did not have the medical, legal, or ethical right to prevent a person from taking his or her own life.

Frederick Crews began his long career at UC Berkeley with a pioneering psychoanalytic study of Nathaniel Hawthorne, *Sins of the Fathers*, repudiated his early book, and devoted himself to proving, at least to his own satisfaction, that Freud was motivated *only* by a nefarious lust for power. Crews's idealization of Freud transformed first into devaluation and then demonization. In the end, Crews saw nothing good about Freud or his creation. Crews feels betrayed by the thinker he had once revered, a man whom he could never get *Out of My System*, to quote the title of his 1975 book. The story of Crews's rejection of Freud reads like a passionate love affair gone horribly wrong, a relationship in which, to recall Bollas's words, hate is not the opposite of but a substitute for love.

There are many other Freudians I could have included here, some of whom I have discussed elsewhere. Norman N. Holland, whom I have called in a 2021 book the "Dean of American psychoanalytic literary critics," was certainly a Freud idolater: one hardly finds a word of criticism in Holland's many books about psychoanalysis and literature. My discussion of another Freudian true believer, Helene Deutsch, appears in *Psychoanalytic Memoirs* (2023). I consider other major Freudian scholars and clinicians in *Psychoanalysis: An Interdisciplinary Retrospective* (2023): Allen Wheelis, Joan Wheelis, Sander L. Gilman, Nancy J. Chodorow, Christopher Bollas, and Adam Phillips. These renowned scholars and clinicians, I should point out, admired Freud but were also aware of his limitations. Deborah Britzman has shown through a series of illuminating books how education is one of the three "impossible professions," to use Freud's felicitous term (the others being government and psychoanalysis). My reviews of two of Britzman's books, *Lost Subjects, Contested Objects* and *A Psychoanalyst in the Classroom*, have appeared in *JPCS: Journal for the Psychoanalysis of Culture & Society* (1998) and the *Journal of the American Psychoanalytic Association* (2016), respectively. I include in *Psychoanalytic Memoirs* discussions of two other leading American psychoanalytic literary critics, Brenda Webster and Madeleine Sprengnether, both of whom were aware of Freud's strengths and weaknesses.

Of the Schadenfreudians, the most notorious is Jeffrey Moussaieff Masson, whom I examine, along with his vexed relationship with Janet Malcolm and Peter Swales, in *Psychoanalytic Memoirs*. Like Crews, Masson began his career as a Freudian, editing and translating a volume of his letters, but then he turned against Freud, judging him guilty of intellectual cowardice. Another Schadenfreudian I could have written about is the psychiatrist E. Fuller Torrey, the author of a book sensationalistically titled *Freudian Fraud: The Malignant Effect of Freud's Theory on American Thought and Culture* (1992). Spying the book in the library, I was dismayed to learn that on the basis of a mild criticism of Freud I had made in my 1985 book *The Talking Cure*, he had enlisted me in his anti-Freudian camp when, in fact, my study is a sympathetic account of the talking cure. Torrey accuses Freud of nearly every imaginable evil ranging from permissive child rearing to the abdication of moral responsibility. As Richard Wollheim noted in his *New York Times* review, *Freudian Fraud* is the "overwrought work of a man who has made no effort to discover whether he is entitled to believe what he wants to believe. It is the unabashed victory of sincerity over truthfulness." Still another Schadenfreudian was the British writer Richard Webster, the author of *Why Freud Was Wrong: Sin, Science and Psychoanalysis* (1995). Webster scornfully refers to Freud as the Messiah who repeatedly deceived himself, projecting onto others his own inhumanity.

A Freudian but Not a Freudist

I began reading Freud when I was a college freshman in 1963 and instantly fell in love with his words. I immediately became a Freudenfreudian, finding joy in Freud's writings, a passion that has continued to this day, sixty years later. I began teaching at the University at Albany in 1973, and after receiving tenure in the late 1970s, I spent three years studying at the National Psychological Association of Psychoanalysis (NPAP), the first nonmedical psychoanalytic institute in the United States, founded by Freud's student, Theodor Reik. I studied at NPAP not to become an analyst but to deepen my understanding of psychoanalysis for my teaching and scholarship. I have never been in psychoanalysis; writing is my therapy of choice, my lifeline, whenever I'm in a crisis. E. M. Forster's observation in *Aspects of the Novel* (1927) conveys how writing can be used as problem-solving: "How can I tell what I think till I see what I say?" (97). Other novelists have made similar statements. "Writing is a form of therapy," Graham Greene declared; "sometimes I wonder how all those who do not write, compose or paint can manage to escape the madness, the melancholia, the panic fear which is inherent in the human situation" (285). The physician-poet William Carlos Williams admitted at the beginning of his *Autobiography* (1951) that time meant nothing to him when he needed to write. "I would be like a woman at term: no matter what else was up, that demand had to be met." Regardless of how late it was at night, regardless of how exhausted he might have been from seeing patients all day, Williams needed to write. "In fact, I couldn't rest until I had freed my mind from the obsessions which had been tormenting me all day. Cleansed of that torment, having scribbled, I could rest" (xiii–xiv).

I have read and reread Freud's writings countless times, always with great pleasure; nearly every page of my copy of the twenty-four-volume *Standard Edition* of Freud's writings is filled with notes, queries, and scribbles. I was, during the early years of my career, a Freud idolater; hardly a word of criticism appears in my early articles and books. At the beginning of my career, I often read literature to see how it confirmed psychoanalytic theory; later I realized that literature helped to create psychoanalytic theory. I would like to think, as a result of my reading, writing, and teaching, that I now have a more nuanced view of Freud's strengths and weaknesses. The creator of psychoanalysis defined himself as a "Freudian but not a Freudist," yet despite the evolution of his thinking, he never realized, as most contemporary analysts now do, that his faith in his creation approached religious dimensions.

My choice of Freud idolaters and Freud bashers is unusual and requires explanation. Trilling, Bloom, Gay, and Crews were academics, like myself. They were among the most influential literature and history professors of their age, and they continue to influence students of psychoanalysis. The decisions made by Kurt Eissler, as the creator of the Freud Archives, continue to stymie contemporary psychoanalytic scholarship. Lawrence and Nabokov are two of my favorite novelists; I teach Lawrence's fiction every other semester (paired with Thomas Hardy, who resembles him in many ways). Do I experience Schadenfreude when teaching these two Schadenfreudian novelists? Perhaps! I believe that authors consciously choose to write on certain subjects, but I also believe that sometimes authors cannot avoid writing about them. This is true of my discussion of Szasz. Once I discovered that no one has commented on how his wife's suicide affected his scholarship, I felt compelled to write about him.

In each chapter, I discuss the extent of the authors' involvement with Freud, showing the continuities and discontinuities of their writings. Whenever possible, I offer snapshots of the writers, suggesting how their personal and professional lives were inextricably related. I explore their attitudes toward the "scientific" status of psychoanalysis; their relationship to later neo-Freudian and post-Freudian theorists; their personal experience, if any, with psychoanalysis and its impact on their work; and the extent to which Freudian or anti-Freudian thinking influenced their own writings. The present book is, in effect, a study of the roller-coaster reception of Freudian theory. Each author interpreted "Freud" in a different and unique way; indeed, Freud's writings are like a projection screen or a Rorschach test, sometimes revealing more about the interpreter than the object of interpretation. *Freudians and Schadenfreudians* has implications for intellectual history, showing how a single man has been ecstatically idealized by his disciples and demonically devalued by his enemies. Whether writing on the Freud idolaters or Schadenfreudians, I try to chart a course between these two extremes, acknowledging that sometimes the murky middle is the most dangerous place. I try to be as balanced as possible, knowing that, as Adam Phillips says in *On Balance* (2010), "there is often nothing more unbalancing than the demand for a balanced view" (xiv). In the conclusion, I suggest the commonalities between the Freud idolaters and Schadenfreudians, and then I discuss the current state of psychoanalysis, the "psychoanalytic credos" by which contemporary analysts live.

Part I

Freud Idolaters

1

Lionel Trilling

Tragic Freud

Seldom does a literary critic's death make the front page of the *New York Times*, but Lionel Trilling's reputation was immense. "In the hands of Lionel Trilling," Thomas Lask enthused in his obituary on November 7, 1975, "criticism became not merely a consideration of a work of literature but also of the ideas it embodied and what these ideas said of the society that gave them birth." Trilling, who died of pancreatic cancer at age seventy, was a trailblazer, becoming the first tenured Jew in Columbia's English department, where he taught his entire life, rising to the rank of University Professor, its most prestigious title. He was not only arguably the most influential American literary critic of his generation but also one of the most impassioned advocates of Freud's work. His seminal essay "Freud and Literature" appeared in *The Liberal Imagination* (1950), the first of several celebrated collections of essays. *The Liberal Imagination* was a literary phenomenon, selling, according to Louis Menand in an article published in the *New Yorker* in 2008, more than seventy thousand hardcover and one hundred thousand paperback copies. In 1955, Trilling delivered the Freud Anniversary Lecture sponsored by the New York Psychoanalytic Institute and Society. The talk was published in the same year as a short monograph, *Freud and the Crisis of Our Culture*, and later revised, under the title "Freud: Within and Beyond Culture," for *Beyond Culture* in 1965. Trilling never became a psychoanalytic literary critic, as some of his contemporaries did, nor did he invent a new approach to literature, but his authoritative essays on Freud became required reading for anyone interested in literature and psychoanalysis.

The story of Trilling's relationship to psychoanalysis begins but does not end with his extensive writings on the subject. It's fascinating to see not only what he reveals about his evolving relationship with psychoanalysis but also what he conceals. Diana Trilling's 1993 autobiography, *The Beginning of the Journey:*

The Marriage of Diana and Lionel Trilling, describes their lengthy experiences in therapy, her husband's protracted struggle with depression, and their strikingly different attitudes toward psychoanalysis. The publication of his correspondence, *Life in Culture: Selected Letters of Lionel Trilling* (2018), also casts light on his experience in analysis. Most surprising of all is the controversial 1999 essay by James Trilling, who calls into question the value of his parents' analysis and suggests a new "diagnosis" of his father's psychological troubles. Psychoanalysis was a family affair for the three Trillings, and there were sharp disagreements over the meaning and benefit of the talking cure.

Reading Freud

Trilling wrote about Freud from the 1940s through the 1960s, the "golden age of psychoanalysis." He recognized that psychoanalysis placed the historian of ideas in a precarious position. "For no system has had to endure more misunderstanding—willed or unconsciously willed—or more intellectual braggadocio from people of normally good and modest intelligence, often while they are themselves making use of Freud's doctrines" (*Speaking of Literature and Society* 218). One may infer from Trilling's cautionary words that *he* will not misunderstand the Freudian system. Indeed, Trilling was confident that he understood the complexity of psychoanalysis, and although he never hesitated to criticize Freud's view of the artist and the nature of art, he didn't doubt that psychoanalysis was scientific, a word that he uses throughout his writings without quotation marks.

Life in Culture enables us to understand when Trilling began reading Freud's works. In a letter written in 1959 to William Gamble, who had requested help with an essay, Trilling explained that the first book by Freud he read with "critical interest" was *Civilization and Its Discontents*. He read the work in 1930, when it appeared in English. In fact, Trilling reviewed the book for *The New Freeman*, but the journal abruptly went out of business before the review was published. Trilling initially characterized *Civilization and Its Discontents* as "ridiculous and even as offensive" (*Life in Culture* 291), largely because, as he now recalls ruefully, he was a Marxist at the time and consequently sought economic and political rather than psychological explanations of the human condition. Less than a decade later, however, when he became disillusioned with Marxism, Trilling revised his thinking about *Civilization and Its Discontents*, concluding that it was one of the most noteworthy books of the age.

Trilling reread *Civilization and Its Discontents* frequently and often required his students to read it. He doesn't explain to Gamble why he admired the book, but presumably it was because he agreed with Freud's central thesis: the inevitable antagonism between the claims of biological instinct and the constraints of civilization. Freud's purpose in writing *Civilization and Its Discontents*, Trilling avers in *Sincerity and Authenticity* (1972), was to "keep all things from becoming 'weightless'" (156), by which he meant Freud's acceptance of the inevitability of suffering. Additionally, Trilling was fascinated with Freud's speculative "death instinct," which, in the literary critic's opinion, contributed to the tragic vision of life. Even if Freud's death instinct has no scientific basis, Trilling wrote in *A Gathering of Fugitives* (1956), "we still cannot miss its grandeur, its ultimate tragic courage in acquiescence to fate" (58). Tellingly, Trilling was never interested in Freud's repetition-compulsion principle, which has far greater clinical significance: the need to repeat a traumatic experience to gain control over it.

Trilling did not disagree with statements in *Civilization and Its Discontents* that readers now find highly problematic, as when Freud contends that the work of civilization "has become increasingly the business of men, it confronts them with ever more difficult tasks and compels them to carry out instinctual sublimations of which women are little capable" (*SE*, vol. 21, 103). Trilling *never* criticized the antifeminist elements of Freudian theory, probably because he shared the patriarchal assumptions of the age.

Trilling cited two other Freud books that had a profound impact on him: *Introductory Lectures on Psycho-Analysis* (1915–17), which he taught with his colleague Jacques Barzun in the Senior Colloquium at Columbia College; and *Beyond the Pleasure Principle* (1920). By 1939 or 1940, Trilling had read nearly everything written by Freud that was published in English, with the exception of *Totem and Taboo*, *The Future of an Illusion*, and *Moses and Monotheism*, "serious omissions," he concedes (*Life in Culture* 292). Curiously, he ignored Freud's "technical" papers, the six essays, written between 1911 and 1915, in which he propounds some of his most far-reaching ideas, such as transference, transference-love, countertransference, clinical resistance, acting out and working through psychological conflict, and ambivalence, a word coined by the Swiss psychiatrist Eugen Bleuler that Freud used for the first time in "The Dynamics of Transference" (*SE*, vol. 12, 106).

Trilling drew a sharp distinction between Freudianism as an intellectual and cultural force, on the one hand, and psychoanalysis as a therapy, on the other. He lauded the former, not the latter. In view of Trilling's admiration of psychoanalysis, Mark Shechner has observed, "perhaps nothing is so remarkable about him as the discrepancy between his zeal for Freud and his use of him" (20). Nowhere in Trilling's writings, Shechner adds, do we find any interest in pursuing the difference between the surface and depth meanings of a text or references to Freud's most revolutionary books, including *The Interpretation of Dreams*, *Jokes and Their Relation to the Unconscious*, and *Three Essays on the Theory of Sexuality*. Trilling's decision not to discuss Freud's case studies is unexpected because they are captivating *literary* stories, generating enormous attention from psychoanalytic and nonpsychoanalytic scholars.

Nor did Trilling write about his many years in analysis, information gleaned from Diana Trilling's autobiography. Trilling never admitted publicly to suffering from depression. It was rare during the middle of the twentieth century for people to talk or write personally about mood disorders, a stigmatized and forbidden subject despite the growing popularity of psychoanalysis. "I have a fairly extensive acquaintance among New York psychoanalysts," Trilling observes neutrally, without elaboration, to Gamble, "but this has but little intellectual value—within the limits of my experience, the best of the analysts are not speculative but clinical" (*Life in Culture* 293). In a letter written in 1956, Trilling remarked that "Americans cannot bear to be unhappy—hence their recourse to psychoanalysis" (257), refusing to include himself among the worried well.

Trilling concludes his 1959 letter to Gamble with the statement that he has recently felt that his relation to Freud's writing has weakened. He expresses the hope to write a short book about Freud as a moralist. He never did. Trilling must have realized, however, that he had written enough about Freud to convince readers that he was one of the most iconic thinkers of the twentieth century.

Idealizing Freud—and Freud's Official Biographer

Trilling was a tough-minded critic who rarely expressed unqualified praise for a book. For this reason, his three reviews of Ernest Jones's multivolume biography, *The Life and Work of Sigmund Freud*, are startling. Published in the *New York Times Book Review* between 1953, the date of volume 1, and 1957, the date of volume 3, Trilling's evaluation can scarcely be more laudatory. He views Jones as Freud's ideal biographer, mainly because he knew Freud for forty years as both friend and associate. Trilling never challenges Jones's authority, singling out the "excellence of his expository style and the scope of his scientific and humanistic learning" (*Speaking of Literature and Society* 270). Trilling's third review, titled "Last Years of a Titan" when it was reprinted in *The Griffin*, characterizes Jones's biography as "one of the most important documents in the cultural history of our time" (*Speaking of Literature and Society* 295).

Trilling endorses Jones's view of Freud as a heroic and indefatigable scientist who pursued the dark truth of human nature despite public opposition and ridicule that would have silenced a less Promethean thinker. A Jewish atheist, like Freud, Trilling invokes a superstitious explanation of the psychoanalyst's destiny. "He was born with a caul, which may in part explain why he took so much pleasure in the history of David Copperfield, who had the same natal sign of good fortune" (*Speaking of Literature and Society* 272). Trilling agrees with Jones's conviction that Freud was betrayed by his earliest colleagues, Alfred Adler and Carl Jung, defectors who tried to dilute Freudian theory. So, too, does Trilling repeat Jones's unfounded claim that the defections of Otto Rank and Sandor Ferenczi were caused by mental pathology at the end of their lives. "It was not only that these two valued coadjutors undertook to revise psychoanalytic theory in simplistic and extravagant ways—both men fell prey to extreme mental illness and they died insane" (297).

Blinded by his faith in a mythic Freud, Trilling cannot see that Jones's biography is a hagiography, abounding in exaggerations convincingly demolished by later scholars. Beginning with Henri F. Ellenberger, scholars no longer accept Freud's claim that his early professional years were spent in a period of splendid isolation. "Contrary to the usual assertion," Ellenberger writes in *The Discovery of the Unconscious* (1970), "his publications did not meet with the icy silence or the disparaging criticism that are said to have existed. Actually the reception was mostly favorable, though at times accompanied by a mixture of surprise and puzzlement" (455). No one now accepts Jones's claim, at the beginning of volume 2, that as a result of his self-analysis, Freud attained in 1901, at the age of forty-five, "complete maturity, a consummation that few people really achieve" (3). Whether sympathetic or unsympathetic to Freud, contemporary biographers present a man who, even late in life, was human, all too human. Freud's voluminous correspondence—he wrote more than twenty thousand letters, most of which were unpublished before Jones's biography—confirms that he repeatedly pathologized dissenters such as Adler, Jung, and Wilhelm Stekel, none of whom were mentally ill. A few examples will suffice. "Adler is a very decent man," Freud wrote to Jung in 1910, "but he is paranoid" (McGuire 373). What's worse than a paranoid? A "malicious paranoid," as Freud described Adler in a letter to James Jackson Putnam in 1912. In the same letter Freud describes Jung, from whom he was not yet completely estranged, as "our friend . . . who apparently has not outgrown his own neurosis" (Hale 217). According to Jones,

Freud referred to Stekel, albeit without evidence, as a case of "moral insanity" (vol. 2, 137). Jones did everything he could to discredit his rivals, such as Otto Rank, a member of Freud's inner circle whom Jones characterizes as "dictatorial" and "manic" (vol. 3, 47).

Trilling was so enamored of Jones's biography that he and his Columbia University colleague (and former student) Steven Marcus published a one-volume abridgment in 1961. Trilling never altered his view of the heroic Freud, the "disturber of the world's sleep," as Freud wryly described himself, a *conquistador*. Trilling ends his final review of Jones's biography by asserting that throughout Freud's final years of unrelenting pain from oral cancer, he "took no analgesic drug and only at the end did he consent to aspirin" (*Speaking of Literature and Society* 299), not realizing, as Freud's physician Max Schur disclosed in his 1972 biography, that he chose at the end physician-assisted suicide, a decision that reminds us that even heroes are human.

Freud Unrevised

Trilling was a Freudian, not a Jungian. He concedes, in his *New York Times Book Review* of *The Correspondence Between Sigmund Freud and C.G. Jung* (1974), that admirers of both men will be disillusioned by their often stinging words to each other, but it's clear where his loyalty lies. Jung's objections to Freud, Trilling declares, are "frankly opportunistic—more people, he believed, would be attracted to psychoanalysis if they were not scared away by sex, and again and again Freud had to insist to him that, as he once put it, there was no way to 'sweeten the sour apple'" (*The Last Decade* 180). Trilling never considers the possibility that Freud overemphasized libido theory, which has largely dropped out of contemporary American psychoanalysis.

Trilling derided the "neo-Freudians," psychoanalysts who sought to revise Freudian theory. In his review of Karen Horney's 1942 book *Self-Analysis*, he ridiculed the idea that, in her words, "life itself is the best therapist," a claim he calls "trivial" (*Speaking of Literature and Society* 182)—despite the fact that Freud constructed psychoanalysis on his own self-analysis, which in contemporary terms yielded Oedipal insights but not pre-Oedipal revelations. Trilling regarded Horney's optimism as shallow:

> It seems to me that her denial or attenuation of most of Freud's concepts is the response to the wishes of an intellectual class which has always found Freud's

> ideas cogent but too stringent and too dark. They have always wanted a less tragic and strenuous psychology, a more reasonable, decent, and cooperative psyche, and Dr. Horney, in all her three books, has given them what they want. (*Speaking of Literature and Society* 184)

If psychoanalysis is a science, as Trilling maintained, it's puzzling that Freud's followers have not made further scientific advances. Yet this is what Trilling avers in his discussion of Horney and other revisionists in *The Liberal Imagination*. "Nor really can it be said that Freudian psychology itself has of late made any significant advances" (255). No one would say that physicists have made no progress after Einstein's discoveries; why, then, has psychoanalytic research stalled after Freud?

The "scientific" status of psychoanalysis remains a vexed question, but the biologist Edward O. Wilson provides a possible solution to the conundrum in his 1998 book *Consilience: The Unity of Knowledge*. An alliance between the arts and science is long overdue, Wilson argues, for neither can be complete without the other. "Science needs the intuition and metaphorical power of the arts, and the arts need the fresh blood of science." The result will be, he suggests hopefully, the "reinvigoration of interpretation," which is the "logical channel of constant explanation between science and the arts" (211).

The Liberal Imagination

The Liberal Imagination remains Trilling's best-known book, partly because it contains two classic essays, "Freud and Literature," first published in the *Kenyon Review* in 1940, and "Art and Neurosis," originally published in the *Partisan Review* in 1947. Trilling opens "Freud and Literature" with a quotation frequently cited by later psychoanalytic scholars:

> When, on the occasion of the celebration of his seventieth birthday, Freud was greeted as the "discoverer of the unconscious," he corrected the speaker and disclaimed the title. "The poets and philosophers before me discovered the unconscious," he said. "What I discovered was the scientific method by which the unconscious can be studied." (32)

As I noted in *The Talking Cure* (1985), because Trilling did not footnote the source of Freud's words—he rarely provides a bibliography for his readers—it was difficult to locate the author and journal in which he had found the quote. After much sleuthing, I found the source of the quotation. In the inaugural issue of *Harofé Haivri* [Hebrew Physician], published in 1940, the Columbia University clinical professor of neurology and psychiatry Philip R. Lehrman wrote an article, "Freud's Contributions to Science," in which Freud responded to a greeting by professor Becker, the Prussian minister of art, science, and education. Trilling may have quoted the words from memory without having a copy of the journal article in front of him, for he slightly misquotes Lehrman. Trilling repeats the quote in "Art and Neurosis," but curiously, he omits the reference to the "philosophers," claiming that it was the literary masters who divined the unconscious (156). The same omission appears in both *Beyond Culture* and *Sincerity and Authenticity*, where he pays tribute to the poets but not to the philosophers as the discoverers of the unconscious. Trilling would have agreed with Lehrman's endorsement of the scientific validity of psychoanalysis and his mistrust of revisionists. "He was careful not to be pedantic," Lehrman concludes his essay, "not to create a strictly defined system, as he recognized and warned that such an attempt might hamper the further development of the science of psychoanalysis" (161).

Freud approached the great philosophers with caution, fearing that if he read them, he would be unduly influenced by their insights, thus compromising his own originality. Wariness of Nietzsche may be seen in Freud's letters to Otto Rank, whom he assures that the philosopher's ideas have had no impact on his own work. Freud explained that he couldn't read past the first page of Nietzsche's autobiographical *Ecce Homo* "partly because of the resemblance of his intuitive ideas to our laborious investigations, and partly because of the wealth of ideas" (Lieberman and Kramer 9). Yet, in recognition of Nietzsche's profound impact on his own and Freud's work, Rank sent Freud a complete edition of the philosopher's writings.

Freud admired literature and was himself one of the great writers of the twentieth century, as Trilling often declared. Near the end of *The Liberal Imagination*, he implies that reading Freud provides him with the same aesthetic delight that he receives from reading literature. "The pleasure I have in responding to Freud I find very difficult to distinguish from the pleasure which is involved in responding to a satisfactory work of art" (282). As Adam Kirsch remarks, "Freud meant at least as much to Trilling as any novelist or poet" (107). Literature and psychoanalysis were, of course, Freud's twin passions. Creative writers are "valuable allies and their evidence is to be highly prized," he affirms in "Delusions and Dreams in Jensen's *Gradiva*" (1907), his first published foray into literary criticism, "for they are apt to know a whole host of things between heaven and earth of which our philosophy has not yet let us dream" (*SE*, vol. 9, 8), the allusion to *Hamlet* confirming Freud's love for literature.

And yet Freud also made derogatory generalizations of art, as Trilling points out in "Freud and Literature." Freud claimed that art is a "substitute gratification," a "narcotic"; asserted that artists, driven by unconscious forces, are unaware of what they are doing; and placed the artist in the same category as the neurotic. Trilling rightly reminds us that there is nothing in the logic of psychoanalysis that demands these troubling conclusions. Trilling is never more eloquent than when he defends art and the artist from reductive psychoanalytic claims. Psychoanalysis can reveal much about the conscious and unconscious meanings of art, but it can tell us little if anything about the mystery of artistic creation. Freud himself acknowledged this at the beginning of his 1928 essay "Dostoevsky and Parricide": "Before the problem of the creative artist analysis must, alas, lay down its arms" (*SE*, vol. 21, 177). This did not, however, prevent Freud and his followers from crudely reducing art to neurosis. Trilling recognized the problem of psychoanalytic reductiveness and avoided it in his own literary writings. As much as Trilling commended Jones's biography of Freud, he criticized Jones's study of *Hamlet*, arguing that there is no single meaning of a work; Jones's "Oedipal" solution to Hamlet's procrastination tells us nothing about the play's greatness. What, then, can psychoanalysis teach us about art? Trilling suggests that of all psychological systems, psychoanalysis is the only one that "makes poetry indigenous to the very constitution of the mind" (*The Liberal Imagination* 49)—an evocative sentence that remains deliberately vague.

Writing in an age when the "New Criticism" was beginning to dominate American literary criticism, Trilling shares its preference for irony, ambiguity, wit, paradox, and complexity. Nevertheless, despite the New Critics' insistence on viewing art as an autonomous object and their rejection of "extra-literary" approaches, Trilling took a biographical approach in his first two books: *Matthew Arnold* (1939), his Columbia doctoral dissertation, and *E.M. Forster* (1943). Trilling shows how biography always intrudes itself on literary interpretations and evaluations. Neither study is particularly psychoanalytic, but it's already apparent that one of his favorite critical words and concepts is "ambivalence," as when he states in the Arnold book that the "story of ambivalent love is a characteristic one of the 19th century" (123). Trilling invokes ambivalence to explain how we may understand and not understand at the same time. In his Forster book, Trilling cites Freud's discussion of the three caskets in *King Lear* to show how love and death are inseparable in Shakespeare's play and Forster's short stories. Forster's stories are not concerned with good and evil, Trilling contends, but rather with good and evil, an improbable paradox difficult to fathom. In *A Gathering of Fugitives*, Trilling maintains that in the "intellectual life there ought to be frequent occasions for the exercise of ambivalence" (119). And he reminds himself in one of his notebooks to write an essay on ambivalent moments—"those moments in our reading when we neither hate nor love what the author is saying but hate and love together: when our mind is poised over a recognition of a truth which attacks other truths, or when the author has brilliantly caught half the truth, and denies the other half. These are the most fertile moments" (W. Phillips 21).

Adept at biography, Trilling was no friend of psychobiography. In *The Liberal Imagination*, he chastises the psychoanalyst Edmund Bergler for claiming to understand "the" psychology of the writer. Trilling expands on his criticisms in a 1948 letter to Bergler, who had implied that writers are masochistic. Not so, Trilling counters. "The number of cases of writers who give no sign of the masochistic pattern you find would be very large indeed" (*Life in Culture* 168). Trilling had no sympathy for Meyer A. Zeligs's 1967 study *Friendship and Fratricide*, a psychobiographical analysis of the relationship between Whittaker Chambers and Alger Hiss. Asked by Viking Press, which had published Trilling's own books, not to speak negatively about its new book, *Friendship and Fratricide*, he found a way to express his judgment in a footnote to the introduction to the reprinted edition of his novel *The Middle of the Journey*, which contains a character based on Chambers: "In my opinion, no other work does as much as this one to bring into question the viability of the infant discipline of psycho-history" (xxii). In an essay on "Literary Psychology," a response to Bernard Meyer's psychobiography on Joseph Conrad, Trilling observes that an understanding of the novelist's neurotic conflicts cannot explain why *Heart of Darkness* remains at the center of the modern literary imagination: "it does not say how neurosis put it there" (*Speaking of Literature and Society* 397).

Illness and Creativity

Trilling long admired Edmund Wilson, the "Dean of American Letters." Wilson's crucial support while Trilling was struggling to write his doctoral dissertation was instrumental in its completion. In his 1947 book *The Wound and the Bow*, Wilson argues that Sophocles's Philoctetes, suffering an incurable wound from a snakebite, acquires power in the form of an invincible bow, an example of creativity arising from psychic injury. Sophocles's play implies to Wilson the idea that "genius and disease, like strength and mutilation, may be inextricably bound up together" (237). Trilling could not accept Wilson's thesis. "I have always resisted Edmund Wilson's wound-and-bow theory," he wrote to the psychologist Saul Rosenzweig in 1944 (*Life in Culture* 113). Trilling was convinced that the artist is no more neurotic than anyone else. The difference, he maintained, is that artists *show* their neurotic conflicts while others—bankers, physicians, professors, lawyers, cabinet ministers—do not. In *The Liberal Imagination*, Trilling elaborated on his objections to Wilson's theory, insisting that genius cannot be reduced to, equated with, or explained by neurosis. "Anyone might be injured as Henry James was, and even respond within himself to the injury as James is said to have done, and yet not have his literary power" (168).

Nevertheless, there is much evidence to support Wilson's theory. Ellenberger was the first to point out the role of "creative illness" in Freud and Jung's lives:

> A creative illness succeeds a period of intense preoccupation with an idea and search for a certain truth. It is a polymorphous condition that can take the shape of depression, neurosis, psychosomatic ailments, or even psychosis. Whatever the symptoms, they are felt as painful, if not agonizing, by the subject, with alternating periods of alleviation and worsening. Throughout the illness the subject never loses the thread of his dominating preoccupation. It is often compatible with normal, professional activity and family life. (447)

George Pickering contends in his 1974 book *Creative Malady* that illness plays a decisive role in the creativity of such otherwise disparate thinkers as Charles Darwin, Florence Nightingale, Mary Baker Eddy, Sigmund Freud, Marcel Proust, and Elizabeth Barrett Browning. The groundbreaking research of Nancy Andreasen (who earned a PhD in English before becoming a psychiatrist) in *The Creating Brain: The Neuroscience of Genius* (2005) and Kay Redfield Jamison in *Touched with Fire: Manic-Depressive Illness and the Artistic Temperament* (1993) demonstrates that a higher incidence of mood disorders exists among literary writers, composers, and artists than in the general population. The poet Robert Lowell grappled with manic-depressive illness, now called bipolar disorder, his entire life. Jamison, who disclosed her own experience with manic depression in *An Unquiet Mind: A Memoir of Moods and Madness* (1995), documents in her 2018 biography *Robert Lowell: Setting the River on Fire* the poet's struggle with mental illness, quoting a question he raises in one of his poems: "'Is getting well ever an art,' he asked, 'or art a way to get well?'" (189). And in my 2019 book *Mad Muse: The Mental Illness Memoir in a Writer's Life and Work*, I show that mental illness is the driving force in the writings of William Styron, Kate Millett, Kay

Redfield Jamison, Linda Gray Sexton, Lauren Slater, Andrew Solomon, and Elyn R. Saks. "One might not have predicted at the beginning of their careers that they were struggling with depression, manic depression, or schizophrenia, but one can see retrospectively, after the publication of their memoirs, how illness catalyzed their work, and how they used their writing in the service of recovery and health" (*Mad Muse* 7).

Those who see a connection between illness and creativity are careful not to imply that "madness" is always a creative act, as R. D. Laing claimed about schizophrenia in *The Divided Self*, or that every act of genius arises from a mood or thought disorder. Trilling never speculates on the origins of art though he hints at its effect on the reader, including a "mithridatic" function: tragic art may help us to "inure ourselves to the greater pain which life will force upon us" (*The Liberal Imagination* 53).

Beyond Culture

One of Trilling's statements about Freud in *Beyond Culture* may have appeared true in the 1960s though certainly not sixty years later: the belief that Freud demonstrated a scientific mind, not a literary one. Now Freud is valued, especially for critics like Harold Bloom, for being primarily a *literary* writer. Trilling's opposition between science and the arts is no longer credible. But there's an even greater surprise about Trilling's discussion of Freud in *Beyond Culture*. For a literary critic who began his career with the hope for social and political change, it's curious that Trilling affirms biology, not culture. But that's what he does in "Freud: Within and Beyond Culture," in which he finds Freud's emphasis on biology liberating. "It is a resistance to and a modification of the cultural omnipotence" (*Beyond Culture* 115). Trilling derives comfort from the idea that there is a "hard, irreducible, stubborn core" of biological urgency within children and adults that culture cannot reach. Conceding that the notion of biological essentialism is pessimistic, suggesting the difficulty of progressive social and political change, Trilling reveals a greater fear in the "growing power of culture to control us by seduction or coercion"; thus, "we must be glad and not sorry that some part of our fate comes from outside the culture" (115). As William M. Chace remarks in his 1980 book, Trilling implicitly argues in *Beyond Culture* against the neo-Freudians who became influential after the Second World War, such as Harry Stack Sullivan, Erich Fromm, and Karen Horney, all of whom deemphasized biological and instinctual drives. Trilling never appears to be troubled by the binary biology *or* culture. Cannot both be shaped for positive change? Trilling's vision of Freud in *Beyond Culture* turns out to be a conservative, even reactionary Freud, a paradoxically illiberal thinker for a literary critic who had once extolled the liberal imagination. If the Freudian superego represents the demands of conscience as shaped by culture, does that mean that Trilling casts his fate with the opposing force, the unruly id? He never answers this question.

Sincerity and Authenticity

Delivered as lectures at Harvard University in 1969–70, when Trilling was the Charles Eliot Norton Professor of Poetry, the six chapters in *Sincerity and Authenticity*, published only three years before his death, represent his final thoughts about psychoanalysis. Much of Trilling's discussion in the final and longest chapter, "The Authentic Unconscious," is a rejection of Sartre's claim in *Being and Nothingness* that psychoanalysis reveals "bad faith" because of its simplistic dualism between the "id" and the "ego." Trilling disagrees, mainly because of Freud's revision of his understanding of the ego, which he now views, in Trilling's words, as "no longer represented as being coextensive with consciousness: some part of the ego is now said to be as far out of sight in the darkness of the unconscious as the id itself" (147). The "momentousness" of Freud's late revision of psychoanalysis is immediately apparent, for he now recognizes that the ego is "no less devious than the id" (148). Freud's revision, in Trilling's view, has restored the "good faith" of psychoanalysis by calling into question its earlier therapeutic optimism.

It should be noted, however, that in his *New York Times* review of Freud's last book, *An Outline of Psycho-Analysis*, written one year before his death, in 1939, Trilling saw a more hopeful Freud. "Freud's positiveness, his belief that truth could actually be found, is also the sign of something particular in his temperament, particular in his vision of the world." What makes Freud preeminent among modern theorists of the mind, Trilling continues, is his "deep therapeutic commitment to the human cause" (*A Gathering of Fugitives* 57). Has Freud grown more pessimistic—or has Trilling? Both, one may answer, but it nonetheless remains true that far from being troubled by Freud's pessimism in *Civilization and Its Discontents* and his late essay "Analysis Terminable and Interminable" (1937), Trilling found something consoling in it, perhaps a sign or symptom of his growing conservatism amid the turbulent events of the 1960s, when the country, in general, and Columbia University, in particular, were torn apart by the Vietnam War and racial tensions. Trilling's characterization of the "Freudian ethos" as a "patrician posture of simultaneous acceptance of and detachment from life in civilization" (*Sincerity and Authenticity* 168) seems a self-characterization.

Diana Trilling: *The Beginning of the Journey*

According to Diana Trilling, her husband began analysis in 1939. In *The Beginning of the Journey*—the title is an allusion to her husband's 1947 novel *The Middle of the Journey*, suggesting their linked destinies—she discloses that he suffered from depression his entire life:

> As pathologies go, his depression was mild but it was nevertheless a clinical symptom and a more troubling phenomenon than mere dejection or downheartedness. For no perceptible reason he would suddenly fall into an extreme bleakness of mood and be unable to function with appropriate spirit. At these times he regarded me as his enemy and acted toward me as if it were I who were the cause of his despondency—there was always anger at the heart of his depression. Yet no one of his acquaintance and no one with whom he worked outside the home was aware that he was subject to these alterations of mood. (161–2)

The Trillings were married for forty-six years, and by most accounts the union was a happy one, yet she discloses his "annihilating verbal assaults," perhaps five or six times a year, when he accused her of being the worst person in the world, having "ruined" his life. "I would come to feel of these scenes that they represented an encapsulated lunacy which from time to time took possession of an otherwise superlatively sane individual" (254).

Lionel Trilling and Diana Trilling were both in psychoanalysis for much of their adult lives, sometimes with the same analyst, other times with different analysts. They had strikingly different attitudes toward Freud. Lionel Trilling was mainly interested in the literary Freud, a giant in the history of ideas, not in the creator of a new system of therapy. By contrast, Diana Trilling was primarily interested in Freud the physician, the man who undertook to heal his patients. She points out an intriguing contradiction in her husband's use of psychoanalysis. "He was absorbed with the literature of human motivation and much gifted in its comprehension, but in the living of his life he was not drawn to the probing of motive. The disinclination probably carried over into his treatment and hindered its progress" (226). In *Speaking of Literature and Society*, she describes her husband as an "overbearing hypochondriac" (414), a problem that did not seem to have been alleviated by analysis.

Diana Trilling's Criticisms of Psychoanalysis

Diana Trilling acknowledges candidly in *The Beginning of the Journey* that she turned to psychoanalysis because she was in "emotional trouble" (49). She never doubts that she would not have become a published author without psychoanalysis. She became early in her career a passionate defender of orthodox psychoanalysis, like her husband, even if it meant distancing herself from feminist efforts to achieve equality. In her essay "Men, Women and Sex," first published in *Partisan Review* in 1950 and then reprinted in *Claremont Essays* in 1964, she assails Margaret Mead's *Male and Female* for "using, bending or discarding the Freudian principles at will" (50). She has no sympathy for Mead's substitution of male womb envy for female penis envy, nor does she support Mead's depathologization of homosexuality. The "homosexual story of this century," Diana Trilling warns, "at least seems to suggest a connection between the increase in women's rights and an increase in inversion" (57). (Diana Trilling's view of homosexuality paralleled her husband's: in *The Liberal Imagination* he criticizes the *Kinsey Report* for its acceptance of homosexuality as a "natural" form of sexuality [233].) Additionally, she takes a dim view of Mead's feminist belief that women should enjoy the same freedom to work as men do, fearing that a society that *permits* women to work *compels* them to "seek extra-domestic occupations in order to feel valued" (62).

Over time, however, Diana Trilling became increasingly critical of psychoanalysis and supportive of the growing feminist movement. Without repudiating her acerbic criticisms of Margaret Mead, Diana Trilling began to argue that women can be mothers and workers. She was particularly censorious of her seven different analysts, all physicians, believing, at the time of the writing of her autobiography, near the end of her life when she was a nonagenarian, that she was never adequately analyzed. She found herself developing an unhealthy dependency on each analyst. An early analyst told her that, as a married woman who delayed having a child for many years, she had chosen to have panic attacks instead of babies, an interpretation the analysand found impossible to believe. Another analyst offered to have a "date" at a speakeasy—this was during Prohibition—an illicit proposal that sabotaged therapy. The third analyst invited her to stay with her family, a boundary violation that doomed therapy. Lionel began seeing the same analyst, which rendered husband and wife, as she sardonically observes in *The Beginning of the Journey,* into "sibling rivals, vying for the attention of the same parental figure" (232). Diana Trilling doesn't name the analyst, but he was Nathaniel Ross, her husband's Columbia classmate.

The next analyst, Paul Schilder, whom she saw five times a week for five years, until his death in an auto accident, had never been himself analyzed. Schilder invited the Trillings to vacation with his family, eliciting her comment, "There is no way to be in the company of one's analyst's family without its interfering in the analytical relationship" (*The Beginning of the Journey* 236). Shaken by Schilder's death, Diana Trilling turned to Bertram Lewin, the president of the New York Psychoanalytic Institute and Society, who told her, to her chagrin, that her previous analysts were not properly trained. Lewin directed her to Ruth Mack Brunswick, who had treated the Wolf-Man, Freud's legendary patient. Brunswick proved to be another disaster, addicted to morphine, emotionally unstable, and irresponsible, canceling many sessions without explanation. Although the five years spent in analysis with Brunswick were the most anguished years in Diana Trilling's life, she reached a transformative insight: the need to fulfill her fierce ambition to become a writer, to see her name in print, and thus to reject her father's advice to avoid self-exposure. After Brunswick's death, Diana Trilling began seeing William Dunn, and following his death, she entered treatment with Marianne Kris, Marilyn Monroe's analyst. Kris was probably Diana Trilling's most effective analyst, but she nevertheless shared the antifeminist assumptions of her profession, including the belief that men are active, women, passive. Kris recommended that she "neutralize" (249) her literary criticism by making it less judgmental, advice that the patient angrily rejected. To Diana's complaint that her husband forgot repeatedly to take out the garbage, Kris replied, reprimandingly, that taking out the garbage was a woman's task.

Diana Trilling's tortuous psychoanalytic odyssey was matched by her husband's—though unlike her, he never wrote publicly about his vulnerability. In a 1937 letter to Nathaniel Ross, Lionel Trilling offers a rosy view of therapy, perhaps telling Ross what he wanted to hear:

> I will not say that I have no more of the old depressions, but when they are intense they are of short duration and these are *very* rare, and when they are of any extended time they are perhaps no more than temperamental. At any rate, I can no longer think of them as a problem. Indeed, for a full year now I have

> been almost impossibly cheerful, very energetic, very concentrated in my work. In part, perhaps, this is the result of good material luck but after all we know what *that* means! My writing has improved a great deal, I consider—and so, I gather, do others; my teaching has gone up; I was able to fight the university to reinstatement, and even to an admitted reversal of opinion and a raise. I was even able to ask a fantastically high price for a hack job and get it! So, if you remember the whole situation, you will see I have come a long way; and that I owe you a lot. (*Life in Culture* 71–2)

Yet according to his wife, Trilling's two recurrent problems, depression and writer's block, continued throughout his life, albeit the frequency and force of the problems may have diminished through analysis. One of his analysts was Rudolph Loewenstein, a leader in ego psychology. He and Diana Trilling loathed each other, and she believed that he harmed Lionel by "colluding" in his ambivalence toward her (*The Beginning of the Journey* 252). Lionel Trilling's final analyst was Grace Abbate, whom he saw sporadically in the last years of his life. Diana conveys a poignant detail of the final meeting between Abbate and Lionel. Visiting him at their apartment when she learned he was dying, Abbate kissed Diana and told her that her husband loved her. "It was not something which she had to say, nor was it much to say, but it was enough" (256).

The Beginning of the Journey captures the private side of Lionel Trilling, highlighting his contradictory attitude toward psychoanalysis. His faith in the "privacy of mind," as Diana Trilling calls it, may help to explain his rejection of the wound-and-bow theory of art. "The privacy of mind, independent of the coercions of social or political fashion, would always be the unannounced premise of his work" (203). Trilling believed that the artist's mental health—or mental illness—was another example of an outside coercion that had no place in the creative process.

And yet outside coercions, including issues of race, class, and gender, always find a way into literary judgments. There were no courses on these subjects when Trilling was teaching, but now there are many in university English departments. There are other lenses through which we see literature, including religion and age. (As a late septuagenarian, I interpret literature differently from the way I did a half century ago: it is now easier for me to identify with an old man's folly, as in *King Lear*, than when I was Cordelia's age.) Diana Trilling became a feminist, a leader in the women's movement. Lionel Trilling did not. "It would have been unthinkable for Lionel and his Columbia friends to be moved by ideology in their judgment of literature" (*The Beginning of the Journey* 84). In many of his books, he writes about "masculine potency" but he never describes "feminine potency," not even when writing about Jane Austen, whom he greatly esteemed. In *The Opposing Self*, he refers to Austen's "masculine ideal," as exemplified by her fictional husbands, but he remains silent about her "feminine ideal" of wives (226).

Diana Trilling comes across as more intellectually combative and contentious than her husband. She was often imperious in her judgments, resentful of her husband's refusal to acknowledge the extent of her contributions to his work, bitter that he destroyed her many edits of his writing. The unspoken message of her childhood, she admits early in her autobiography, bred in her an "intellectual confidence—an arrogance, if you will—which I have never lost" (*The Beginning of the Journey* 20). Outspoken and often provocative, she makes statements that she knows will be controversial. "Lionel taught me to think; I taught him to write" (19).

Natalie Robins's 2017 biography, *The Untold Journey: The Life of Diana Trilling*, offers another perspective of the couple. The young Diana comes across as a Freudian true believer, advised by her husband and friends to take down her shingle. When her young son, James, developed a fear of elevators, she was certain she knew the reason: because of his "fear," as she wrote, of "male genitalia being lost on the endless chasm of female genitalia" (142). Later in her career, Diana Trilling became a trenchant critic of Freudian orthodoxy, rejecting his theory of penis envy and female passivity. Robins's biography is sometimes racy, as when she speculates on whether Diana Trilling had extramarital affairs. She fails to probe the depth of the Trillings' marital conflicts and the extent to which psychoanalysis changed their lives. There are also factual errors, as when she misspells the name of "Dr. Grace Addabte" (139). Despite these problems, Robins records much about her biographical subject's life that does not appear in *The Beginning of the Journey*, including the Trillings' parenting style, which she describes as "remotely enlightening, with more than a touch of self-absorption" (181).

"Of This Time, of That Place"

Trilling was known for being a literary and cultural critic, but he always wanted to be a creative writer. "Trilling's celebration of Freud," Adam Phillips remarks in *Equals* (2002), "may be a cover-story for his failure as a novelist" (168). Trilling published only one novel and left another incomplete; *The Journey Abandoned: The Unfinished Novel* appeared in 2008. His most popular short story, "Of This

Time, of That Place," first published in *Partisan Review* in 1943 and frequently reprinted, including in Trilling's own anthology, *The Experience of Literature: A Reader with Commentaries* (1967), interrogates the link between intellectual brilliance, if not genius, and madness. Given Trilling's admiration for Freud and his many years in analysis, the story reaches a conclusion that radically calls into question the possibility of the talking cure.

"Of This Time, of That Place" focuses on the difficulty of moral and psychological judgments, a theme that appears throughout Trilling's writings. The authorial figure, Joseph Howe, is beginning his career as a poet and English professor at a midwestern school, Dwight College, where he encounters in his freshman literature course a student, Ferdinand R. Tertan, whose literary and philosophical erudition marks him as different from his classmates: "'Some professors,' he said, 'are pedants. They are Dryasdusts. However, some professors are free souls and creative spirits. Kant, Hegel, and Nietzsche were all professors.' With this pronouncement he paused. 'It is my opinion,' he continued, 'that you occupy the second category'" (76).

No undergraduate student speaks this way on the first (or last) day of the semester, and Howe doesn't know how to respond. Tertan's motive is not to impress or manipulate his professor, which are the motives of another student in the class, the unctuous Theodore Blackburn, but to express his love for learning. Tertan is intellectually dazzling but also unquestionably odd, speaking in convoluted sentences that defy clarity. Trilling captures Tertan's singularity in a few lines of dialogue: "I think, therefore I am (cogito etc.) but who am I? Tertan I am, but what is Tertan? Of this time, of that place, of some parentage, what does it matter?" (78). Tertan seems to inhabit another realm of being, unlike the others in the story who are bound by time and place. Trilling invests Tertan with a psychological insight that enlivens the story. Howe, who has published three books of poetry, ruminates over a negative review of his most recent volume, but Tertan points out that the poet's inevitable fate is to be misunderstood and underappreciated. Tertan's words comfort the insecure Howe, revealing an unforeseen role reversal between teacher and student.

Howe's dilemma arises when he must grade Tertan's work. Notwithstanding Tertan's insights on life and literature, his devotion to arts and letters, Howe concludes that the boy is "mad," a word that he believes suddenly illuminates everything that mystified him about Tertan, including his faulty rhetoric. Worried about Tertan's "florid leaps beyond fact and meaning" (99), Howe consults with the dean, who shares with him a letter from Tertan expressing deep pedagogical gratitude toward Howe. Because of Howe's intervention, a physician, presumably a psychiatrist, is called in to diagnose Tertan; the prognosis is not good. "A classic case, a classic case," he repeats pitifully, "sure to take a perfectly predictable and inevitable course to a foreknown conclusion" (104). Howe realizes that he has betrayed Tertan, and the story ends with Tertan's haunting appearance at graduation. More isolated than ever, Tertan reflects an image of "perverse majesty" that only deepens Howe's guilt.

"Of This Time, of That Place" is tightly structured, contrasting the madness of two entirely different students, one clinically insane, the other cunning and malicious. The story calls into question "instruments of precision": cameras that record reality, grades that evaluate academic achievement, and psychiatric diagnoses that measure sanity. Trilling succeeds in conveying Howe's dilemma, and as readers, we wonder how we would have reacted to his situation.

The main problem with Trilling's story is that the young English instructor has no clinical authority on which to base his grim judgment of Tertan's madness. There's no evidence of pathology or a psychiatric disorder. That's why the psychiatrist can only refer, maddeningly, to a "classic case." A classic case of what? Tertan never exhibits symptoms of depression, manic-depression, obsessive-compulsive disorder, paranoia, grandiosity, or less common psychiatric disorders, such as derealization/depersonalization. Because we have no access to Tertan's inner thoughts, Howe forms his judgment based solely on the student's spoken and written language and his eccentric physical appearance. Tertan is never a threat to others or to himself. His comments in class bore or amuse his classmates, but he is never disruptive or rude. Why, then, is he clinically insane? He is certainly unusual, odd, bizarre, even freakish—but this does not necessarily betoken neurosis or psychosis. Mark Krupnick suggests in *Lionel Trilling and the Fate of Cultural Criticism* (1986) that the teacher and student in "Of This Time, of That Place" are psychological doubles reminiscent of Joseph Conrad's short story "The Secret Sharer": "the romantic extremist Tertan is disavowed, not integrated into Howe's identity as the outlaw Leggatt is integrated into that of Conrad's young captain" (83). Insofar as Trilling never ironically undercuts Howe's judgment of madness, the latter reflects the authorial point of view. Reading the story oppositionally, against the grain, we can say that Howe is mad for presuming to have clinical expertise that he lacks. It's true that one can imagine teachers becoming crazy reading their students' poorly written essays—perhaps this explains why teachers give up in despair when trying to correct their students' writing—but Tertan's florid prose never becomes a word salad reflective of schizophrenic thought.

Trilling must have recognized this problem with "Of This Time, of That Place," for in his commentary to the story in *The Experience of Literature* he admitted that soon after the story's publication, readers wrote and telephoned him expressing disappointment that he never demonstrated Tertan's insanity. Trilling defended the story, admitting that he based Tertan on one of his own students who "suffered from a deep disturbance" of mind symptomatic of an "extreme mental pathology." Like Howe, Trilling communicated this judgment to his own dean; again like Howe, Trilling felt remorse and disloyalty over his perceived betrayal. Trilling concludes his commentary with certainty over his student's tragic insanity. "Nothing, I fear, can reverse the diagnosis of Tertan's illness" (*The Experience of Literature* 784).

There is an unusual sidebar to this story. In his 1988 book *Lionel Trilling: The Work of Liberation*, Daniel T. O'Hara asserts that "Of This Time, of That Place" is closely based on Trilling's experience with his own undergraduate student Allen Ginsberg, the future visionary poet and author of such groundbreaking works as *Howl* and *Kaddish*, who had a stormy relationship with his teacher. Trilling denied the connection, stating that he had written the story before Ginsberg became his student. Interestingly, in 1946, Trilling wrote a letter to Abram Kardiner, a therapist who cofounded Columbia's psychoanalytic clinic for training and research, housed in the department of psychiatry, urging Ginsberg's admission to the clinic. In the letter Trilling characterizes Ginsberg as a "young man of quite exceptional intellectual gifts" and expresses the hope that a "healthy Ginsberg would have a good chance of becoming a person of real intellectual distinction" (*Life in Culture* 143). It is impossible to know why Trilling believed that the troubled Ginsberg would benefit from verbal therapy while his other student, the model for Tertan, would not.

Regardless of the provenance of Tertan, "Of This Time, of That Place" is psychologically flawed. As Robert Boyers points out in his 1977 book *Lionel Trilling: Negative Capability and the Wisdom of Avoidance*,

> Freud would not have turned away so readily from Tertan, had the young man been his patient and shown himself resistant to a proper transference relationship. Was it not Freud, in fact, surely Trilling's intellectual hero, who taught us to be wary of normative judgments, who urged the most careful distinctions be made between "worthless persons" and "resistant patients?" (14)

Although Boyers's observation is the *only* criticism in his otherwise sympathetic study of Trilling, Diana Trilling denounced the comment in *The Beginning of the Journey*, referring to Boyers's "strangely personal championship of Tertan" and his "attack upon Lionel for mistreating Tertan" (383). One can only conclude that there may have been a degree of truth in Marianne Kris's recommendation to Diana Trilling to "neutralize," or soften, her literary criticism.

"My Father and the Weak-Eyed Devils"

Controversy returned to Lionel Trilling's life, nearly a quarter of a century after his death, when James Trilling published an article in 1999 in *The American Scholar* titled "My Father and the Weak-Eyed Devils." An art historian in Providence, Rhode Island, and the author of two books on the history and language of ornament in the arts, James Trilling writes about his lifelong struggle with attention deficit disorder, ADD, now called attention-deficit/hyperactivity disorder, ADHD. The symptoms, which began when he was around four, included "rages, inability to stay on task," and, as he grew older, "procrastination, daydreaming, insatiable cravings, insensitivity, and disorganization" (23). Only when James Trilling was in his late thirties, after having read an article about ADD, did he apply the diagnosis to himself. After consulting several doctors, he began taking Ritalin (methylphenidate) under a neurologist's supervision. Medication has dramatically improved his life. "The day-to-day effects are perceptible; the long-term effects have transformed my life" (24). The ADD diagnosis came as a revelation to James Trilling, partly because he had spent much of his life in psychoanalysis: eleven years in child analysis, beginning when he was seven years old, and five years in analysis as a young adult, when he almost flunked out of Harvard as a freshman. None of his analysts had mentioned the possibility that his behavioral difficulties could be cured by medication.

ADD remains a contentious psychiatric category, with many mental health professionals believing that it is a catchall label and overdiagnosed. Inattention, hyperactivity, and impulsivity are common problems, critics assert, not a distinct psychological difficulty. But what makes James Trilling's article controversial, even polarizing, is the claim that his father suffered from the same problem, wasting years in psychoanalysis searching for a psychological explanation of a neurological disorder. "It dawned on me that my father had had ADD soon after I recognized the disorder in myself" (24). Invoking Joseph Conrad's *Heart of Darkness*, from which he draws the title of his article, James Trilling maintains that his father, like the haunted Kurtz, confronted violent demons, including a "flabby, pretending, weak-eyed devil." ADD, he concludes, is the "key, the one insight," that makes sense of his father's conflicted life. "All my father's personality flaws," he insists, underscoring his epiphany, "which continued to haunt my mother almost twenty years after his death, were symptoms of attention deficit disorder" (25).

James Trilling's metaphor, *key*, recalls *The Key to All Mythologies*, the book Edward Casaubon devotes his lifetime to writing in George Eliot's masterpiece, *Middlemarch* (1871). The Dryasdust Casaubon never completes the book, symbolizing the failure of his grandiose ambitions. Lionel Trilling also felt like a failure for not fulfilling his own ambitions: the biggest disappointment in his life, according to his son, was his failure to write so little fiction. But the question remains, can a son who is not a clinician accurately diagnose his father decades after his death? Can any psychiatric diagnosis, especially a contested one such as ADD, be retrospectively applied with any degree of accuracy? ADHD made its first appearance in the second edition of the American Psychiatric Association's (APA) *Diagnostic and Statistical Manual of Mental Disorders* (*DSM*), published in 1968; the diagnosis was retheorized in the third edition, published in 1980. James Trilling concedes that although there are a few serious studies of ADD, most of the information about the disorder comes from the self-help literature, which is not always authoritative. Undeterred by the vagaries of psychiatric diagnosis, James Trilling conjectures that his paternal grandfather also suffered from ADD because he "botched" the reading at his bar mitzvah, in England, and was so disgraced that he fled to the United States. In short, the son sees pathology everywhere in his extended family. Perhaps most troubling, he regards his father's writings as symptomatic of illness rather than as efforts toward health and recovery. "My father's 'character-drive to an Olympian or royal position' [words Lionel Trilling had written about himself in a notebook entry] was less an affectation than a defense mechanism. He needed a way to block out unaccustomed or unmanageable stimuli, and he found one, or it found him" (35).

James Trilling never told his mother about his diagnosis because he knew she would be furious: "It would have struck her as a self-serving evasion of reality, and would have made me as alien and degraded in her eyes as if I had joined a cult" (21). One can only imagine how Lionel Trilling would have responded to his son's psychiatric diagnosis. "The horror! The horror!" he might have sputtered, Kurtz's dying words in *Heart of Darkness*. Throughout his life Lionel Trilling pilloried psychoanalytic reductiveness of art, and it's likely that he would have been mortified by his son's psychiatric reductiveness. Father and son were temperamentally opposite; James Trilling seems unaware that his father's weaknesses were also his strengths: "During his entire career as an interpreter of literature, I doubt that my father ever solved a problem, in the sense of marshaling evidence to prove or disprove a theory. On the contrary, he built his career on the mistrust of certainties and was rarely content with a simple answer when a complex one could be found" (36). I suspect that Lionel Trilling would disagree vehemently with the first sentence and concur unapologetically with the second, reminding us that literature and history always call into question conventional wisdom, challenging the pieties of an age. Speak for yourself, the father might have added, not for others. And he might have reminded his son of F. Scott Fitzgerald's observation in the posthumously published *The Crack-Up* (1945), a statement that appears in *The Liberal Imagination*: "The test of a first-rate intelligence is the ability to hold two opposed ideas in the mind at the same time and still retain the ability to function" (238).

James Trilling's article predictably ignited a firestorm of criticism. The *American Scholar* published a dozen responses from academics, ranging from admiration to condemnation. Those who have worked with patients suffering from ADD/ADHD praise the author's honesty and bravery, while others believe that his essay is egotistical and self-serving. The two scholars who have written books on Lionel Trilling reach opposite conclusions: Mark Krupnick, whom James Trilling cites in his article, is largely persuaded by the accuracy of the ADD diagnosis, while Robert Boyers believes that the author's motives were vengeful. The response that generated the most attention came from Paul R. McHugh, director and psychiatrist-in-chief in the department of psychiatry and behavioral sciences at Johns Hopkins University. Enraged by the "pseudo-psychiatric" article, McHugh resigned from the editorial board of the *American Scholar*—a resignation that was reported in the *New York Times*. Diana Trilling's biographer, Natalie Robins, fully accepts the diagnosis, stating confidently that "Lionel was always able to make his ADD work to his advantage" (352).

It's worth noting that James Trilling's attitude toward psychiatry could not be more different from that of the psychiatrist in "Of This Time, of That Place." The former's supreme faith in psychopharmacology contrasts the latter's bleak prognosis of Tertan. Paradoxically, in the final analysis, psychoanalysis as a clinical therapy has no place for James Trilling or Tertan's psychiatrist.

Which Freud?

Freud's writings are so vast, complex, and contradictory as if to suggest many different Freuds. Trilling chose to see the tragic Freud, the man who urged heroic acceptance of the ineluctability of suffering. The tragic Freud, as Trilling proclaims in *Sincerity and Authenticity*, insists upon the "essential immitigability of the human condition as determined by the nature of the mind" (156). Walter Kaufmann (1921–80), the renowned German-American Princeton philosophy professor, saw Freud in the same way, one of the greatest men of the century and the embodiment of what he calls in *The Faith of a Heretic* (1961) the "tragic virtues." Thinking of Freud, Kaufmann remarks that there is no teacher of humility like ambition. In Kaufmann's view, humility and ambition are not admirable by themselves, but fused, they represent a cardinal virtue. Kaufmann then coins a felicitous neologism to describe thinkers like Freud, a word with which Trilling would likely agree: "humbition" (318).

Trilling honored the tragic Freud, but he also acknowledged the hopeful Freud, the man who, though he was not gifted with an abundance of empathy, a concept he often mistrusted, nevertheless believed that his creation, psychoanalysis, could make a difference in his patients' lives. Sometimes the tragic and hopeful Freuds were inextricably linked, as we see at the end of *Studies on Hysteria* (1893–1895), when he provides wry comfort to a patient: "[M]uch will be gained if we succeed in transforming your hysterical misery into common unhappiness. With a mental life that has been restored to health you will be better armed against that unhappiness" (*SE*, vol. 2, 305). One can imagine Professor Howe quoting Freud's words to Tertan, who would appreciate his teacher's insights, compassion, and pedagogical love.

2

Harold Bloom

Agonistic Freud

Like Trilling, with whom he had much in common, culturally, intellectually, and aesthetically, Harold Bloom always celebrated the "literary" Freud, never the "clinical" Freud, the man who founded a new approach to therapy—despite the fact that Bloom, like Trilling, suffered from depression that drove him into therapy in the 1960s. Freud idolaters, Trilling and Bloom believed that he was one of the greatest writers of his age, of any age, yet they disdained psychoanalytic literary criticism, rejecting it as an abomination. Trilling and Bloom saw Freud differently, the former as "tragic," the latter as "agonistic," but both found inspiration in his writings.

Bloom was, arguably, the most famous—and infamous—literary critic of the past half century. He was certainly the most influential and prolific. The *New York Times* printed two separate obituaries: the first, by Dinitia Smith, appearing on the day of Bloom's death, October 14, 2019, at age eighty-nine; the second, by Dwight Garver, published one day later. Bloom called himself, as Smith reported, a "monster" of reading, capable of memorizing a four hundred-page book in an hour. He could recite from memory all of Shakespeare's poems and plays; John Milton's *Paradise Lost*, nearly eleven thousand lines long; and much of nineteenth-century British Romantic poetry. Garver cited a story about a graduate student who, telephoning Bloom's home, was told by his wife that he was writing a book. "That's all right," the student said, "I'll wait." Blessed with a photographic memory that contributed to his encyclopedic mind, Bloom devoured literature. He was the author of over forty books, not to mention the editor of six hundred books published by Chelsea House. Several of Bloom's tomes, some of which were over seven hundred pages long, were bestsellers, including *The Western Canon: The Books and Schools of the Ages* (1994), *The Book of J* (1990), *Shakespeare: The Invention of the Human* (1998), *How to Read and Why* (2000), and *Genius: A Mosaic of One Hundred Exemplary Creative Minds* (2002). Bloom's *The Anxiety of*

Influence, published in 1973 and translated into forty-five languages, remains the single most noteworthy—and hotly debated—theory of artistic creativity.

A Department of One

The son of struggling immigrant parents born in Eastern Europe, Bloom was raised as an Orthodox Ashkenazi Jew in the Bronx, the youngest of five children. His mother was "intensely religious," as he indicated in the posthumously published *The Bright Book of Life* (2020), while his father, a garment maker, was "indifferent to such 'foolishness'" (511). Yiddish was his first language, Hebrew, his second. Bloom didn't begin speaking English until he was six. He went to Cornell as an undergraduate on a full scholarship and then earned his PhD in English from Yale, where he taught his entire life, rising to Sterling Professor of Humanities, the most prestigious academic rank at Yale, in a "department of one," as he wryly observed in *Genius*, a "teacher without colleagues." While remaining in the Yale English Department, he was Berg Professor of English at New York University from 1988 to 2004. If genius is the capacity to absorb everything, then he was undeniably one himself. Indeed, Bloom was the recipient of a MacArthur "Genius" fellowship as well as many other awards and honors, including the American Academy of Arts and Letters Gold Medal for Belles Lettres and Criticism. Passionate about reading, writing, and teaching, he vowed that he would leave the classroom in a body bag—a large one, he sardonically added. He taught his last class from home four days before his death.

Bloom was sui generis, a force of nature, a larger-than-life figure because of his unsurpassed knowledge, his fierce devotion to Shakespeare (he called himself Bloom Brontosaurus Bardolater), his championing of the aesthetic pleasure of literature, and his unfashionable belief in literary character in an age that proclaimed, in Roland Barthes's words, the death of the author. He was contemptuous of those who advocated feminist, post-structuralist, multicultural, or historical approaches to literary study, all of which he pilloried as the "School of Resentment." Bloom asserted repeatedly that Hamlet was the greatest character in literature, but he most closely identified with Falstaff, albeit a Jewish version, whom he resembled in his exuberance, girth, vitality, and mordant wit. Combining high and popular culture, Bloom viewed himself as a Marxist, referring to Groucho, not Karl. Bloom did not suffer fools—or unfriendly literary critics—gladly; but no one could deny his intimidating erudition or his lifelong love for literature.

Bloom was a compulsive writer, and he wrote to the end of his life, dying in harness, like his hero Freud, working to live and living to work, not only to keep death at bay but also to remain connected to his readers and pay tribute to the poets and novelists, living and dead, who made life worthwhile. Bloom's final books have a deeply moving elegiac quality. The title of *The Bright Book of Life*, an allusion to D. H. Lawrence's affirmative vision of the novel, conveys Bloom's reverence for life and literature, which he believed were inseparable. The other book published posthumously in 2020, *Take Arms Against a Sea of Troubles: The Power of the Reader's Mind Over a Universe of Death*, words spoken by Hamlet in his "to be or not to be" soliloquy, offers fascinating insight into Bloom's final years.

An Overview of Bloom's Writings on Freud

Throughout his career, Bloom insisted that Freud was among the greatest writers of all time; he mentions the founder of psychoanalysis in nearly all of his books. Yet Bloom was, paradoxically, no fan of psychoanalysis. Given Bloom's astounding literary productivity—he claimed that he wrote *The Anxiety of Influence* in three days—it's remarkable that the one book he could not complete was on Freud. "From 1970 through 1985," he confesses in *The Daemon Knows: Literary Greatness and the American Sublime* (2015), "I attempted to complete a large study of Freud, to be called *Transference and Authority*, but my own gathering ambivalence toward Freud's work finally defeated me. A huge unfinished manuscript rests abandoned up in my attic, testifying to what I no longer seem to know" (452–3). It was, as far as I know, Bloom's only failure to complete a manuscript.

Freudian references suffuse Bloom's writings. Although there are citations to Jung but not to Freud in Bloom's first book, *Shelley's Mythmaking* (1959), an expansion of his Yale doctoral dissertation, Freudian references abound in his next books on British romanticism: *The Visionary Company* (1961), *Blake's Apocalypse: A Study in Poetic Argument* (1963), *Yeats* (1970), and *The Ringers in the Tower* (1971). It was in *The Anxiety of Influence*, as we shall see, that Bloom used Freudian concepts to advance a new theory of poetic creativity. Bloom continued to appropriate Freudian theory throughout the 1970s and early 1980s in such books as *A Map of Misreading* (1975), *Poetry and Repression* (1976), and *Agon: Towards a Theory of Revisionism* (1982). Unlike some literary critics who highlight only a handful of Freud's texts, or who seize upon a single psychoanalytic idea, Bloom refers to nearly all of Freud's writings. His last books recall in their funereal tone and expression of grief Freud's 1917 essay "Mourning and Melancholia," but the literary critic seems to reject the psychoanalyst's injunction that we must terminate our relationship with the dead, suggestive of Bloom's continuing bond with Freud.

Freud remains for Bloom a "greater dialectical critic of Romanticism than any analyst who has emerged from Structuralism, including Lacan," Bloom avows in the epilogue to *The Visionary Company* (464). Blake's contraries anticipated Freud's "civil war" between the ego and the id, he observes in *Blake's Apocalypse* (91). Freud understood that "poetry might be a discipline roughly parallel to psychoanalysis," Bloom avers in *Yeats*, "one in which the poet and his reader, like the analyst and his patient, would find not cure but a balance of opposites, not ultimates beyond knowledge but self-knowledge, not a control over fate but self-control" (215). In *The Ringers in the Tower*, Bloom suggests that, like Blake and Wordsworth, Freud provides "both a map of the mind and a profound faith that the map can be put to a saving use" (13). Sometimes Bloom quotes Freud from memory, not bothering to look up a passage or footnote it, as when he writes in *The Ringers in the Tower*, "Somewhere Freud has a splendid sentence that anyone unhappy in love can take to heart: 'Object-love was at first ego-libido and can be again transformed into ego-libido'" (23). The quote comes from Freud's 1917 essay "A Difficulty in the Path of Psycho-Analysis" (*SE*, vol. 17, 139).

Bloom often quotes in several books the same Freudian passages. In a single paragraph in *Kabbalah and Criticism* (1975) he cites Freud; Isaac Luria, the sixteenth-century mystical rabbi identified with the Kabbalah, the Jewish esoteric tradition; Sandor Ferenczi, the Hungarian-born psychoanalyst who became a close friend of Freud and then, falling out of favor, an enemy; and Gershom Scholem, the German-born Israeli philosopher regarded as the founder of modern Kabbalism:

> Scholem theorizes that Luria saw the whole function of creation as being God's catharsis of Himself, a vast sublimation in which His terrible rigor might find some peace. This is not unlike Freud's extraordinary explanation as to why people fall in love, which is to avoid an over-filled inner self. As man must love, in Freud's view, in order to avoid becoming sick, so Luria's God had to create, for His own health. But He could create only by catastrophe, in Luria's judgment, an opinion again very like that of Freud's disciple, Ferenczi, whose book *Thalassa* also ascribes every act of creation to a necessary catastrophe. (41)

Bloom was thinking of Freud's passage in his 1914 essay "On Narcissism: An Introduction": "A strong egoism is a protection against falling ill, but in the last resort we must begin to love in order not to fall ill, and we are bound to fall ill if, in consequence of frustration, we are unable to love" (*SE*, vol. 14, 85). Part of Bloom's boundless interdisciplinary scholarship is seeing prefigurations and postfigurations of Freudian doctrine everywhere—and offering his own synthetic insights to produce new knowledge.

The Anxiety of Influence

Bloom's signature work, the book by which he will best be remembered, *The Anxiety of Influence*, is indebted to Freud's 1909 essay "Family Romances," in which he argues that a son wishes to replace his father to earn his mother's love. "The liberation of an individual, as he grows up, from the authority of his parents," Freud writes in the opening sentence, "is one of the most necessary though one of the most painful results brought about by the course of his development" (*SE*, vol. 9, 237). Bloom offers six "revisionary ratios" in his theory of influence, all but one of which contain obscure names: *Clinamen*, poetic misreading or, to use the word Bloom popularized, misprision; *Tessera*, completion and antithesis; *Kenosis*, repetition and discontinuity; *Daemonization*, a word Bloom defamiliarizes as the counter-sublime; *Askesis*, or purgation and solipsism; and *Apophrades*, the return of the dead. Bloom's "ephebe," the young poet who must misread precursors to achieve greatness, puts into practice these six revisionary moves. In Bloom's Oedipal interpretation of influence, strong poets always struggle against their precursors, recreating themselves, self-begotten, as in Freud's family romance. Revising one of Freud's iconic sentences, "where id was, there ego shall be," Bloom defines *Kenosis* as "Where the precursor was, there the ephebe shall be" (91); similarly, he limns *Daemonization* in two ways: "Where my poetic father's *I* was, there *it* shall be" or "there my *I* is, more closely mixed with *it*" (110).

In the preface to the second edition of *The Anxiety of Influence*, published in 1997, Bloom includes Shakespeare in his discussion, asserting that the bard experienced anxiety toward his major precursor and literary rival, Christopher Marlowe. Bloom rejects critics who argue that the anxiety of influence is simply a reworking of Oedipal rivalry, a charge he probably believed detracted from his own originality. Cultural belatedness is never acceptable to strong poets, Bloom asserts, nor is it acceptable, one infers, to strong literary critics like himself.

Bloom's Freud was relentlessly agonistic, as was Bloom himself. He refers to Freud's "beautiful humaneness" (107), but this is not what most impresses Bloom. Rather, he admires Freud the agent provocateur, a role that Bloom himself performed in the embattled world of literary criticism.

Bloom denied that he was revising Freudian theory, but his attitude toward repression could not have been more different from Freud's. The psychoanalyst viewed repression pejoratively to describe unacceptable feelings and desires banished into the unconscious, where they sometimes developed into neuroses, but Bloom had no use for the unconscious. Repression for Bloom became an honorific literary term for the creation of great poetry. A "strong poem" is a "triumph of repression," Bloom enthuses in *Poetry and Repression*, "*not* of sublimation" (*Poetry and Repression* 135). Unlike repression, which forms the cornerstone of Bloom's theory of the anxiety of influence, sublimation never interested him; it remains an "underdeveloped and intellectually unsatisfactory notion," he laments in *Poetry and Repression* (232), a concept he disregarded. Sublimation implies for Freud a successful redirection or resolution of sexual or aggressive energy, a process responsible for the highest achievements of humankind, but Bloom's theory of poetic influence envisions ceaseless warfare. It's impossible to avoid the conclusion that in revising if not misinterpreting Freud, Bloom was engaged in his own creative misprision.

It's ironic that Bloom rejected psychoanalysis as a master narrative yet propounded in *The Anxiety of Influence* his own grand narrative, based not on psychology but on figuration. Bloom's Freud is a highly rhetorical one. As Steve Polansky pointed out in 1981, Bloom sought to "rhetoricize Freudian psychology," seizing back what he thought Freud had taken from poetry (234). Whereas Freud had colonized literature, using it to confirm psychoanalytic theory, believing, as he wrote in "A Short Account of Psycho-Analysis" (1924), that his young science "is in a position to speak the decisive word in all questions that touch upon the imaginative life of man" (*SE*, vol. 19, 208), Bloom struck back, colonizing psychoanalysis, insisting that it was a branch of literature. Both Freud and Bloom were thus engaged in a titanic struggle to dominate the other's domain.

Bloom concedes in *The Anatomy of Influence* (2011), a companion piece to *The Anxiety of Influence*, that an "undersong of foreboding" pervades the earlier work, a hard book for even Bloom to reread because it is "tense with anxious expectations, prompted by the signs of times, which it avoids mentioning" (5). Bloom notes drolly that influenza derives from the Latin word *influential*, evoking the "influence of the stars." Bloom's 1973 study served as an irritant to many who read it. In retrospect, Bloom realized that *The Anxiety of Influence* was a "weapon" against the growing cultural wars of the 1960s and 1970s.

Bloom never seemed troubled by the theory's essentialism, upon which literary critics immediately pounced. Combining psychoanalytic defense mechanisms, rhetorical theory, and Jewish mysticism, Bloom's anxiety of influence "is one of the most baroque constructions in literary critical history," Arthur Bradley complains, "and by the end of the 1970s the critics were already queuing up to demolish it" (262). Elizabeth Wright does not demolish Bloom in *Psychoanalytic Criticism* (2002), but she points out the irony that although poems are for him relational events, an example of intertextuality, dependent upon the poet's projection and introjection, he never discusses the British object-relations theorists, such as Melanie Klein. Nor does Bloom discuss the creation of poetry as an act of reparation, arising from the need to mourn and heal conflict. Bloom's arcane terms have not become household words in literary criticism, and Bloom himself stopped using them in his later writings.

Appropriating Freud's Death Instinct

Beyond the Pleasure Principle (1920) holds special interest to Bloom, not because of the "repetition-compulsion principle," the need to repeat traumatic events for the purpose of mastery, but because of the highly speculative "death instinct," where Freud conjectures the existence of an "*urge inherent in organic life to restore an earlier state of things* which the living entity has been obliged to abandon under the pressure of external disturbing forces" (*SE*, vol. 18, 36; italics in original). The "*aim of all life is death*," Freud adds paradoxically two pages later: "*inanimate things existed before living ones*." Bloom quotes the last sentence in *A Map of Misreading* (91) and then shows its relevance to poetry and literary criticism. In Bloom's view, the literal meaning of a text is death insofar as the former represents anteriority, an earlier state of existence, whereas a trope represents a defense against death, a "*willing error*, a turn from literal meaning in which a word or phrase is used in an improper sense, wandering from its rightful place. A trope is therefore a kind of falsification, because every trope (like every defense, which is similarly a falsification) is necessarily an interpretation, and so a mistaking" (93).

Unlike most clinicians (with the exception of Kleinians and Lacanians), who have rejected Freud's death instinct, Bloom admires "Freud's most audacious hypothesis" (*A Map of Misreading* 91). He regards Freud's insights into narcissism as a defensive movement against the death drive. Bloom preferred Freud's late writings, including *Beyond the Pleasure Principle* and *Civilization and Its Discontents* (1930), both of which are admittedly speculative and philosophical, to Freud's early writings. Freud's radical dualism in his late writings appealed to Bloom, himself the author of a radical theory of poetic originality.

Curiously, Bloom was never interested in Freud's case studies, which have commanded great attention from literary scholars. Nor was he interested in Freud's most popular books, *The Interpretation of Dreams* (1900) and *The Psychopathology of Everyday Life* (1901). Bloom ignored *Jokes and Their Relation to the Unconscious* (1905), one of Freud's most lively and entertaining books. Bloom regarded *Inhibitions, Symptoms and Anxiety* (1926) as Freud's greatest book for students of literature, a judgment with which few if any literary scholars would concur.

Praise for the Creator, Not the Creation

In lauding the literary Freud, Bloom dismisses nearly all psychoanalytic literary critics. Most of his comments are not only critical but also mocking, as when he tells us in *Poetry and Repression* that he doesn't blame Freud for "what is now called psychoanalytic literary criticism, since none of it that I have read merits being called either psychoanalysis or literary criticism" (212). Bloom was, ironically, a Freudian when he spoke about the creator and a Schadenfreudian when he spoke about the creation. He was fond of quoting the Viennese satirist Karl Kraus's aphorism that psychoanalysis is the disease it purports to cure. Bloom considered Freud as one of the most tendentious of writers, but the same observation can be made about Bloom himself, except, perhaps, in his last books, where he shows a less intellectually aggressive side. Bloom has no use for neo-Freudians like Herbert Marcuse and Norman O. Brown, whom he calls in *Figures of Capable Imagination* (1976) "false prophets" (xii). He never mentions his exact contemporary, Norman N. Holland, who, like Bloom himself, was a Shakespeare scholar. One of the few psychoanalytic critics Bloom praises is Lionel Trilling, whom he cites in *Wallace Stevens* (1977). In 1940, Lionel Trilling, in his ambivalent and moving essay *Freud and Literature*, remarked that "it was left to Freud to discover how, in a scientific age, we still feel and think in figurative formations, and to create, what psychoanalysis is, a science of tropes, metaphors and its variants, synecdoche and metonymy" (376). Unlike Trilling, however, Bloom did not regard psychoanalysis as a science; it was, instead, a scientism, a mythology that did not recognize the metaphorical nature of its own storytelling.

Bloom often goes out of his way to interject a facetious comment about Freudian enthusiasts, as when he observes in *Genius* the number of times in his youth when he had dinner or went to a movie with them as they "carried along a volume or two by the founder of psychoanalysis" (749). Yet most of Bloom's criticisms were not of the creator but of the creation. "Though a frustrated crew of current resenters stigmatize Freud as a charlatan," he opines in *Genius*, "they do him violence, he being so majestical" (179), an oblique allusion, possibly, to the leading contemporary Schadenfreudian, Frederick Crews.

Bloom's theory of the anxiety of influence was based on early Freud, but in *Agon* he questions his early belief in the accuracy of the family romance. He admits that while writing a book on transference and authority in Freud's writings—the book he never completed—he realized that Freud's most important work is *Totem and Taboo* (1913)—despite the fact that Freud "dissimulated, productively and shrewdly, by using his own mythopoeic versions of taboo and totemism as the covert models for the analytical transference" (*Agon* 44). Freud is still Bloom's prophet of agon and ambivalence, still among the greatest of twentieth-century writers, but whatever belief Bloom may have had in psychoanalysis as a healing therapy is gone. Applying the anxiety of influence to Freud, Bloom suggests that the psychoanalyst's darkest precursor in *Beyond the Pleasure Principle* is Freud himself, for he says one thing but means another in his 1920 book. "Against his own drive for scientific authority, he now swerves into a purely speculative authority" (130). Bloom also asserts in *Agon* that because Freud is such a strong writer whose books and articles lend themselves to multiple interpretations, there are no "true" or "correct" interpretations of his work. Freud is, like the greatest poets, astonishingly original. In *The Breaking of the Vessels* (1982), published in the same year as *Agon*, 1982, he declares that Freud is "*the* inescapable mythologist of our age," a figure whose claims to science "should be shrugged aside forever; that is merely his mask" (62). By contrast, Jung is, in Bloom's view, a "mere literalizer of anterior mythologies" (*Agon* 108).

Freud's Jewishness

The ghostly Freud haunted Bloom's dreams, as he wryly concedes in *Ruin the Sacred Truths* (1989), one of his many books on religious criticism. Freud appears in Bloom's dreams as "Yahweh the Father, complete with cigars and Edwardian three-piece suit" (106). Freud's Jewishness became increasingly important to Bloom. The center of Freud's work, Bloom asserts, repression, appears to be "profoundly Jewish" (158). Moreover, in Freud's tripartite map of the mind, the superego is the most Jewish, according to Bloom. "In his late book that we know as *Civilization and Its Discontents*, Freud writes a kind of tragicomedy or even apocalyptic farce, in which the superego compels the ego to abandon its aggressivities, but then goes on punishing the ego for supposedly manifesting precisely those aggressivities" (159). It's surprising that Bloom never cites, in support of the role of Freud's Jewishness in the construction of psychoanalytic theory, the pioneering work of Sander L. Gilman, who has written more convincingly about this subject than any other scholar. Bloom would have little sympathy for Gilman's argument in *Freud, Race, and Gender* (1993) that to understand Freud's Jewishness, one must grasp the association between Jews and disease in fin de siècle Vienna. Nor would Bloom have been receptive to Gilman's idea that Freud's emphasis on the castration complex derived in large part from the belief that circumcision, the Jewish marker of difference, reflected the prevailing anti-Semitic view of the "feminized" Jewish male.

Bloom returns to the Jewish superego in his next study, *The Book of J*, where he argues that the Hebrew Bible was written by an author who was likely a woman. In one of the greatest of ironies, Bloom suggests, "Freud is J's descendant and is haunted by J's Yahweh in the figure of the Superego. The Punch and Judy Show element in Freud's scenario of the relations between Superego and hapless Ego is precisely like J's dark comedy of the relations between Yahweh and the hapless Israelites in the Wilderness" (305–6). In *The American Religion: The Emergence of the Post-Christian Nation* (1992), Bloom derides the hapless ego and its equally hapless proponents, housed in fanatical Institutes for Psychoanalysis. "The Freudian Fundamentalists (of the Ego Psychology sect) are as literal minded as the Southern Baptist Fundamentalists, and both groups believe that their sacred texts, the [authorized] Standard Edition of Freud and the Holy Bible, somehow interpret themselves and are inerrant" (24). Curiously, Bloom never caricatures Anna Freud, the leader of ego psychology and the author of *The Ego and the Mechanisms of Defense* (1937; rev. 1976), which Bloom praises in several books. Had Anna Freud not written *The Ego and the Mechanisms of Defense*, he admits in *The Anatomy of Influence*, he never would have been able to write *The Anxiety of Influence*.

Bloom condemned multicultural approaches to literature, believing that discussions of race, class, and gender destroyed the aesthetic pleasure of reading. Yet in his later writings, he paid attention to religion as a lens through which readers interpret and evaluate literature. He regarded T. S. Eliot as a virulently anti-Semitic poet and literary critic, along with Ezra Pound. Reading Shakespeare's portrait of Shylock in *The Merchant of Venice* was a wounding experience for Bloom, so much so that he asserted it might have been better for Jews had the play never been created.

Freud and *The Western Canon*

In *The Western Canon*, his best-known book after *The Anxiety of Influence*, Bloom devotes a chapter to a Shakespearean reading of Freud, an interpretation that he develops five years later in *Shakespeare: The Invention of the Human*. Bloom begins the chapter in *The Western Canon* with a characteristic dismissal of Freudian literary criticism, comparing it to the Holy Roman Empire: "not holy, not Roman, not an empire; not Freudian, not literary, not criticism" (371). Unimpressed with the Freud–Jones interpretation that Hamlet delayed in following the ghost's injunction to kill Claudius because of an unresolved Oedipus complex, Bloom maintains that Shakespeare induced intense anxiety in Freud that led to a reductive Oedipal interpretation of *Hamlet*. Additionally, Freud's anxiety, in Bloom's view, led to his crazy belief that the Earl of Oxford wrote Shakespeare, a theory propounded by a man aptly named J. Thomas Looney. "How could Freud," Bloom asks, "possibly the best mind of our century, have fallen into such zaniness?" (373). Bloom adds a gratuitous comment, remarking that "[a]s a therapy, psychoanalysis is dying, perhaps already dead: its canonical survival must be in what Freud wrote" (376).

Bloom's Depression—and Therapeutic Fury

Bloom never wrote a memoir, unlike his close friend and colleague Geoffrey Hartman, the author of *A Scholar's Tale: Intellectual Journey of a Displaced Child of Europe* (2007), but his last books, though mainly literary criticism, read in part like a spiritual autobiography. His most personal disclosure appears first in *Omens of Millennium* and then, in more detail, in later books, including *Take Arms Against a Sea of Troubles*. Bloom devotes only a paragraph in *Omens of Millennium* to the event, telling us that in the "middle of the journey," in 1965, at age thirty-five, he found himself "immersed in acute melancholia," lost the ability to read and teach, and then, at the suggestion of his Yale psychiatrist, traveled to London where he saw an eminent Pakistani psychiatrist, whom he immediately despised and stopped seeing after only three sessions. Bloom's "fury was therapeutic" and partly dislodged him from his dark night of the soul (24–5). That's all he discloses about the experience.

One can only speculate why Bloom returns to the troubling event in *Take Arms Against a Sea of Troubles*: perhaps the book's title, which refers to Hamlet's melancholy, reminds him of his own depressed state of mind in 1965. For a year and a half, he acknowledges, he was in analysis with Theodore Lidz, a "shrewd and humane practitioner" who terminated treatment because Bloom was paying him "so that he could endure endless lectures on the right way of reading Freud" (564). Bloom then summarizes his three disastrous sessions with the anti-Semitic Masud Khan, who insulted Bloom's intelligence and physical appearance. Bloom's account of therapy is not without caustic humor: Ridiculing Bloom's uncombed hair, Khan gave him a comb to which the unkempt analysand responded by saying he didn't use one.

In a biographical study published in the *New Yorker* in 2002, Larissa MacFarquhar offers additional information about Bloom's depression in the mid-1960s. During this time, he stopped teaching a popular graduate course on psychoanalysis because of a problem he called Uncle Siggy's Revenge.

> Each year, as the semester progressed, Bloom gradually lost control in the most rococo way. "My transference to Freud got more and more dubious," he says, "and the parapraxes [Freudian slips] would become so monstrous that in the final two classes everything was an unintended pun or double-entendre or some terrible self-revelation. I wasn't saying what I meant to say at all. It became occult!"

Bloom never reveals the origins of his depression nor why he was so argumentative with Lidz (1910–2001), who was Sterling Professor of Psychiatry at Yale and known primarily for his research on the interpersonal causes of schizophrenia, a subject that Bloom unexpectedly mentions, in passing, in several books, including *The Anxiety of Influence*, *Kabbalah and Criticism*, *Agon*, *Omens of Millennium* (1996), and *Fallen Angels* (23). Bloom had a personal interest in schizophrenia; as Kate Maltby reported in her obituary of Bloom, one of his sons suffers from the thought disorder.

Why did Bloom remain in analysis with Lidz for so long, one wonders, merely arguing about reading Freud? Was he not interested in reading himself, understanding his conflicts and defenses? Did he consider the possibility that arguing over how to read Freud might betoken clinical resistance, something to be overcome before he could confront deeper conflicts? How did Bloom's wife, Jeanne, a school psychologist presumably sympathetic to verbal therapy, feel about her husband's combativeness in analysis?

There's no evidence Bloom feared, as did Rilke, that being in analysis would destroy his creative angels as well as his demons. Nor did he reject a lengthy and expensive analysis for shorter forms of psychotherapy. Nowhere does he comment on other forms of verbal therapy. Words apparently never failed Bloom in the classroom or when he was lecturing publicly, as he often did. Nevertheless, it's hard to imagine Bloom in psychoanalysis, for although in his later books he writes about his mentors and friends, he never discloses much about the formative influences on his life. He reveals little about his parents and siblings, and nothing about his wife or children. We can only guess how he thought about himself as a child, adolescent, and young man. Bloom never writes about the personal (as opposed to intellectual) influences on his life. Nor does he discuss what he began to learn about himself and others through the study of psychoanalysis. In *Omens of Millennium* he is unsure when his identity came into existence. "At sixty-five, I find myself uncertain just when my self was born. I cannot locate it in my earliest memories of childhood, and yet I recall its presence in certain memories of reading" (15). Preferring to analyze texts to analyzing himself, Bloom would make an unlikely candidate for psychoanalysis.

The talking cure did not help lift Bloom's depression. Rather, it was the reading cure (and the writing cure) that raised his spirit. Bloom never directly wrote about, much less theorized, the ways in which literature can have a therapeutic influence on a reader in crisis. Geoffrey Hartman raises this question in *A Scholar's Tale*, albeit without attempting to answer it. The Yale literary critics—Bloom, Hartman, Paul de Man, J. Hillis Miller, and the French philosopher Jacques Derrida, who often taught at Yale—were interested primarily in the literary Freud, and although they emphasized the difficulty of reading, particularly reading as an act of crisis leading to an aporia, an irresolvable internal contradiction, they were wary of the ways in which literature could be therapeutic for writer and reader alike.

Bloom's experience with Lidz and Khan convinced him that psychoanalysis did not work. Nor does he recommend any other form of psychotherapy. It seems unlikely that any analyst could have persuaded Bloom to lay down his guard and open up about his life, something he hints at but never does in his other books. A week before his death, Bloom was scheduled to give a talk on Freud to the American Psychoanalytic Association (APsA) in New York City. The psychoanalysts might have appreciated his enthusiasm for Freud the writer, but it's not likely they would have been pleased by his devaluation of their own profession. One can only imagine how Bloom would have responded to the statement expressed by Geoffrey Hartman in *A Scholar's Tale* that psychoanalysis is, "above all, the creation of a humane treatment for those needing medical attention of a psychological kind and who had been neglected or even abused" (126). Bloom never concedes this in his own writings.

Healing Through Reading and Writing

To my knowledge, Bloom never used the words bibliotherapy or "scriptotherapy," coined by the psychoanalytic literary critic Suzette A. Henke in her 1998 book *Shattered Subjects: Trauma and Testimony in Women's Life-Writing*. Since the last quarter of the twentieth century, literary critics as well as clinical, experimental, and social psychologists have explored the therapeutic value of reading and writing, a subject Bloom never theorizes but enacts in his late writings. The University of Texas psychologist James Pennebaker showed in his 1990 book *Opening Up: The Healing Power of Expressing Emotions* how writing facilitates well-being, including heightening the immune system. Louise DeSalvo reaches a similar conclusion in *Writing as a Way of Healing: How Telling Our Stories Transforms Our Lives* (1999). Two books with the same titles albeit different subtitles—Mark Bracher's *The Writing Cure: Psychoanalysis, Composition, and the Aims of Education* (1999), and *The Writing Cure: How Expressive Writing Promotes Health and Emotional Well-Being* (2002), edited by Stephen J. Lepore and Joshua M. Smyth—affirm the healing benefits of personal writing. More recently, Judith Harris shows how elegy writing is a therapeutic strategy for coping with grief; she makes the important distinction in *The Poetry of Loss* (2023) between writing *about* bereavement and writing *through* bereavement. It's likely that the early Bloom would have been unimpressed with these writings, though the later Bloom would have acknowledged that reading and writing can lead to self-healing.

Reading Emerson was transformative to Bloom during his psychological distress. Earlier in *Take Arms Against a Sea of Troubles*, he characterizes himself as a "devout Emersonian since 1965" (9), the onset of his midlife crisis. Next to Walt Whitman, Emerson was the American writer Bloom admired the most. It is not an exaggeration to say that reading Emerson may have saved Bloom's life. He refers to this fraught time in *Where Shall Wisdom Be Found?* (2004), declaring that during his depression he read "backward and forward everything that Emerson and Freud had written, finally choosing the Concord sage as lifetime guide, because he speaks to me so directly, more so even than Freud" (120). Why was reading Emerson healing? Bloom never addresses this question, but we may infer from his many discussions what he loved about Emerson. One of Bloom's favorite Emerson passages, which he cites in *Poetry and Repression*, affirms resiliency: "I am Defeated all the time; yet to Victory I am born" (243); the same quote appears in *Figures of Capable Imagination* (64). Another cherished Emerson quote, Bloom's favorite, appears in *Agon*, affirming creativity: "In every work of genius we recognize our own rejected thoughts; they come back to us with a certain alienated majesty" (170). Still another favorite, which Bloom quotes in *Kabbalah and Criticism*, testifies to Emerson's embracing of contradiction: "a foolish consistency is the hobgoblin of little minds" (109). Emerson's writings, particularly his 1841 essay "Self-Reliance," spoke to Bloom in ways that Freud's writings never did.

Although Bloom asserts in *Agon* that we read to usurp, we also read to be inspired and strengthened, to find wholeness and well-being, to connect with others, to overcome loneliness, to discover how we are similar to and different from others. To judge from Bloom's writings, loneliness was a major, perhaps *the* major problem in his life. "As the years pass," he remarks in *Ruin the Sacred Truths*, "I develop an even greater horror of solitude, of finding myself having to confront sleepless nights and baffled days in which the self ceases to know how to talk to itself" (131). Self-talk is a cognitive strategy used to create an inner dialogue to facilitate positive thinking, but for Bloom, self-talk involved the chanting of literature to overcome solitude.

The anxiety of influence dominated Bloom's thinking, but how did he feel about separation anxiety, the stress that children feel when separated from their parents, apprehension that can later develop into anxiety or depression? The British pediatrician and psychoanalyst D. W. Winnicott, whom Bloom must have read, coined the term "transitional object" in 1953 to describe any object, such as a teddy bear, blanket, or doll, that allows a child to remain connected to his or her mother. Arguing that a transitional object is a symbolic breast, Winnicott conjectures that it is the bridge between subjectivity and objectivity, the space between self and other. Books can also be a transitional object. Whenever I travel, I carry my briefcase filled with books; they are my security blanket: nothing is more comforting or soothing than reading during times of stress. I'm not suggesting that Bloom's theory of the anxiety of influence can be reduced to or is commensurate with separation anxiety, but it is significant that in his late books Bloom soothes himself by reciting his favorite poets. "When I am alone and read aloud to myself," he writes in *The Western Canon*, "it is almost always Whitman, sometimes when I desperately need to assuage grief. Whether you read aloud to someone else or in solitude, there is a particular appropriateness in chanting Whitman" (289). Chanting Shakespeare to himself, day and night, has the same self-soothing role, he admits at the beginning of *Take Arms Against a Sea of Troubles*, reminding him of "voices lost and found" (5).

The word *healing* seldom appears in Bloom's early books, but it occurs with increasing frequency in Bloom's later ones, as when he observes in the preface to *How to Read and Why*: "Reading well is one of the great pleasures that solitude can afford you, because it is, at least in my experience, the most healing of pleasures" (19). We read *Great Expectations*, he continues later in the book, "to go home again, to heal our pain" (165). The healing pleasures never disappoint, for unlike cherished relatives and friends who inevitably die, books survive. They also embody timeless insight. Bloom refers to the three criteria in *Where Shall Wisdom Be Found?* that compel him to read and teach: aesthetic splendor, intellectual power, and wisdom, all of which help him withstand the traumas of aging, recovering from life-threatening illness, and the loss of relatives and friends.

A Wounded Storyteller

Beginning around the turn of the twenty-first century, when he became a septuagenarian, Bloom expressed with growing urgency the *personal* need to read, write, and teach. Self-healing is one of the main motives behind his late work. He remarks in the beginning of *Genius* that he resumed writing a week after September 11, 2001. "I cannot know whether I helped my students at all, but I momentarily held off my own trauma, by freshly appreciating genius" (3). He ends *Genius* by lamenting the number of his friends dying or dead. He declares on the opening page of *Where Shall Wisdom Be Found?* that the book "rises out of personal need, reflecting a quest for sagacity that might solace and clarify the traumas of aging, of recovery from grave illness, and of grief for the loss of beloved friends" (1). He mentions, without being specific, returning to teaching after a year spent recovering from ill health. "At the gates of death, I have recited poems to myself, but not searched for an interlocutor to engage in dialect" (62). He begins *The Anatomy of Influence* by suggesting that like the seventeenth-century author of *The Anatomy of Melancholy*, Robert Burton, he too writes to cure his own learnedness, in his case, the sense of "having been overinfluenced since childhood by the greatest Western authors" (ix). An inveterate reader and insomniac, Bloom reveals lying in bed at night, having not recovered mentally from a traumatic injury years earlier, trying to reassure himself that he was still alive. He informs us that in the previous year he was in the hospital for five months with a broken back and other maladies. Bloom returns to his litany of woes in the coda to *The Daemon Knows*, remarking on a "recent three-month delay [that] was involuntary, with a protracted illness followed by an accident" (493). Bloom writes, to use the sociologist Arthur W. Frank's expression, as a wounded storyteller, a person who transforms illness into a narrative. He writes despite illnesses, accidents, and injuries that would silence a less resilient author. Poems are "apotropaic litanies," Bloom avers in *Kabbalah and Criticism* (111), but so are other forms of writing. Bloom's late books eloquently show how writing is part of his *ongoing* self-healing.

In his last three books, published in 2019 or posthumously in 2020, Bloom continues to draw attention to his mortality. He wonders in *Possessed by Memory* whether he continues to read and teach to "hold off death" (66). He finds his deteriorating body a source of both pain and sublime pleasure. Despite the tremor in his fingers, macular degeneration, and growing deafness, we sense pride in his ability to write, to survive any emergency. Pages of *Possessed by Memory* read like a dated diary entry. "I write these paragraphs," he records in the chapter on Tennyson, "on June 13, 2017, barely twenty-four hours back from six weeks' hospitalization and rehabilitation after two serious operations. I am so deeply exhausted that I scarcely speak" (268). Not too exhausted to write, however. But he writes now in a wheelchair, through dictation. Ghosts surround him and soon he will become one himself. Mourning these spectral losses does not lessen grief but it does, significantly, make it less disabling. He asks near the end of *Possessed by Memory* a rhetorical question: "Is there a relation between a writer's immortality and a reader's search for consolation in regard to the death of friends or family and intimations of the reader's own impending mortality" (505). Notice how Bloom doesn't directly express his *own* quest for immortality. No one can accuse Bloom of an excess of modesty, but he doesn't wish to call attention to his immense ambitions and accomplishments. It's doubtful that Bloom would have used Walter Kaufmann's neologism "humbition" to describe the great poets or himself. No less than the great writers in the canon, he craves to be remembered. Writing involves in his late books mourning the dead. "Our beloved dead live only as long as we absorb them into our daily thoughts and feelings" (506). These esteemed colleagues include, as a partial list appearing in *Possessed by Memory*, the poets A. R. Ammons, Robert Penn Warren, John

Hollander, Mark Strand, Alvin Feinman, and John Ashbery, as well as the philosopher Richard Rorty and the literary critic Angus Fletcher. In *The Bright Book of Life* he pauses on June 12, 2018, one month short of his eighty-eighth birthday, to memorialize his parents; four siblings; and colleagues, friends, and students who are no longer alive. In the middle of a discussion of Shelley in *Take Arms Against a Sea of Troubles*, Bloom recalls visiting with his wife the dying Paul de Man every other day in the hospital during his final two weeks. In the same book Bloom honors the memory of Geoffrey Hartman and William Merwin.

The Work of Mourning

By reciting these names, Bloom engages with what clinicians call grief work. He creates a dialogue with deceased colleagues and friends, bringing them to life through his own writings, maintaining an ongoing relationship with them, celebrating their work. He doesn't speak for the dead, but he speaks about them, forging a lasting bond with them. These colleagues and friends are always present in Bloom's imagination, and now in his readers' imagination as well. Another reason he writes—and teaches—is to preserve his identity as a writer and teacher. "I'd feel totally useless if I couldn't write," he told MacFarquhar, "And it's the same thing with teaching."

Isn't it odd that Bloom, the master theorist of the anxiety of influence, fails to theorize mourning? He refers often to "Mourning and Melancholia," but whereas Freud argues that the living must withdraw from the dead, declaring the object to be lost so that the ego can continue to live, Bloom implicitly argues to the contrary. He never overtly breaks from Freud, however. Bloom observes in *The Bright Book of Life* that, in Freud's words, "the work of mourning" must be relinquished lest it be transformed into melancholia, but then Bloom adds that Proust does not obey this injunction. Nor does Bloom retreat from the dead. He *must* write about the beloved dead, both to bear witness and to keep the dead alive. (One of the revisionary ratios, we recall, *apophrades*, is the "return of the dead.") In his final two books, *The Bright Book of Life* and *Take Arms Against a Sea of Troubles*, the latter of which could have been titled "Whatever Does Not Kill Me, Makes Me Stronger," Bloom continues to write about death, continues to express grief for lost loved ones. One suspects that his reading and writing at the end of his life lessened rather than heightened his melancholy. "When I say to myself and to others that reading helps in staying alive," Bloom writes on the opening page of the latter, "I am aware that I am being metaphorical" (1–2). True, a reader may agree, reading and writing are lifelines, a powerful metaphor, but I doubt that Bloom would disagree that reading and writing were *literally* necessary for his survival and well-being.

The intensely personal quality of Bloom's last books recalls academic memoirs such as George Steiner's *Errata: An Examined Life* (1998). The Franco-American Steiner, a polymath like Bloom, bewails at the end of his memoir that too often his activity as a writer, critic, teacher, and scholar has been, consciously or not, an "*in memoriam*, a curatorship of remembrance" (174). One can make the same observation about Bloom's late books, albeit without an apology.

Bloom's final books allow him to engage in a life review of his work, a phenomenon that often occurs, as I suggest in *Dying in Character* (2012), in end-of-life memoirs. To give only one example, in *The Anxiety of Influence* Bloom recalls with deep regret the beginning of his teaching career when the only way he could survive in the classroom was to subdue his "gentle nature" by using an "aggressivity and hostility" to teach his "barbarous students." Encountering former students a half century later, he is told that they would have learned more had he manifested "even an iota of affection" (30). Many students, such as Andrew Solomon, have spoken glowingly of Bloom's teaching, but Bloom is still pained by his early pedagogical style.

Two great Blooms dominate twentieth-century literature. James Joyce's Leopold Bloom, "Poldy," in *Ulysses*, is probably the century's most complex and fully realized fictional character. Harold Bloom remains the century's most colorful literary critic. To date, no biography has yet appeared, but when it does, the mythic Bloom will continue to draw attention. Bloom never tired of repeating, as he does in *The Book of J*, the Blessing: "more life, into a time without boundaries" (283); his own writings, like Lawrence's, are part of the bright book of life.

Bloom's Blindnesses

Fading Bloom is a marvel, but he still has the same blindnesses near the end of his life as at the beginning. He never comments on Freud's self-confessed limited understanding of female psychology, such as his claim that women have a less fully developed superego than men and his emphasis on "penis envy." Bloom remains unapologetic about the School of Resentment. "They resent literature," he huffs in *The Western Canon*, "or are ashamed of it, or are just not all that fond of reading it" (521). Given his lifelong role as a provocateur, he must have known, on some level, that he was being outrageously unfair, yet he remains unrepentant in his demonization of feminist and multicultural approaches to literature. He takes a perverse pride in his prejudice, and his utterances are, like Falstaff's, irrepressible and unstoppable. But Bloom is also willing to acknowledge, in his last books, the truth of some of his detractors' criticisms, as when he quotes in *The Anatomy of Influence* the statement made about him by his former professor and then colleague, William K. Wimsatt, Jr., who abstained from voting when Bloom came up for tenure at Yale: "He is an eighteen-inch naval gun, with tremendous firepower but always missing the cognitive target" (16). However much the criticism may have stung Bloom, he nevertheless dedicated *The Anxiety of Influence* to Wimsatt.

Bloom remained a canny reader of Freud, but he never qualified some of his inaccurate or misleading statements about the founder of psychoanalysis. He states in *Yeats*, for instance, that Freud "does not quest after a cure that cannot be found" (215); only the second part of that statement is accurate. In *The Book of J*, he claims that Freud believed "character is fully formed in your infancy" (320), an exaggeration. In *Poetry and Repression*, Bloom cites Freud's remark that "The poets were there before me" (53), neglecting to add that the philosophers were also there. And in *Genius*, Bloom insists that Freud maintained "there were no accidents" (657), a misreading.

It's easy to parody Bloom's writings, particularly near the end of his career. "He wrote ceaselessly, torrentially, and as he churned away he easily became vatic, windy, merely reckless where he had once been adventurous," James Wood grumbled in the *New Yorker* immediately after Bloom's death. "Late Bloom repeated and recirculated his favored obsessions, cross-referencing himself in ecstasies of unearned fulfillment." And yet Wood concedes that Bloom was a wonderful stylist and that one never mistook him for another writer: "the late, popular style was a faded fan, but it was still recognizably Bloom's old peacockery."

Late Style

The Columbia University postcolonial literary scholar Edward Said offers two examples of "late style" in his posthumously published book (2006) of the same title. One example of late style involves the artist's inability or unwillingness near the end of life to resolve, reconcile, or harmonize inner tensions; the other example reflects a new spirit of reconciliation or serenity not found in his or her earlier work. Bloom's late style reflects the latter example. Less agonistic and polemical in his late books than in his earlier ones, Bloom is beholden to those who helped him in the beginning of his career. Gratitude lies at the center of Bloom's final books. In *The Daemon Knows* he describes his younger self, entering graduate school, as "[r]ough, shaggy, parenthetical, self-conscious, and amiably polemical" (197). He alienated most of his professors and would not have survived without the encouragement and kindness of two distinguished scholars, Dean William Clyde DeVane and Professor Frederick Albert Pottle. Sixty-three years later and still at Yale, Bloom hopes to play the same role to his students as his two mentors did for him. In *Take Arms Against a Sea of Troubles* he regrets wasting time denouncing the School of Resentment, adding dryly that time now wastes him.

Bloom imagines expressing admiration to those with whom he intellectually quarreled. He no longer holds grudges, he says, not even against Masud Khan. He declares that he is only an "amateur student of psychoanalysis" and, therefore, cannot make a contribution to it beyond pointing out that psychoanalysis and literary criticism are both "ancient modes of speculation" (*Take Arms Against a Sea of Troubles* 565). Apart from the questionable accuracy of this statement, we can say that Bloom's noteworthy contribution to psychoanalysis includes not only *The Anxiety of Influence* but also the concept of "self-overhearing," a phenomenon he attributes to Shakespeare. Bloom elaborates on the four aspects of self-overhearing in *Possessed by Memory*: (1) to see one's own other selves, (2) to see (by glimpses) the shattering reality of others and of otherness, (3) to see nothing that is not there and the nothing that is, and (4) to see everything that could be there and the plenitude that already is (85). This is precisely what happens in effective psychoanalysis: with an analyst's guidance, analysands are constantly engaged in self-overhearing. As I suggest in the conclusion, Bloom's concept of self-overhearing resembles what contemporary analysts call "listening to listening."

Freud's Superstitiousness—and Bloom's

Despite his belief in reason and his disbelief in religion, Freud was highly superstitious, as his biographers have remarked. He was certain he would die at a certain age, though he kept pushing back the year when he survived it. Ernest Jones pointed out Freud's "disconcerting habit" of parting with the words, "Good-bye; you may never see me again" (vol. 3, 279). To the dismay of his disciples, Freud believed in prophetic and telepathic dreams. If he were at the beginning of his career rather than near the end, he wrote in a 1921 letter, he might choose to study occult phenomena (*Letters* 334).

Bloom was also, strangely enough, superstitious. In an essay published in the *Jewish Chronicle* immediately after his death, his former undergraduate student Kate Maltby confides that he told her and her classmates in 2007 that once in his youth he had visited a medium to understand Yeats's fascination with the occult.

> She had prophesied a youthful expiration date for Bloom; when he returned years later to taunt her with his survival, she grudgingly revised this to tell him he would die instead at 89. "The good lady promises I have twelve years left," Bloom would tell my classmates. "So do not consider handing in that essay two days late and hoping that I've dropped dead in the meantime."

Being eighty-nine must have spooked Bloom, for *three* times in *Take Arms Against a Sea of Troubles* he refers to himself as *ninety* years old. But he was not destined to be a nonagenarian. Near the end of the book Bloom recalls the date of his predicted demise and cheerfully vows to outlive it:

> This book had its beginning in a cavalcade of illnesses and accidents, so that much of it was dictated to generous assistants in hospitals and rehabilitation centers. Happily, it is ending a few months after my eighty-ninth birthday, and I seem so far to be holding together. I am rather superstitious, and three charming ladies of Gypsy descent—in Wales, Jerusalem, and Los Angeles, each ten years apart—read my palm and granted me eighty-nine years, three months, and eleven days. Once that cheered me, but I have no intention of departing on October 22, 2019, though I will be particularly careful that day. (577)

The prediction, it turned out, was off by eight days.

3

Kurt R. Eissler

Faultless Freud

Lionel Trilling and Harold Bloom wrote book after book extolling Freud's greatness as a writer, but they were never the defenders of the faith, keepers of orthodoxy, the popes of psychoanalysis, protecting their revered hero from criticisms, accurate or not. Nor were the two literary critics the royal archivists, the creator of the Freud Archives, restricting biographers and other scholars from reading the creator's private papers. That role fell to Kurt R. Eissler. Freud could do no wrong for Eissler, who spent his entire career resisting every opportunity to modify or revise Freud's theorizings.

"We are witnessing what is evidently a piecemeal destruction of Freud's psychological achievement, which was based on introspection and interpretation," Eissler bemoans. "By insidiously changing methods, falsifying concepts, and simplifying issues, the corrupters of psychoanalysis are transmogrifying it into what they call more exact science and a therapeutically more effective treatment. Yet all these changes, allegedly undertaken for the sake of improvement, make out of psychology a behavioristic science forever divorced from man's living soul." The lament, buried in a footnote in his two-volume 1963 tome, *Goethe: A Psychoanalytic Study, 1775–1786* (1163–4, n.22), bespeaks Eissler's worshipful attitude toward Freud.

Eissler doesn't specify in the footnote who the corrupters of psychoanalysis are, nor the nature of the corruptions they propose, but his remark betrays all-or-nothing thinking, also called dichotomous or binary thinking. To Eissler, psychoanalysis, as divinely inspired by Freud, is irrevocably true, pure unadulterated science; any effort to change or reform it will lead to inferior behavioristic science, shallow and watered down. It's ironic that Eissler identifies Freudian psychoanalysis with "man's living soul" when Freud was militantly opposed to all forms of religion and spirituality. Why did Eissler believe that Freud alone knew the full extent of his creation—particularly since Freud often changed his mind, contradicting earlier theorizings? Why wouldn't Freud and Eissler wish psychoanalysis to become more therapeutically effective? Doesn't our understanding of every science grow over time, requiring new thinking? It has often been said that contemporary college physics students know more about the theory of relativity than Einstein did a century ago. Wouldn't the same be true of psychoanalysis? Why, then, was Eissler so fearful of change?

Eissler was the leading figure in what Anna Freud called, in a letter to Masud Khan in 1975, the "Defense League" to protect her father's increasingly damaged reputation. The expression appears in Elisabeth Young-Bruehl's 1988 biography of Anna Freud (431). But as Young-Bruehl notes, Eissler "cried 'anti-Freud' so often that no one would listen should a significant anti-Freud come along." Yet he was also, she added, a "publisher's dream—a man who helped book sales by bestowing psychoanalytic concern on hostility to psychoanalysis" (433).

Eissler was born in Vienna in 1908, received his PhD in psychology at the University of Vienna in 1934 and his medical degree in 1937. He trained at the Vienna Psychoanalytic Institute but left for Chicago in 1938 when the Nazis rose to power in Austria. In 1943, he became a Captain in the U.S. Army Medical Corps. The same year his brother, Erik, was killed in a concentration camp, an event he never wrote about in his dozen books and nearly one hundred articles. After the war, Eissler went into private practice in New York, and in 1952, he was one of the founders of the Sigmund Freud Archives, housed in the Library of Congress in Washington, DC. In his capacity as its creator and secretary, which was tantamount to being its director, Eissler earned both praise for preserving Freud's writings and condemnation for refusing to allow some of this material, hidden for decades, to be made public. In his 1988 biography *Freud: A Life for Our Time*, Peter Gay accused Eissler of an "addiction to secrecy" (784), a criticism with which every Freud scholar would agree. From the beginning Eissler was at the center of the psychoanalytic community, befriending Anna Freud by setting up a tax-free foundation to fund her Hampstead child therapy clinic, helping Ernest Jones pen his three-volume hagiographic biography of Freud, and assisting James Strachey with the *Standard Edition* of Freud's psychological writings. Eissler's wife, Ruth, also a psychoanalyst, edited *The Psychoanalytic Study of the Child*, dying in 1989. Eissler died a decade later at age ninety. Sarah Boxer ends her *New York Times* obituary of Eissler by quoting his friend and fellow analyst George Gross. "Dr. Eissler, he said, 'was disappointed that he had not found a person who understood Freud the way he did.' In that, he was a little like Freud. Mr. Gross said, 'Freud was constantly disappointed.'"

In the Freud Archives

A shy, reserved man embodying old-world charm, equally at home in literature, the arts, and mythology, Eissler was highly erudite and spent most of his time writing long scholarly psychoanalytic studies. He was uncomfortably thrust into the public eye when he consented to be interviewed by Janet Malcolm for her 1984 book *In the Freud Archives*, based on two long articles that had appeared the previous year in the *New Yorker.* "He is tall, gaunt, and unmistakably European," Malcolm observes, "with an underlying, insistent, almost pathological kindheartedness" (*In the Freud Archives* 4–5). The kindheartedness no doubt misled Eissler into adopting his two maverick protégés, Jeffrey Moussaieff Masson and Peter Swales, to his everlasting regret. It's likely that Eissler also regretted speaking so forthrightly to Malcolm, who promptly washed the Freud Archives' dirty laundry in public. Musing aloud to Malcolm—always a dangerous activity because her loyalty to telling a gossipy story overcame whatever scruples she might have had about causing pain to her biographical subjects—Eissler wondered whether his catastrophic blunder of hiring Masson betrayed his own unconscious "ambivalence" toward Freud (74), something he could not imagine. Malcolm captures the contradictions of Eissler's character: "its singular mixture of brilliance, profundity, originality, and moral beauty on the one hand, and willfulness, stubbornness, impetuosity, and maddening guilelessness on the other" (8). Among Eissler's best qualities, in Malcolm's judgment, was his freedom from self-justification, but he was startlingly uncritical of Freud. No one was more of a true believer than Eissler, and no American analyst was more influential in affirming and reifying psychoanalytic orthodoxy. He may have chosen to write a biography of Goethe not only because he was the greatest German writer but also because he was one of Freud's heroes; indeed, Freud quoted Goethe more than any other writer.

Goethe: A Psychoanalytic Study, 1775–1786

Three of Eissler's books were on geniuses—Goethe, Leonardo da Vinci, and Hamlet—and like Freud, he loved to speculate on the subject of creativity. It was always male genius, however, that piqued Eissler's interest, never female genius, which he implies, as did Freud, does not exist. Eissler conceded, in the appendix to *Goethe*, that many women have the same skills, talents, abilities, and endowments that appear in their talented male counterparts, but for some reason, he avers, one doesn't see genius in women. Thus, he cites, admiringly, the late nineteenth-century novelist George Eliot, not realizing that she is one of the great geniuses of English literature. Eissler rejects cultural explanations of genius, concluding that biological and psychological reasons must be responsible. "In the male the potential generative material is practically unlimited," unlike in the female, where the creative function is "bound up in the generative material and is therefore less accessible to the diversion of which the male creative function seems extremely capable" (*Goethe* 1402).

Eissler's patriarchal views are palpable in Brenda Webster's wry memoir *The Last Good Freudian* (2000), where she chronicles her many years spent and misspent on the analytical couch. Of her three analysts, she was most sympathetic to the courtly, urbane Eissler. "If Freud was King Arthur," Webster quips, "Eissler was Launcelot, a quixotic but fiercely loyal defender of the faith" (82). Throughout her four years in treatment with Eissler, beginning in 1956, when she was twenty, she could not convince him to change his mind about the absence of female geniuses. Eissler comes across as concerned for Webster's welfare but trapped in a Freudian straitjacket. The daughter of Ethel Schwabacher, an artistically gifted albeit troubled woman whose luminous abstract expressionist paintings appear in the permanent collections of major museums, and herself an acclaimed psychoanalytic literary scholar and creative writer, Webster felt only consternation when Eissler recommended that she devote her life to a husband and children rather than to a professional career. Nor could she change his conviction that women were innately masochistic, passive, and envious, as he believed, following Freud. As I wrote in *Psychoanalytic Memoirs* (2023), in one revealing exchange in *The Last Good Freudian*, Eissler and Webster disagreed over Cordelia's refusal to tell her father what he wanted to hear.

> Eissler was impressed by Cordelia's honesty, but Webster was annoyed by Cordelia's infuriating bluntness. Both positions are understandable and equally valid, but Webster's therapy was less a dialogue than a monologue, with an authoritarian teacher instructing a resistant student. Ironically, Eissler was Webster's father surrogate, and she was thrust into the position of Cordelia, reluctant to play the role of obedient daughter. (83)

Psychoanalysis worked for Webster as a hermeneutic, enabling her to analyze literary texts, but it did not work for her as a therapy.

Eissler was "no idolater of Freud," Clifford Yorke, a fellow psychoanalyst who knew him well, claimed in an obituary published in the *Guardian*. But this was untrue. The orthodox Eissler never challenged *any* of Freud's theorizings, including his Victorian sentimentalization of the mother–son relationship, as can be seen in Eissler's Goethe biography.

> The absence of ambivalence in the relationship of Goethe's mother to him is conspicuous. Freud's statement that "the only thing that brings a mother undiluted satisfaction is her relation to a son; it is quite the most complete relationship between human beings, and the one that is the most free from ambivalence" . . . can be applied *in toto* to Goethe's mother. (vol.1, 77)

Women who do not accept motherhood as a natural fulfillment aroused Eissler's suspicion, as when he writes about Goethe's long relationship with Charlotte von Stein, who regarded motherhood as a torture. "No matter how much one takes cognizance of the hardships under which women suffered in the eighteenth century because of medical and hygienic ignorance," Eissler avows, "one cannot refer Charlotte von Stein's complaints to reality factors. There comes to the fore, rather, the envy of male prerogatives, or, at least, what Charlotte von Stein considered as such, as well as the feeling that being a female condemns one to suffering" (144–5).

Leonardo da Vinci: Psychoanalytic Notes on the Enigma

On at least one occasion, in his 1961 book *Leonardo da Vinci: Psychoanalytic Notes on the Enigma*, Eissler had no choice but to point out a problem in Freud's writing, as in his embarrassing mistake in *Leonardo da Vinci and a Memory of His Childhood* (1910), where he mistranslates the Italian word *nibbio*, which means "kite," for "vulture." Yet even here Eissler puts a positive spin on Freud's error. "The fact that Leonardo actually did not write of a vulture but of a kite gives occasion to demonstrate how sensitive an instrument psychoanalysis really is. It would have called psychoanalysis seriously into question as a reliable method if further historical research had confirmed conclusions that Freud deduced from premises later proved wrong" (22–3). Eissler remained discreetly silent about Freud's bizarre idea that the Earl of Oxford was the real author of Shakespeare's writings, a conjecture that Freud's fellow analysts tried vainly to convince him was looney, which happened to be the man's unfortunate name, J. Thomas Looney, who proposed the idea.

Several of Eissler's books were written as counterblasts to those who disagreed with Freud. Eissler singles out the art historian Meyer Schapiro's critique of Freud's study of Leonardo. For example, Schapiro doubts that

Leonardo's kindness to animals is a sign of repressed sadism, as Freud insisted. Eissler defends Freud's interpretation of a conflict in Leonardo between "massive sadistic (aggressive) impulses. These were partly absorbed in strong reaction formations, such as pity and orderliness" (58). But cannot a child's kindness to animals, or other children, be viewed as instinctual and inborn as aggression? In this view, kindness is coequal with cruelty, not a "reaction formation," as Freud theorized. "Kindness" does not appear in the index to the *Standard Edition* of Freud's writings, and there is only one entry under "compassion"; tellingly, the entry is listed under "compassion, narcissistic origin of," indicating that Freud rarely thought about these words, and when he did, he viewed them as reversals of "cruelty" or "sadism," of which there are *dozens* of entries in the index.

Eissler also defends in his study of Leonardo Freud's theory of homosexuality. Freud did not pathologize homosexuality, as did many other thinkers of his time; he regarded homosexuality not as an illness but as a developmental arrest, a fixation at an earlier state of psychosexual development. "Homosexuality is assuredly no advantage, but it is nothing to be ashamed of, no vice, no degradation," Freud wrote in a 1935 letter: "it cannot be classified as an illness; we consider it to be a variation of the sexual function, produced by a certain arrest of sexual development." Freud believed that many of the greatest men of history were homosexual, including Plato, Michelangelo, and Leonardo. "It is a great injustice to persecute homosexuality as a crime—and a cruelty, too" (*Letters* 423). Nevertheless, Freud maintained, in Leonardo's case, that (in Eissler's words), the "aggression against the female, inherent in homosexuality, is thus denied and the claim set forth that respect and esteem for women force the subject to seek gratification with the coarser sex" (Eissler, *Leonardo* 106). It cannot be denied, Eissler continues, that the "ingredients of homosexuality as asserted by psychoanalysis" include the "active impulses toward an effeminate contemporary that disguises conflict in the parental relation, the passive submission to a father and a distant adoration of a revered mother" (106–7). The American Psychoanalytic Association (APsA) supported the American Psychiatric Association (APA) in its decision to include homosexuality as a "sexual deviance" in the 1968 edition of the *Diagnostic and Statistical Manual of Mental Disorders* (*DSM-III*); but whereas the APA decided in 1973 to eliminate the homosexuality diagnosis from the *DSM*, APsA refused to endorse this decision. It was not until 1991, when confronted with an antidiscrimination lawsuit, that APsA allowed for the training of gay and lesbian analysts.

Medical Orthodoxy and the Future of Psychoanalysis

It's doubtful that Eissler realized the irony in the title of his 1965 book *Medical Orthodoxy and the Future of Psychoanalysis*, his attempt to encourage the medical community to allow "lay" or nonmedical analysts to join the American Psychoanalytic Association. In protesting medical orthodoxy, he seems oblivious to his own psychoanalytic orthodoxy. One can only speculate on how Eissler would have thought about this question had Freud not written *The Question of Lay Analysis* (1926). "Doctors have no historical claim to the sole possession of analysis," Freud observes (*SE*, vol. 20, 229). Freud offers several prescient ideas, including the hope that the United States, a country he detested, would allow social workers to receive psychoanalytic training, turning them into a "band of helpers for combating the neuroses of civilization" (*SE*, vol. 20, 250). Receiving a master's degree in social work is now one of the most popular paths to becoming a psychoanalyst.

Eissler begins the preface to *Medical Orthodoxy and the Future of Psychoanalysis* with a combative sentence, and perhaps an apologetic one. "On rereading the manuscript, I asked myself whether this is an angry book" (vii). Regretting that good manners prevent him from calling a spade a spade, he declares that defending Freud is one of his highest goals: "misrepresentations with regard to Freud's life and character that could easily have been avoided, if the available sources had been studied with even a modicum of objectivity, deserve a far more bitter reply than I have in any case allowed myself to indulge in" (viii). There are many examples of Eissler's idolatry of Freud. In likening the birth of psychoanalysis to Athena's springing fully armed from the head of Zeus, Eissler refers in passing to Freud's "fatherly friend" Josef Breuer, his collaborator in *Studies on Hysteria* (1893–5). One can use the word "fatherly" only if it is fraught with intense ambivalence. It's true that in "On the History of the Psycho-Analytic Movement" (1914), Freud praises Breuer. "[I]t was not I who had brought psycho-analysis into existence: the credit for this was due to someone else, to Josef Breuer, whose work had been done at a time when I was still a student engaged in passing my examinations (1880–82)." Freud then mentions that colleagues believed his gratitude was hyperbolic, expressed "too extravagantly on that occasion" (*SE*, vol. 14, 7–8). Expressing gratitude, on the one hand, followed by faint/feigned praise, on the other, highlights Freud's ambivalence that he could not bring himself to confess, especially when it came to the talking cure, to which he unapologetically (and possessively) referred, in

"On the History of the Psycho-Analytic Movement," as "my creation" (*SE*, vol. 14, 7). Freud could not tolerate being financially indebted to Breuer, who had loaned him money, and when the latter generously offered to cancel the debt, Freud felt doubly indebted—and doubly troubled. "Recently Breuer pulled another brilliant stunt," Freud confided to Fliess on January 16, 1898. After describing in a long paragraph the details of Breuer's "deeply hurt feelings" when his younger colleague tried to pay him back, Freud concludes, "It is genuine Breuer. It is enough to make one extremely ungrateful for good deeds" (Masson 294).

"The Poison of Eclecticism"

As in his other books, Eissler resists nearly all the changes in psychoanalysis that were not authorized by Freud. In an extended footnote, he inveighs against the developments in theory and practice effected by Karen Horney, Erich Fromm, Harry Stack Sullivan, Franz Alexander (whom he spends the most time denouncing), and others, dismissing their "further developments" as empty phrases. Nor was he impressed with Melanie Klein. Eissler rejects the "extreme biologism of the English school, whose founder was a lay analyst, yet whose theories were such as one might perhaps have expected from a mind that had suffered the strait-jacket training of a medical school with a rigid biological orientation" (*Medical Orthodoxy* 103). Later he makes a more censorious statement. "Klein carries out a piece of legerdemain that makes it possible to ignore in theory the full impact of social reality on psychic development and structure" (355–6). In one of his most strident expressions, Eissler refers to the "poison of eclecticism" (84, n.11).

Eissler was on the right side of psychoanalytic history, however, as was Freud, in urging the American Psychoanalytic Association to accept nonphysicians for training. Both realized, in Eissler's words, the desirability of the early Viennese situation where there was a "regular and intensive cross-fertilization, *within the psychoanalytic society*, between medically trained analysts and lay analysts representing the humanities" (196). But it was not until 1989 that APsA, under pressure from a lawsuit filed by four members of the American Psychological Association, permitted nonmedical clinicians to study at APsA-approved institutes. The American Psychoanalytic Association is much more inclusive than it was in the past, though its membership is graying: the average age of the members is seventy (Almond 13).

Near the end of *Medical Orthodoxy and the Future of Psychoanalysis*, Eissler defends the Freud Archives by stating that it was not created to honor or idealize Freud but to preserve irreplaceable documents that might be lost to future biographers. Nevertheless, certain documents continue to be closed to the public, extending to the year 2113, fueling speculation that they portray Freud in an unfavorable light. The current executive director is the historian Louis Rose, the former editor of *American Imago*, a journal cofounded by Freud and Hanns Sachs in 1939. A search of the Sigmund Freud papers in the Library of Congress does not indicate how many of the 48,600 items remain closed to the public.

Discourse on Hamlet and HAMLET

Scattered throughout Freud's writings are references to *Hamlet*, a play that holds a privileged position in the history of psychoanalysis. Of the more than twenty thousand letters Freud penned, the most important was to Fliess on October 15, 1897, which begins with the announcement that Freud's self-analysis is the most noteworthy event in his life. Freud then refers to what he always thought was his greatest discovery, one that led to the creation of psychoanalysis. "A single idea of general value dawned on me. I have found, in my own case too, [the phenomenon of] being in love with my mother and jealous of my father, and I now consider it a universal event in early childhood" (Masson 272). If this is true, Freud continues, the Oedipus complex helps to explain the "gripping power" of *Oedipus Rex* as well as the meaning of Hamlet's hesitation to avenge his father's murder. A key difference between the two plays, Freud suggests in *The Interpretation of Dreams* (1900), his voice tinged with sarcasm, is the "secular advance of repression in the emotional life of mankind. In the *Oedipus* the child's wishful phantasy that underlies it is brought into the open and realized as it would be in a dream. In *Hamlet* it remains repressed; and—just as in the case of a neurosis—we only learn of its existence from its inhibiting consequences" (*SE*, vol. 4, 264).

Freud did not have much else to say about *Hamlet*. In "Psychopathic Characters on the Stage," written in 1905 or 1906 but published posthumously in 1942, Freud conjectures that Hamlet is not psychopathic but only *becomes* so during the course of the play. The same Oedipal complex lies in everyone, Freud contends, creating intense resistance; Freud then adds, immodestly, "the conflict in *Hamlet* is so effectively concealed that it was left to me to unearth it" (*SE*, vol. 7, 310). Elaborating on Freud's idea, Ernest Jones offers in *Hamlet and Oedipus* (1949) a compelling interpretation of Hamlet's delay. Jones can be faulted, however, as a number of literary critics have pointed out, beginning with Lionel Trilling and later Norman N. Holland, for believing, with Freud, that he has "solved" the "mystery" of the play. The greatest mystery of *Hamlet* lies in its incomparable genius, which psychoanalysis can do little to explain.

Not that Eissler fails to try. Throughout the 656-page tome *Discourse on Hamlet and HAMLET* (1971), he offers one speculation after another about the nature of genius. Typical is the following comment expressed in a footnote: "One aspect of the greatness of dramatic works (and perhaps of art in general) may well be measurable in terms of its ability to overcome resistance and to set in motion some grasp of reality even when the viewer's disbelief is at its height" (19, n.8). Speculations like this recur throughout Eissler's writings.

No psychologist, in Eissler's opinion, approaches Freud in greatness, but, sounding like Harold Bloom, he has no problem in conceding priority to the creator of *Hamlet*. "Here Shakespeare really went beyond Freud, in making the [Oedipus] complex the fountainhead of a poison that has pervaded the whole fabric of society" (162). Eissler sees *Hamlet* as confirming (if not originating) Freud's controversial theory, advanced in *Beyond the Pleasure Principle* (1920), of a death instinct, but some of Eissler's other comments about Freud, while intended to be laudatory, are problematic, such as the following:

> When a physician who was in analysis with Freud, and whose character Freud apparently did not esteem highly because of his insincerity, once complained about having been impotent with his wife, Freud is said to have replied: "*Herr Kollege*, this is the first thing you have told me about yourself that is a manifestation of sincerity." If this story is not "legend" (it rings true to me, and was related to me by a person for whose reliability I feel inclined to vouch), I regret that Freud never published it, for it covers a chapter of psychopathology that is generally ignored. (500)

Most contemporary readers would find this rejoinder to an analysand, a fellow physician, no less, deeply insulting, an empathic failure that would cause patients to terminate treatment. Why did Eissler find this story so praiseworthy? Because of Freud's honesty? Surely Freud could have found less offensive language to encourage his patient's self-disclosures. Because of Freud's insight into impotence? Surely he must have known the vulnerability of a patient confessing to this problem. Why would Freud want to heighten this vulnerability? Curiously, the same incident appears in *Freud as an Expert Witness* (1986) but with two significant changes: Eissler omits any mention that Freud's patient was a physician, and a footnote indicates that he cannot vouch for the correctness of the report (255, n.8).

Eissler did not write *Discourse on Hamlet and HAMLET* as a rebuttal to another scholar's work, as he did, for example, in his books on Victor Tausk's suicide, but he is surprisingly disapproving of other psychoanalytic critics' approaches to Shakespeare. He has little use, to give one example, for Holland's pioneering work on reader-response criticism. Holland wrote two books on Shakespeare. The first, *The Shakespearean Imagination* (1964), is steeped in the assumptions of New Criticism, explication de texte, the dominant theory of literary criticism of the age. Holland's second book, *Psychoanalysis and Shakespeare*, published only two years later, represents a sea change in his thinking. Holland's major focus is on *Hamlet*, where, after summarizing nearly hundred commentaries on the play, including Eissler's, to which he refers respectfully, he offers his own approach, based not on the Oedipus complex, which struck Holland as the rock upon which Freud founded psychoanalysis, but on a developmentally earlier pre-Oedipal approach. Holland also begins to adumbrate an approach to reading, articulated in his next book, *The Dynamics of Literary Response* (1968), that would become reader-response criticism, for which he is best known. Eissler refers to both *The Shakespearean Imagination* and *Psychoanalysis and Shakespeare*, and while he praises Holland for providing a methodological justification for the use of psychoanalysis in the interpretation of fictional characters, he cannot accept Holland's statement that we need to grasp the mind of the reader or audience to understand literature. "Would we have to conclude that psychoanalytic interpretations are wrong," Eissler asks rhetorically, "if empirical testing were not able to show that any of the contents claimed by psychoanalysis have ever become relevant in audience response?" For Eissler, psychoanalytic interpretations of Shakespeare (and other writers) are "valid statements about something objectively given" (18), a dictum that denies the subjectivity of reading and the reader's role in the creation of meaning.

Notwithstanding this fundamental difference between them, Eissler and Holland had much in common, beginning with their idealization of Freud, their lifelong devotion to classical psychoanalysis, and their aggressive intellectuality. Holland was one of the first literary scholars to graduate from a psychoanalytic institute and undergo a full training analysis. Both men could be personally warm, witty, and charming, but they were doctrinaire Freudians when it came to defending his reputation. "I think that only the analyzed can truly decide on matters of psychoanalytic training and practice," Eissler asserts in *Medical Orthodoxy and the Future of Psychoanalysis* (204). In *Psychoanalysis and*

Shakespeare, Holland makes an even more astonishing pronouncement, one that would offend every literary critic:

> It is a little surprising that there should be any literary critiques of this kind, that is, attacking the Freud-Jones analysis of *Hamlet*, not from a literary but a psychological point of view. With all due respect to my literary colleagues, it seems to me that they are somewhat out of their depth, psychologically. Surely criticisms of a psychoanalytic diagnosis as such are the province of the expert—in psychoanalysis. For literary critics not trained in psychoanalysis there are plenty of cogent criticisms of the Freud-Jones view of *Hamlet* that can be made from the point of view of an expert in literary criticism: misreadings, misunderstandings of tone, treating a play as a puzzle, reading back to Shakespeare, treating the characters as real people, and so on. It seems to me the purely literary critic would do well to confine himself to those, if he wishes to object. (185)

In light of Eissler's and Holland's statements, one can appreciate the truth of Erik H. Erikson's statement in *Young Man Luther* (1958) that a training analysis is like monastic penitence: it "takes greater chances with the individual's relation to himself and to those who up to then have shared his life, than any other professional training except monkhood" (151). One can go further than this by suggesting that however insightful a training analysis may be, it poses the danger of indoctrination, enforcing orthodoxy.

Deviations from Orthodoxy

Eissler often goes out of his way to fault psychoanalysts whose thinking departs from orthodox Freudian theory. Many of these criticisms appear in the footnotes or appendix, which become like personal asides, allowing him to vent. Eissler's sharpest criticisms are directed against Erik H. Erikson, arguably the most famous American psychoanalyst, the author of several bestsellers, including *Childhood and Society* (1950), *Young Man Luther* (1958), *Insight and Responsibility* (1964), and *Gandhi's Truth* (1969). While some of Eissler's disagreements are with Erikson's interpretation of *Hamlet*, including his belief that the Prince lives in a society that requires rejuvenation, his harshest comments are reserved for Erikson the analyst. Eissler singles out a comment Erikson made in his 1958 essay "The Nature of Clinical Evidence" in which he communicates his emotional response to a patient. In Eissler's summarizing words, the patient, who had been showing signs of improvement, was in a "state of excitement that might well have been ominous, brought about by a most disturbing dream." Erikson reviewed the patient's associations to the dream and then responded: "I also told him, without anger but not without some honest indignation, that my response to his account had included a feeling of being attacked." Eissler then offers his own response, a stern rebuke of Erikson's behavior:

> Whatever the reaction may actually have been—anger or indignation—the reason for my citing this episode is not that emotional derailments of this kind are rare among analysts. No one is, of course, immune to them: my concern is that Prof. Erikson justifies his anger, takes it as a constructive response and informs the patient about it, as if such responses were indeed legitimate and had to be tolerated by the patient. In truth, there is no justification for an analyst's anger, not to speak of his indignation, when he feels disappointed or accused by a patient. If such derailments occur, it is high time for the analyst to aim at some enlightenment with regard to what his own unconscious relationship to the patient may be. (*Discourse on Hamlet and HAMLET* 517)

How is Erikson's behavior different, we wonder, from Freud's, who, Eissler discloses in *Discourse on Hamlet and HAMLET*, challenged his patient's "sincerity?" Why does Eissler extol Freud's confession while he condemns Erikson's? Reading Erikson's essay, one has a much more positive attitude toward him than Eissler allows. Although Erikson does not use words like "intersubjectivity," "relational therapy," or "two-person psychology," which characterize the theory and practice of many contemporary psychoanalysts, he foregrounds the element of subjectivity in all forms of psychotherapy. Erikson urges a *disciplined* subjectivity, one that is in the patient's best interests. Erikson's approach is in many ways classical: he affirms what Freud calls the analyst's "free-floating attention"; the role of free association in the interpretation of dreams, which, for both Freud and Erikson, is the "royal road to the unconscious"; and the analyst's avoidance of undue interference. A traumatic moment in therapy occurred when, during the third month of treatment, Erikson had an "emergency operation," the details of which he doesn't disclose to the reader (nor, presumably, to the patient). The untoward event resulted in the patient's fear of being "abandoned" and found its way into his dreams, reinforcing earlier fears. Thus, the face in the dream symbolized Erikson's, among others. The main theme of the dream under question involved the patient's fear that through an act of "horrible anger," either his own or Erikson's, he would lose the therapist's help and end his chance for recovery. To reassure the patient that he would not leave him, and that everything can be discussed in analysis, Erikson shares his thoughts and feelings with him. The patient was "delighted" and "left the hour—which he had begun with a sense of dire disaster—with a broad smile and obvious encouragement" (85).

Eissler concludes his discussion in *Discourse on Hamlet and HAMLET* by noting that Erikson's deviation from orthodoxy is so radical that future historians will not call him a psychoanalyst but rather a psychotherapist, a term that is distinctly inferior to Eissler. This is in itself testimony, according to Eissler, "to the fact that psychoanalysis did *not* lose its vitality after the death of its founder" (518). But Eissler was writing during the waning years of the "golden age" of psychoanalysis, before its precipitous loss of popularity and prestige. Erikson's writings retain their vitality, testimony to his brilliance if not genius.

Victor Tausk's Suicide

It is unusual for a psychoanalyst to include in the appendix of a book about another analyst's suicide a rebuttal by the deceased analyst's son who claims that the author is wrong about nearly all of his interpretations and reconstructions of his father's life. It is more unusual when the son disagrees with the author's assertions of the suicide's impact on his *own* life. Such is the strange provenance of Eissler's *Victor Tausk's Suicide* (1983). Even more bizarre is that this is Eissler's *second* book about Tausk, the first one, *Talent and Genius: The Fictitious Case of Tausk Contra Freud*, having been published in 1971. One can only imagine the son's anguish in reading two books by the same author—indeed, three books, if we consider Paul Roazen's *Brother Animal: The Story of Freud and Tausk* (1969), which initiated the bitter controversy surrounding Freud's complicity in Victor Tausk's death.

According to Roazen's chronology, Tausk was born in 1879 in Žilina, Slovakia, and began to study law in 1897 at the University of Vienna. In 1900, he married Martha Frisch, a distant cousin of the theologian Martin Buber, and two years later he completed his legal training. Tausk found the practice of law unfulfilling, however, and after the births of his sons Marius in 1902 and Victor Hugo in 1903, he and his wife agreed to separate. They moved to Vienna in 1905, and a year later, Tausk traveled to Berlin and worked as a journalist, his father's profession. Suffering a breakdown in 1907, Tausk spent twenty-five days in a sanatorium, after which he returned to Vienna in 1908 and began the study of medicine at the University of Vienna. At Freud's invitation, to whom he had written a letter expressing admiration, Tausk started attending meetings held at the Vienna Psychoanalytic Institute. He wrote a number of insightful clinical papers on schizophrenia, manic-depression, masturbation, and the psychology of the war deserter. In 1912–13, Tausk had a sexual relationship with Freud's confidante Lou Andreas-Salomé, with whom Nietzsche and Rilke had earlier fallen in love; her *Journal* conveys much information about the "Tausk problem." After serving in the First World War as an army psychiatrist, Tausk resumed his psychoanalytic practice in Vienna and sought to enter analysis with Freud. The founder of psychoanalysis turned him down, however, and referred him to Helene Deutsch, who was at the time in analysis with Freud. He also refused Tausk's request to analyze his son Marius. Roazen, later the biographer of Helene Deutsch, asserts that Tausk spent most of the analysis talking about his convoluted feelings toward Freud. The analysis, which began in January 1919, lasted only for three months; Freud persuaded Deutsch to end the "incestuous situation" (101), believing that Deutsch's analysis of Tausk interfered with Freud's analysis of her. In 1919, Tausk became engaged to marry Hilde Loewi, who was pregnant with their child, but the night before the wedding, Tausk committed suicide, on July 3, 1919.

The facts of Tausk's life are not controversial, but the interpretation and meaning of his suicide are, as well as Freud's role in the death. Many of Roazen's interpretations of the Freud–Tausk relationship are persuasive, and he tries, without entirely succeeding, to be fair to both men. There's little doubt that Tausk was one of Freud's most talented students and that their relationship was stormy. Tausk believed that Freud had plagiarized his ideas, including the conviction that a melancholic's reproaches against others reflect self-reproaches. Roazen never doubts Freud's genius, but he acknowledges that Freud "felt uncomfortable with someone like Tausk around, a man bright enough even to anticipate some of his own concepts. Freud did not like the uncertainty lest Tausk have an idea before he did" (Roazen 55). Other Freud scholars have made similar observations. George Makari remarks in *Revolution in Mind: The Creation of Psychoanalysis* (2008) that Freud always used the same strategy when encountering opposition: "he would fight bitterly to hold his ground, and then after rebuffing a foe, he would quietly incorporate those aspects of the challenge he most admired into his ever-expanding models. The Freudian field grew fat on a host of vanquished opponents" (160).

No event is more difficult to fathom than suicide, even when a person leaves a suicide note, as Tausk did. Except for "rational" or physician-assisted suicide, in which one ends life primarily because of irremediable pain, there are almost always a multitude of reasons for suicide: it is perhaps the most "overdetermined" action, caused by many factors. Even if Roazen is correct that one of the motives for Tausk's suicide was Freud's rejection, there were other reasons, including ambivalence over remarriage. Part of the legacy or "illegacy" of suicide is finding others to blame. Most people who attempt or commit suicide are highly ambivalent, wishing both to die and live, but Tausk made sure he would succeed. He placed a cord around his neck, shot himself in the temple with his army pistol, and strangled himself as he was falling. He also left instructions to have all of his papers destroyed, similar to his contemporary Franz Kafka, though fortunately Kafka's future biographer, Max Brod, did not comply with the request.

Should one accept, at face value, Tausk's final letter to Freud, written immediately before the suicide, in which he expresses only positive feelings? "I thank you for all the good which you have done me. It was much and has given meaning to the last ten years of my life. Your work is genuine and great, I shall take leave of this life knowing that I was one of those who witnessed the triumph of one of the greatest ideas of mankind" (Roazen 127). Nor is there a hint of anger or bitterness in Tausk's farewell letter to his family. On the other hand, if we accept the psychoanalytic interpretation of suicide as internalized aggression—the desire to murder another turns inward, resulting in the symbolic death of the other along with the expiation of guilty feelings—then Tausk *was*, notwithstanding his suicide note to the contrary, furious with Freud. There is a shocking disconnect between Tausk's words and actions. Suicides are unlike other deaths; the closer one is to a person who commits suicide, the more guilt and anger one feels.

And Freud's feelings toward Tausk? Freud wrote a three-page obituary of Tausk, the longest of the nine he penned, in which he spoke movingly about Tausk's talents and accomplishments. Freud referred to Tausk's inner struggles, implying that he was psychologically wounded from his war service. Freud affirmed eloquently the value of Tausk's life and work. In private, however, Freud conveyed darker feelings, confessing in a letter to Lou Andreas-Salomé that "I do not really miss him; I had long taken him to be useless, indeed a threat to the future" (Roazen 140). In *The Psychiatrist and the Dying Patient* (1955), Eissler tries to talk a patient out of committing suicide, reminding her of how her physician would feel. "I asked her whether she ever thought what it meant to a physician when a patient dies by his own hand" (189). One can understand Freud's anger and his fear that the suicide would discredit psychoanalysis.

Given Freud's unmistakable ambivalence, he was right not to accept Tausk into analysis: the negative countertransference would have doomed therapy. It's problematic, though, that Freud pressured Deutsch into terminating her treatment of Tausk. There's little question that the precipitating cause of Tausk's suicide was his fear over remarriage, but was Freud's rejection of Tausk also a major factor? Roazen has no doubt that this was a key reason. Nevertheless, Tausk had a history of depression and possibly manic depression. Should one conclude, as Roazen does, that Freud's letter to Lou Andreas-Salomé was "inhuman" (Roazen 140)? Ironically, Roazen sounds as harsh and judgmental here as Freud appears in his letter to Lou Andreas-Salomé. Roazen makes other disputable allegations, including the conjecture that Tausk's suicide was an acting out of Freud's evolving theory of a death instinct. Roazen further suggests, in a more speculative assertion, that Freud might have postulated the existence of a death instinct as a way to absolve himself of responsibility for Tausk's suicide. Roazen finally accuses Freud of damaging if not destroying his analysands' and students' lives. "How could Freud have ever gotten so much power over those people?" (Roazen 156), a rhetorical question that conjures up the existence of a Rasputin, an evil genius. After his father's suicide, the seventeen-year-old Marius Tausk visited Freud, who was courteous to him and promised to return Tausk's final letter to him, which the son treasured for the remainder of his life. But Roazen then offers a gratuitous reproach of Freud: by returning the letter, Freud "was finishing getting rid of Victor Tausk" (Roazen 127).

Eissler's two books on Tausk contain largely similar arguments and information, and one wonders why the author felt a second book was necessary. Eissler may have thought that if he couldn't demolish his opponent the first time, he would the second time. Much of the first book, *Talent and Genius* (Tausk representing the former, Freud the latter), is an ad hominem attack. Thus, Eissler writes, in one place, about the "grandiose fantasies" that Roazen projected onto Freud, "as if he were almighty" (111), and, in another place, how Roazen "identified with Tausk's aggression against authority" (193). Sometimes Eissler's tone sounds threatening. "The author had better be terribly sure of everything he is saying here, because what he is doing is nothing less than accusing Freud of actions that are abominable" (86). Other times, Eissler's tone is condescending, as when he writes about Roazen's "uncanny journalistic flair, an art of which he is an estimable master" (148). Throughout the book he accuses Roazen of intellectual dishonesty. "I would not like to play poker with the author; I am almost certain that, with each round, he would announce the rules of the game anew, after every player had put his cards on the table" (182). In the appendix, Eissler characterizes Roazen's book as a folie à deux between the biographer and his subject, shared madness. Eissler never considers whether his lifelong overidentification with Freud, who can do no wrong, is another example of folie à deux.

Talent and Genius is objectionable in other ways. Eissler does not limit his disapproval to Roazen; he also blames those who have reviewed Roazen's book favorably. In a footnote, he singles out for censure Roy M. Whitman, a "member of the American Psychoanalytic Association and active in a university Department of Psychiatry." According to Eissler, "Whitman leaves all of Roazen's errors uncorrected"—and adds a new one (207, n.12). In another footnote, Eissler quotes from an unpublished letter in the Sigmund Freud Archives. "It is the Archives' policy not to make its collection accessible, for the time being, to the public. The Board of Directors [of which he was the head] has given me special permission to deviate in this instance from this policy" (156, n.2). Despite or because of the use of this privileged information, Eissler cannot understand other scholars' indignation over not having access to the same material.

"Enough," Eissler exclaims midway through *Talent and Genius*. "If I have not convinced the reader by now that the author's book is a biased and malicious attack against Freud, I never shall—even if I should pile on more examples" (194). But he cannot help himself write another book on the subject. In his first book, Eissler never refers to Victor Tausk's son Marius, an omission he rectifies in his second book. Eissler sent Marius Tausk, whom he refers to as "Prof. Dr. Tausk," a copy of the manuscript and invited him to respond to it. Although Eissler tells us little about Marius Tausk (1902–90), he was an influential endocrinologist and pharmacologist who was involved with the discovery of the adrenal steroids, oral contraceptive pills, and corticosteroids. Marius Tausk received his medical training at the University of Graz in Austria and then left for Amsterdam to work in an institute of pharmacology and later joined a pharmaceutical company. He received several scientific awards, two honorary doctorates, and was honored with the Knighthood of the Order of the Netherlands Lion. He spoke five languages—and often he disagrees with Eissler's English translation of his father's writings in German. Acknowledging that he knows little about psychoanalysis, Marius Tausk invokes the words of a famous German chemist, A. Windus, who advised his doctoral students, "Make yourself an enemy of your own theories!" (301). From Marius Tausk's point of view, Eissler never heeded that advice.

Eissler agreed to Marius Tausk's request not to respond to his criticisms, though throughout the book Eissler tries to anticipate his objections. Eissler's two books offer largely the same interpretation of Tausk's psychopathology, albeit the second is more detailed and conjectural. Additionally, *Victor Tausk's Suicide* is a more disturbing portrait than its predecessor, which accounts for Marius Tausk's belief that Eissler wrote it not as an empathic physician but as a severe judge and moralist. Apart from the vexed question of why Tausk killed himself, which we can never know with certainty, the question is how Eissler defends Freud from Roazen's accusations—and Marius Tausk's involvement with the controversy.

Eissler maintained that the motives for Victor Tausk's suicide haunted Marius Tausk's life, an allegation with which the son vigorously disagrees. He denies Eissler's other claims, such as the severity of his father's psychopathology. Marius Tausk does not comment in the appendix on his father's relationship to Freud, nor on Roazen's belief that Freud's rejection of Victor Tausk played a causative role in the suicide, but he discusses these two issues in his article "Victor Tausk as Seen by His Son" in a 1973 issue of *American Imago*. The article conveys the author's resentment over Roazen's characterization of his "masochistic Jewish mother" (Roazen 9), his interest in becoming a psychoanalyst until his father's suicide, and his attitude toward Roazen's book. The crucial sentence is the following: "When Dr. Roazen presented me with his 'rejection hypothesis' I was utterly incredulous but I confess when I read the complete story, it impressed me as far more convincing than I had anticipated" (Marius Tausk 333). "More convincing" does not imply "fully convincing." Ironically, in writing two books exonerating Freud's role in Tausk's suicide, Eissler succeeds only in calling further attention to it. Eissler protested too much, doing harm to both Freud and himself.

Three Instances of Injustice

Having spent his entire adult life defending Freud, Eissler defends himself in his 1993 book *Three Instances of Injustice*, which might have been more accurately titled *J'Accuse*. In the third and last chapter, "The Maligned Therapist *or*, An Unsolved Problem of Psychoanalytic Technique," the aggrieved author is determined to settle scores, engaging in psychoanalytic payback. Or, to use Anna Freud's defense mechanism, Eissler identifies with the aggressor, seeking to wound the two psychoanalytic biographers, Peter Gay and Elisabeth Young-Bruehl, who have wounded him. The result is not pretty.

First, though, Eissler inveighs against gossip and rumor, remarking on the self-destructive motivation of those engaged in this behavior. Anyone who has read *In the Freud Archives* will be able to identify the anonymous author whom he describes:

> A writer who had an uncanny ability to induce the subjects of her interviews to make unintentionally self-damaging statements succeeded in one instance in amassing a collection of highly compromising confessions. In one of her publications she included, without any ostensible necessity, a few statements that her victim had never made. She was so unwise as to put them in quotation marks—that sacred stamp of absolute veracity—which got her into trouble. Those remarks had been supererogatorily added to an otherwise excellent and accurate piece. (*Three Instances of Injustice* 195)

Did Eissler believe that he was rising above the fray by not naming Janet Malcolm? That anonymity allowed him to psychoanalyze Malcolm with impunity? He may have thought so, for in the next paragraph he refers to the "denigrator's masochistic tie to the object of her attack." Did he exempt himself from her chief victim, Masson? Probably, insofar as he claims to have admired the rest of her book, despite the fact that Malcolm skewers him as well as Masson and Swales. Malcolm, whose writings confirmed Freud's self-fulfilling prophecy that psychoanalysis brings out the worst in everyone, died in 2021 at age eighty-six. In her *New York Times* obituary, Katharine Q. Seelye cites Robert S. Boynton's warning in 1992: "Don't ever eat in front of Janet Malcolm; or show her your apartment; or cut tomatoes while she watches. In fact, it probably isn't a good idea even to grant her an interview, as your every unflattering gesture and nervous tic will be recorded eventually with devastating precision."

Eissler next defends his role as secretary of the Freud Archives. Distressed by the many mistakes in translation and interpretation of Freud's correspondence, he insists on the need to impose restrictions on its holdings. "Never-sagging vigilance was to make sure that such literary felonies were not repeated" (*Three Instances of Injustice* 203–4). The main object of Eissler's attack is Peter Gay, whom he accuses of violating a patient's confidentiality in the biography of Freud, misreading a letter by Freud, blaming Eissler for the gaps in the biography, and overlooking Freud's identification with Hamlet and Macbeth. Unable to deny the biography's critical and popular success, Eissler offers an unlikely explanation: "a book that contains so many quotations from Freud's letters as Gay's does cannot but leave the reader deeply touched" (214). The statement reminds me of Norman Holland's quip in *Psychoanalysis and Shakespeare* (1964) about a remark of Freud's. "One of his students was giving a seminar paper on *Hamlet*, and he began by apologizing for the number of quotations from Shakespeare he would have to use. 'Bring as many quotations as you can,' Freud dryly remarked. 'They will certainly be the best part of your paper'" (152). Holland, like Freud, had a droll sense of humor; by contrast, Eissler's comment is mean-spirited. As if his denigration of Gay were not (self-)damning enough, Eissler adds, using a metaphor of impotence, "When Gay read his manuscript it may have dawned on him that his text fell flat and could not rival the letters in sparkle; the limpness of his own contribution might well have frightened him, and the shift to rage at me could then have given him relief" (214).

Eissler's animus toward Elisabeth Young-Bruehl arose from a comment in her biography about Anna Freud, who, returning to Vienna in 1971 after an absence of thirty-three years, "escaped," in her biographer's words, the "hour-by-hour schedule Kurt Eissler had prepared for her in his self-appointed role as her manager—a role she did not want him to assume but which she could not bring herself to refuse him" (Young-Bruehl 402; Eissler 209). One can understand Eissler's pain and disappointment over Anna Freud's criticism, but why call further attention to it? He sees this as part of the "detractor's"—by which he means Young-Bruehl, not Anna Freud—"self-betrayal of unreliability" (209). In the final analysis, Eissler calls Gay and Young-Bruehl "confabulators" because "their detractions do not reveal anything of either an external or an internal reality" (211).

The truest statement in *Three Injustices* occurs when Eissler admits, to his puzzlement, that he was not immune to the criticisms of others. The reader infers this, however, without his explicit confession. Eissler ends the book by discussing how malicious statements about him have undermined his analysands' faith in him. The maligned therapist has several options, he adds, including, in his own case, suing Gay and Young-Bruehl for defamation of character. "The verdict, assumedly favorable, would come to the patients' attention eventually and restore their faith, albeit after long delays" (237). He rejects this option only because he did not wish to expose himself to the tribulations of years of litigation. Eissler never imagines the simplest and best choice for the maligned therapist: dignified silence.

Freud and the Seduction Theory: A Brief Love Affair

Eissler's last book, *Freud and the Seduction Theory: A Brief Love Affair*, published posthumously in 2001, might have been called *Eissler and Freud: A Lifelong Love Affair*. The book demonstrates Eissler's axiom that no criticism of Freud, or himself, goes unchallenged—despite his doleful recognition, as stated in the preface, that "Friend and foe agree that my polemics are a waste of time and effort" (ix). The main targets of Eissler's attack are, no surprise, the usual suspects: Masson, whom he characterizes, in an allusion to Don Quixote, as one who "tilts at imaginary windmills, for the Freud he spars against never existed" (215), and, to a lesser extent, Peter Gay, an "uncannily misguided biographer" (19), but he also pillories other scholars, such as Marianne Krüll, the author of *Freud and His Father* (1986). Additionally, Eissler defends his long relationship with Sergei Pankejeff, better known as the "Wolf-Man," Freud's most famous patient. Yet unexpectedly, for the first time Eissler offers substantial criticisms of Freud, highlighting his hostility toward his early collaborator and benefactor, Josef Breuer. Eissler's uncharacteristic criticisms of Freud, however, do not alter his unshakable faith in psychoanalysis, but in his final book he may have been brooding over Nietzsche's cautionary warning that one repays a teacher badly by remaining a student—and so for the first time the disciple admits that the master was occasionally wrong not in his theory but in his behavior.

"Ingratitude was not a trait of Freud's character," Eissler avers, "but he was notably ungrateful to Breuer" (*Freud and the Seduction Theory* 170). He acknowledges that Freud's ambivalence toward Breuer was everlasting and that in his writings Freud presents a false version of his coauthor. As always, Eissler puts the best possible spin on the fraught relationship:

> It was particularly fortunate that Breuer could serve as a superego figure who, through his own excellent personality, stimulated sublimation. This was an incalculable blessing since it protected the creative process in Freud. Often it happens that valuable creative energy is wasted in hostile acting out against the father. Freud's relationship with Breuer walled in that possibility and served like a guardian angel over the integrity of Freud's creativity. (178)

Breuer benefited from this ambivalence, Eissler maintains, in a rationalization of rare wit: "After all, the ingrate hooked his monumental work to his benefactor's modest beginnings and thus secured him fame that would last as long as his own" (180).

Eissler's discussion of the Wolf-Man occurs in a chapter titled "Alice Miller's Prosecution of Freud," a metaphor that allows Eissler to serve as the impassioned defense attorney. To grasp his series of rebuttals, the reader must first know something about Freud's most iconic patient and the multiple stories surrounding the Wolf-Man, the only Freudian case that we can follow from infancy to death in 1979 at age ninety-two. We have several clashing accounts, each with its own insights and blind spots: Freud's *From the History of an Infantile Neurosis*, written in 1914 and published four years later; the Wolf-Man's *Memoirs* (*The Wolf-Man by the Wolf-Man*), edited and translated by the psychoanalyst Muriel Gardiner, published in 1971; Ruth Mack Brunswick's "A Supplement to Freud's 'History of an Infantile Neurosis,'" published in 1928 and included in Gardner's 1971 volume; Gardner's impressions of her meetings with the Wolf-Man; and the Viennese journalist Karin Obholzer's startlingly candid book *The Wolf-Man: Conversations with Freud's Patient—Sixty Years Later*, published first in German in 1980 and then in English in 1982. The entire story has a Rashomon-like quality, offering conflicting interpretations of the same enigmatic patient.

Freud's affection for the Wolf-Man is striking throughout the case study. Less convincing is Freud's conviction that the origins of his patient's obsessional illness arose from traumatically witnessing his parents having coitus *a tergo* (from behind). For orthodox psychoanalysts, the case study proved the existence of the "primal scene," the first time Freud referred to this term in his published writings. Freud inferred from the Wolf-Man's analysis that his two-year-older sister Anna had "seduced him into sexual practices" (*SE*, vol. 17, 20), but her suicide was far more consequential to him. Freud and the Wolf-Man's later analyst, whom he never liked, Ruth Mack Brunswick, placed greater emphasis on the impact of Anna's seductive behavior than on the lifelong consequences of the suicide on her brother's life. Nor was this the first suicide in the Wolf-Man's life. His father's sudden death at age forty-three from an overdose of veronal was likely a suicide, as was the Wolf-Man's paternal grandmother's death. Decades later, his wife, Theresa, also committed suicide, an act that left him devastated and bereft. Unable to understand why his sister and wife killed themselves, the Wolf-Man became suicidal himself, an example of the contagious nature of self-inflicted death.

The Wolf-Man took great pride in being, as Freud called him, a "piece of psychoanalysis" (*The Wolf-Man by the Wolf-Man* 150). Tellingly, there is not a word in the Wolf-Man's memoirs about witnessing the primal scene or about castration fear. The Wolf-Man's story is sharply different from Freud's story. Freud remains a heroic figure for the Wolf-Man not because of the analyst's dubious dream interpretations but because of the quality of the therapist–patient relationship. This becomes abundantly clear in Obholzer's interviews of the Wolf-Man, which took place between 1974 and 1979. Admiring the creator but not the creation, the Wolf-Man admits to Obholzer that throughout his memoirs he was telling psychoanalysts what they wanted to hear. By contrast, he now describes his life-story to Obholzer as a "propaganda piece for psychoanalysis" (185). Both Gardiner and "Dr. E."—a reference to Eissler—objected strenuously to the Wolf-Man's conversations with Obholzer, though Eissler eventually withdrew his objections. "They made a showpiece of me," the Wolf-Man twice observes, sardonically, to Obholzer (135, 186).

The Wolf-Man's bitterness toward psychoanalysis cannot be dismissed as the result of failing physical and mental health, as Eissler attempts to do in *Freud and the Seduction Theory*. Eissler has nothing kind to say about Alice Miller (whose name is so objectionable that he refers to it as "AM"), Obholzer, or the Wolf-Man himself. The Wolf-Man "formed the illusion of being another Dostoevski and was pained when this was not confirmed during the initially enthusiastic review of his memoirs," Eissler opines. "He never forgave me for expressing the opinion that he was better as a raconteur than as a writer, an opinion shared by Muriel Gardiner" (391). But if one looks at Gardiner's comment in *The Wolf-Man by the Wolf-Man*, one sees heartfelt praise. "His great gift of storytelling and of portrayal of character, although more evident in conversations than in writing, is not missing from his letters" (343). Instead of openly endorsing, if not celebrating the Wolf-Man's memoirs, which reveal the therapeutic nature of writing, Eissler refers to it as providing "considerable narcissistic gratification for Pankejeff" (391), implying a degree of psychopathology. Why not simply say that writing provided the Wolf-Man with healthy pleasure? The only value of Obholzer's publication, according to Eissler, is that one can hear the "decaying personality" of the patient (398). But the book is valuable in other ways, showing not only that Freud was a "genius" but that his interpretation of the lupine dream was "terribly farfetched" (Obholzer 35). The Wolf-Man's characterization of Eissler as a "fanatic of psychoanalysis" (174) would be endorsed by nearly every analyst who was not an orthodox Freudian.

Eissler ends *Freud and the Seduction Theory*—and his writing career—with a rueful reference to contemporary analysts like himself. "The classical analyst who follows Freud is in a precarious situation. Burdened by the doctrine of infantile sexuality and the Oedipus complex and perhaps even crushed by the death drive, which unleashes destruction, he sees dark clouds" (434). Alice Miller's book, like Marianne Krüll's, is part of what Eissler calls the "Freud-Bashing International" (458). Psychoanalysis has "fallen apart," he bewails on the last page (488). Eissler's pessimism exceeds Freud's at the end of his life. Earlier in the book Eissler cites Freud's fervent wish, invoking Macbeth, to "die in harness" (235), a wish that was no less true for Eissler himself, who continued to write to the end of his life, receiving whatever narcissistic gratification he could in his relentless war against perceived Schadenfreudians.

4

Peter Gay

Rational Freud

One might think that two distinguished psychoanalytic scholars, Kurt Eissler and Peter Gay, both of whom revered the same man, Sigmund Freud, to the degree of idolatry, and who did everything they could to enhance his reputation, would respect each other's work, especially if the two men had much in common: secular Jews, born in Europe, who both emigrated to the United States to escape the Nazis, and who were gifted with great intelligence, linguistic ability, and a prodigious work ethic. Moreover, Eissler and Gay were children of the Age of Reason who believed that Freud's creation was scientific. Yet admirers of the same man, and the same profession, psychoanalysis, do not necessarily admire each other.

"All life weighed in the scales of my own life," the poet William Butler Yeats remarks in his autobiography, "seems to me a preparation for something that never happens" (94). This was not true for Gay, Sterling Professor of History at Yale University and, following his retirement in 1993, director of the Center for Scholars and Writers at the New York Public Library. All of Gay's life seemed a preparation for writing his acclaimed 1988 biography *Freud: A Life for Our Time*. Five of Gay's twenty-five books were on Freud, whom he saw as the first psychologist to chart the workings of ambivalence. In 1976, the same year he published *Art and Act*, Gay entered the Western New England Institute for Psychoanalysis as a research candidate and began his training analysis. His goal, as he admits in *Freud for Historians* (1985), was to transform himself from an "informed amateur in the Freudian dispensation into something of a professional" (xiv). Gay never practiced psychoanalysis, but he became a leading psychoanalytic cultural historian and biographer, "one of the major American historians of European thought, period," as Sander L. Gilman stated in the *New York Times* obituary on May 12, 2015, which marked Gay's death at the age of ninety-one. Gay's Freud was, like Gay himself, a loyal son of the Enlightenment, on which Gay had written several books, a rationalist with a "wry respect," as he claims in *Reading Freud* (1990), "for the tenacity of human irrationality" (123).

My German Question

Born in 1923, Peter Joachim Fröhlich spent his childhood and early adolescence in Berlin. He and his parents were fortunate to flee the Nazi menace weeks before escape became impossible. As he recalls in his 1998 memoir *My German Question: Growing Up in Nazi Berlin*, he was doubly lucky, for his father had first booked passage from Germany to Havana on the *St. Louis* in May 1939, but then, presciently anticipating a problem, he found another steamer, the *Iberia*, that left two weeks earlier. As it turned out, Cuban officials refused to allow the *St. Louis* to enter the country, and when the United States also denied the ship entry, the *St. Louis* returned to Europe, where many of the Jewish refugees were deported to concentration camps and eventually murdered. He entered the United States in 1941, changed his surname to "Gay" (the English translation of Fröhlich), and received a full scholarship to the University of Denver in 1943. For years Gay could not speak about his rage toward Germans. Recalling the 1936 Olympic Games held in Berlin, which Hitler used as a showcase for rising German imperial power, Gay describes the satisfaction he experienced when a German sprinter dropped the baton, a sight that filled him with Schadenfreude, which he says dryly can be "one of the greatest joys in life" (83). It took Gay many years before he stopped believing that the only good German was a dead German.

My German Question remains Gay's most self-disclosing work, helping us understand his evolving interest in psychoanalysis. Citing Freud's formulation of the return of the repressed, Gay refers to his "childhood rage" that became a theme in his training analysis—rage that seems to have preceded Hitler's rise to power. He never knew, he told his analyst, whether his mother was angry at him for a reason or whether she was ill. "In retrospect, I know that I mistook the latter for the former, and I confess that I value this conjecture as an important insight for me" (41). He acquired "through some mysterious process of osmosis" some of his mother's physical and psychological ailments. It took him several years to recognize what her "partial invalidism" had done to him. "It seems brutally unfair to my mother, but to this day she remains entrenched in my superego; she makes me uncomfortable. She almost never appears in her own voice, but I recognize her in all her disguises" (42). His mother appeared to be the first, though not the last, to accuse him of being "thin-skinned" and lacking a sense of humor. If this is true, he continues, the problem began in his childhood. Years later, in 1958, when he told his mother that he wanted to marry a divorced woman, Ruth Slotkin, with three young daughters, she welcomed the news: "If I chose such a woman, was her reasoning, she must be all right" (43).

Gay speaks more positively about his father, the "hero" of the memoir, a businessman who was self-educated, cultured, liberal, and fiercely antireligious. Recalling a painful memory, Gay reveals that in the early 1950s, while under the spell of an anthropology course he had taken as a graduate student at Columbia, he lectured his father on the "vulgarity of atheism and the need to understand the social function of religion." The tirade sent his father to bed weeping. At around this time Gay began reading Freud, who "promptly restored my unbeliever's equilibrium by his teaching and by his example" (50). Gay remained, like his parents, a secular Jew, committed to rationality and European Enlightenment values. Gay's first experience with psychiatry occurred when he was a graduate student, filled with self-doubts about his sexuality as a result of a Cuban soldier who had tried to pick him up in 1940, when he was sixteen. "When you have fantasies about sex," a "sensible psychiatrist" in New York asked him, "what do you think about?" Gay replied, without hesitation, "Women," and "that was that" (90). Gay credits his lifelong interest in psychoanalysis—"assisted self-help"—to this event.

Selected as a Notable Book of the Year by the *New York Times Book Review*, *My German Question* "accentuated the negative at the expense of the positive," as Gay concedes (x). Perhaps his most surprising admission, in light of his faith in the talking cure, is that writing the book brought no therapeutic relief. "The intimates who cheered me on virtually promised me that writing my memoir would afford me a long-needed catharsis, that the exploration of my early years would bring me peace of mind. But the promise was not fulfilled" (x). While writing the memoir, however, Gay realized that he had largely freed himself from the poisons of the past, discovering the truth of Freud's observation that, in Gay's own words, "the most effective—or, rather, the least ineffective—way of dealing with misery is work" (204).

Reading is "largely a Rorschach test," Gay declares near the end of *My German Question*. "It is disheartening but true: we get out of texts largely what we put into them" (202). Gay's observation, which is the guiding principle of reader-response criticism, can be seen in his vast scholarship on Freud. Gay does not specify the ways in which his experience growing up in anti-Semitic Berlin shaped his understanding of Freud, who spent nearly his entire adult life in anti-Semitic Vienna, but both men were driven by the search for truth. Both saw psychoanalysis as a young science. Both believed in knowledge as power. Gay never doubts that the major aspects of psychoanalytic theory—the existence of the unconscious; the influence of childhood experiences; transference and countertransference; and defense mechanisms such as repression, projection, and identification—are universal. Gay's Freud was a heroic Freud, a larger-than-life Promethean thinker committed to the pursuit of dark truths regardless of the consequences.

Freud, Jews and Other Germans

Gay's first book on psychoanalysis, *Freud, Jews and Other Germans* (1978), presents us with the essential aspects of the "master," a word he uses throughout his writings. The opening chapter, "Sigmund Freud: A German and His Discontents," envisions psychoanalysis as both the "science of candor" and the "science of suspicion" (46). Tellingly, Gay does not regard psychoanalysis as the "hermeneutics of suspicion," an expression formulated by Paul Ricoeur in *Freud and Philosophy* (1970). Gay never doubts that psychoanalysis is a science, albeit a "peculiar science" (53). He regards Freud's self-analysis as a "masterpiece of the scientific imagination, a masterpiece of the highest order" (82). Gay uses the word *scientific* repeatedly, without qualification: "his scientific works provide sketch maps to his innermost nature" (36). The opening paragraph of *The Freud Reader* (1989), edited by Gay, affirms the founder of psychoanalysis as a "great stylist and equally great scientist" (xi), a conviction that appears throughout Gay's scholarship.

Gay's admiration of Freud is boundless even when he describes character traits that others may view negatively. Sometimes Gay uses subtle irony to convey these qualities. "It is true, and helpful, that Freud was not afflicted with the vice of modesty" (36). Nor was Gay. It is not likely he would have endorsed Kaufmann's concept of humbition. In *My German Question* he recalls suffering from short bouts of depression in 1938, shortly before leaving the country, and visiting a doctor who diagnosed him with an "inferiority complex" (144), an opinion he vigorously protested. ("Inferiority complex" was an idea generated by Freud's rival Alfred Adler, not one of Gay's heroes.) Gay regards Freud as sincere, honest, and guileless, a man whose character was beyond reproach. "Freud was most forceful, most amusing, most reasonable, most persuasive when he was most himself" (50)—a statement that comes close to idealization. Gay minimizes the role of culture in Freud's life and in the creation of psychoanalysis. "Freud lived far less in Austrian Vienna than in his own mind" (33), words that seem odd coming from a cultural historian.

Gay is quick to defend Freud from other historians and biographers who have criticized his originality. Witness the following footnote about Henri F. Ellenberger's prodigious *The Discovery of the Unconscious: The History and Evolution of Dynamic Psychiatry* (1970), a tome nearly one thousand pages long: "Self-important and opinionated, the book dishes out verdicts of approval and disapproval much like an old-fashioned schoolmaster, though it is, necessarily, full of historical information" (31, n.4). Interestingly, Gay defends Freud against his own self-criticisms. Thus, when Freud famously claimed in a letter to Wilhelm Fliess written in 1900 that he was not a man of science but rather a "conquistador" by temperament, "an adventurer, if you want it translated—with all the curiosity, daring, and tenacity characteristic of a man of this sort" (Masson 398), Gay responds that although Freud was being candid, he was "not his own best judge" (37). Gay uses the same strategy in his biography. "It is one thing to treat Freud's self-appraisals with respect; a responsible biographer can do no less," he writes in the preface. "It is quite another thing to treat his pronouncements as gospel. As will appear more than once in these pages, Freud was not his own best judge" (*Freud* xvi).

In the other chapters of *Freud, Jews and Other Germans*, Gay anatomizes Jewish self-hatred, a phenomenon found often in *Ostjuden*, Eastern Jews, who internalized the poisonous anti-Semitism that could be seen throughout Europe. But Gay never sees Freud in this way, not only because he lived mainly in his interior self but also because his mind "was as large, as free, as his physical habitat was constricted" (35). It may be impertinent to suggest that as a German-born Jew, Gay could not imagine the feelings of inferiority of Eastern European Jews, but for whatever reason, as Gilman remarks in *Freud, Race, and Gender*, being a Jew meant for Freud being a member of a race. "The importance placed on the rhetoric of race in the science of Freud's time is a quality missing in Gay's biography" (7). Gilman and Gay are arguably the two major American psychoanalytic cultural historians, each prolific and persuasive, but there is a fundamental difference between them. Gilman delineates in his many books on psychoanalysis how Freud constructed his theory through his largely unconscious assumptions about race, class, and gender. Gilman highlights the subjectivity of the human sciences, demonstrating how Freud converted the rhetoric of race in his scientific writings into the construction of female gender, where he theorized that women are inferior to men. Gay, by contrast, argues that if psychoanalysis is a science, as he maintains, then the origins of Freud's ideas—or his feelings about race—do not determine their validity or lack of validity. Tellingly, Gilman gives specific reasons for his criticisms of Gay's work; Gay doesn't explain his objections to Gilman's work, as when he states in passing, in *A Godless Jew*, that he found Gilman's 1986 book *Jewish Self-Hatred: Anti-Semitism and the Hidden Language of Jews* Gay "thoughtful" but "overstated" (171). Gilman would never say, as Gay does, that Freud's Jewishness was "inessential" to the creation of psychoanalysis.

A Godless Jew

A warmup for his biography, published one year later, *A Godless Jew: Freud, Atheism, and the Making of Psychoanalysis* (1987), offers three central propositions: Freud created psychoanalysis as an atheist; he imagined no common ground between faith and unbelief; and it was as a Jewish atheist that he made his monumental discoveries. Gay then shows how both the Jewish and Christian responses to Freud's view of religion revealed a wide spectrum of responses, ranging from rejection and condescension, on the one hand, to approval and appropriation, on the other hand.

No less than Freud, Gay believed in the inevitable hostility between psychoanalysis and religion, and he was skeptical of analysts or theologians who sought common ground. Gay insisted that Freud's iconoclasm, along with his refusal to accommodate religious faith, enabled him to create psychoanalysis. One wonders whether Gay himself, also an "infidel Jew," an expression Freud used in English to characterize himself in his 1928 essay "A Religious Experience" (*SE*, vol. 21, 170), would have devoted so many years to writing about Freud had he not shared the same sense of being a secular Jew, a son of the Enlightenment, like his father, whom he describes in *My German Question* as "bluff and outspoken [who] left no doubt where he stood in the historic battle between reason and unreason" (50). To be sure, Gay wrote books about non-Jews, including a study of Voltaire and a biography of Mozart. Nevertheless, it was the atheistic Freud who seized Gay's imagination, partly because Gay was sympathetic to the idea, which he first acquired from his parents, that one could live without religious faith. On the penultimate page of *A Godless Jew*, Gay shares an anecdote, acquired from "a private communication to the author" in 1984, about a guest who visited Sigmund and Martha Freud on a Friday afternoon in the summer of 1938 and was told, by the latter:

> "You must know that on Friday evenings good Jewish women light candles for the approach of the Sabbath. But this monster—*Unmensch*—will not allow this, because he says that religion is a superstition." Freud gravely nodded and agreed: "Yes," he said, "it *is* a superstition," to which the Frau Professor, addressing her visitor, rejoined, "You see?" (153)

Gay dutifully captures the husband's and wife's conflicting views (Martha Bernays, the granddaughter of the Chief Rabbi of Hamburg, was raised in an observant Orthodox Jewish family), remarking that the guest found the latter's indignation funny, and perhaps, we may add, painful and sad. Gay's voice is indistinguishable from Freud's when it comes to religious disbelief. A few pages earlier, Gay rejects the temptation to "exaggerate" Freud's rigidity (143), yet Freud's unbending nature is conspicuous in this anecdote. Gay then ends his book with the stirring conclusion to *The Future of an Illusion* (1927), allowing Freud's words to speak for himself—and for Gay, too: "No, our science is no illusion. But an illusion it would be to believe that we could get anywhere else what it cannot give us" (154).

Freud: A Life for Our Time

Whenever I begin a book, I first turn to the Acknowledgments page, from which one can learn a great deal about the author. Gay's acknowledgments in *Freud: A Life for Our Time* are full, rich, generous, and sometimes rueful. After praising Kurt Eissler for his diligence in creating the Freud Archives, of incalculable significance to psychoanalytic scholars, Gay then chides him for keeping some of the material closed for decades. Noting Eissler's argument that some scholars have used the available material to besmirch Freud's reputation, Gay responds with a simple counterargument: "bad history or bad biography can be driven out only by better history or better biography, and these can be written only if documents are accessible to scholars." Gay then adds, dolefully, describing his nearly twenty-year correspondence with Eissler on this vexed issue: "total defeat" (784–5).

Notwithstanding this defeat, Gay's *Freud* was the best biography of its age, building upon and superseding Ernest Jones's pioneering three-volume biography published in the mid-1950s. Unlike Jones's idealized biography, Gay's is more balanced though equally laudatory. Encyclopedic in its scope, Gay's biography seems to refer to everything written by and about Freud. Gay read Freud's writings in the original German; most of the translations in the biography are his own. A biographer writing for the general public but also for other scholars, Gay often cites the differences between his own translations and those of James Strachey, the general editor of the *Standard Edition* of Freud's works in English. One can disagree with Gay's conclusions on the many contentious issues of Freud's creation of psychoanalysis and of Freud himself, but Gay's biography, written in the spirit of the Enlightenment, is itself a tribute to science, rationality, and order.

Gay's image of the rational Freud is both a strength and weakness of the biography, as Gilman remarks in his review of *A Godless Jew* and *Freud* published in *The Jewish Quarterly Review*. Gilman opens his review with lavish praise: "Peter Gay's grand biography of Sigmund Freud is without any doubt the definitive 'Freud for our times.' It is a major work of scholarship and erudition which presents the reader with a clear and crisp image of the life, works, and times of 'the father of psychoanalysis'" (251). Yet at the same time, Gilman contends, the biographer sanitizes Freud by avoiding the many ambiguities, particularly on the troubled subject of the "Jewish race," that "complicate Gay's image of Freud as the great rationalist" (253).

Freud's Self-Analysis

Freud's self-analysis is central to any study of his life and work. Widespread agreement exists on the basic facts of the self-analysis; the controversy arises over what Freud learned and failed to learn from his introspective voyage. The self-analysis began around October 1896 and involved what Freud thought was his greatest discovery, the universality of the Oedipus complex. Freud viewed the writing of *The Interpretation of Dreams*, his most revolutionary book, as part of his self-analysis, which was based on free association, his most noteworthy discovery. In the 1908 preface to the second edition of *The Interpretation of Dreams*, Freud reveals the precipitating event of his self-analysis. "For this book has a further subjective significance for me personally—a significance which I only grasped after I had completed it. It was, I found, a portion of my own self-analysis, my reaction to my father's death—that is to say, to the most important event, the most poignant loss, of a man's life" (*SE*, vol. 4, xxvi). Gay uses a felicitous metaphor to convey the impact of Jacob Freud's death on his son's self-analysis: "it acted like a pebble thrown into a still pond, making successive rings of unsuspected magnitude" (89).

Ernest Jones was the first biographer to mythologize the singularity of Freud's self-analysis. "It is hard for us nowadays to imagine how momentous this achievement was," Jones enthuses in volume 1 of *The Life and Work of Sigmund Freud*, "that difficulty being the fate of most pioneering exploits. Yet the uniqueness of the feat remains. Once done it is done forever. For no one again can be the first to explore those depths" (vol. 1, 319). Jones regards Freud's self-analysis as not only unique in history but also leading to an almost saintly disposition, a supremely self-disciplined scientist who was single-mindedly devoted to the pursuit of psychological truth. "There emerged the serene and benign Freud, henceforth free to pursue his work in imperturbable composure" (vol. 1, 320). Lest we forget, the opening sentence of volume 2 of Jones's biography highlights the extraordinary inner change produced by this self-analysis. "By 1901 Freud, at the age of forty-five, had attained complete maturity, a consummation of development that few people really achieve" (vol. 2, 3). Jones's word *consummation* may be an allusion to Hamlet's words, "'tis a consummation/Devoutly to be wish'd"; if so, the allusion would be apt because in his October 15, 1897, letter to Fliess, Freud refers to the gripping power of the two best-known literary examples of a son's love for his mother and jealousy of his father: *Oedipus Rex* and *Hamlet*.

Gay is more skeptical than Jones of Freud's self-analysis. To begin with, he calls into question the value of self-analysis without an analyst to supervise the process. "No matter how one-sided, the psychoanalytic situation is a dialogue. The analyst, though largely a silent partner, offers interpretations that the analysand presumably could not have reached on his own" (*Freud* 97). Additionally, Gay cites Freud's statements that complete self-analysis is impossible. There were depths to his mind that Freud could not reach, Gay suggests, such as his fatal addiction to cigars. "Freud's inability to give up smoking vividly underscores the truth in his observation of an all-too-human disposition he called knowing-and-not-knowing, a state of rational apprehension that does not result in appropriate action" (427). Despite these qualifications about the value of Freud's self-analysis, Gay nevertheless endorses his predecessor's evaluation: "Ernest Jones's hyperbole has much to commend it" (98).

Not according to a later biographer, however. Louis Breger argues in *Freud: Darkness in the Midst of Vision* (2000) that Freud never came to terms in his self-analysis with the many early losses in his life, including the death of his baby brother Julius, who died from an intestinal infection a few months after birth. Julius was named after Amalia Freud's brother, who died when he was twenty. Freud's other losses, in Breger's view, included the withdrawal of his mother's attention following the birth of six more children before he reached the age of ten. The fear of maternal loss, compounded by the departure and arrest of his Catholic nanny, to whom he was devoted, provoked too much anxiety for Freud to confront in his self-analysis. Breger's view of Freud as traumatized by these early losses remains highly controversial, but it helps to explain his neglect of the mother's role in the raising of children. Freud's refusal to acknowledge maternal ambivalence—both a child's ambivalence toward the mother and her ambivalence toward the child—also allows us to understand Freud's Victorian sentimentalization of the mother–son relationship. "A mother is only brought unlimited satisfaction by her relation to a son," he avers in *New Introductory Lectures on Psycho-Analysis* (1933); "this is altogether the most perfect, the most free from ambivalence of all human relationships" (*SE*, vol. 22, 133).

Breger respects Gay's scholarship on Freud but offers several convincing criticisms. "One comes away from this biography believing that Freud was on the right side of all the controversies, that he was the hero and the others cowards, petty, or mentally disturbed" (381). Breger points out, moreover, that Gay never takes seriously psychoanalytic theorists other than Freud, such as John Bowlby and Heinz Kohut. And Gay has little to say about the most salient aspect of psychotherapy, the quality of the patient–analyst relationship. In a brief footnote in his Freud biography, Gay remarks that analysts have recently begun to call this rapport a working alliance or a therapeutic alliance but then adds, condescendingly, "it is not ancestor worship for them to reread Freud's papers on technique and conclude that they have been largely anticipated once again" (300). This is not true, however. The contemporary emphasis on the therapeutic relationship is radically different from the early analysts' practice, where they often attempted to be a blank screen to their patients, a technique Freud advised but did not follow himself.

Madelon Sprengnether does not cite Breger in her 2018 book *Mourning Freud*, but she agrees that Freud never came to terms with his early losses, resulting in his inadequate understanding not only of women but also of grief. For example, after Freud's daughter Sophie died suddenly in 1920 from the Spanish influenza, he refused to mention any sorrow that his grandson Ernst must have felt, as is evident in an astonishing footnote that appears in *Beyond the Pleasure Principle*. "When this child was five and three-quarters, his mother died. Now that she was really 'gone' ('o-o-o'), the little boy showed no signs of grief" (*SE*, vol. 18, 16, n.1). Sprengnether characterizes Freud's next sentence as a "stunning *non sequitur*" (52): "It is true that in the interval a second child had been born and had roused him to violent jealousy" (16). In Sprengnether's view, Freud's interpretation of the fort/da ritual probably reveals more about his own efforts to deny grief than it does about his grandson's anguish. Sprengnether's characterization of the differences between Jones's and Gay's attitude toward Freud's self-analysis is persuasive. "What Jones accomplishes through a rhetoric of hero-worship, Gay conveys through a tone of sophisticated rationality and urbanity" (37).

Gay is aware of Freud's many troubling statements about women, his belief that women were largely a "dark continent," yet the biographer consistently casts a positive spin on the negative. "He said some deeply offensive things about women, but not all of his theoretical pronouncements and private opinions were antagonistic or patronizing" (501). In *A Godless Jew*, Gay characterizes Freud's notorious query to Marie Bonaparte—"what does woman want?"—as "virtually a cry of despair, the desolate exclamation of a decoder staring at a document he cannot decipher" (151). The touching metaphor ignores Freud's other callous or insensitive judgments on female psychology.

Another Biography

As Gay's subtitle suggests, his biography of Freud is "A Life for Our Time," reflective of the closing decades of the twentieth century. A more timely biography is Adam Phillips's *Becoming Freud: The Making of a Psychoanalyst* (2014). One of England's most celebrated psychoanalysts and literary critics, Phillips is a witty provocateur, and he opens his slender biography, only 178 pages long, with an astounding claim: "The story of Freud's life is easily told" (1). Unlike Gay, Phillips sees Freud as an anti-Enlightenment thinker who, as he grew older, found it harder to believe in reason and science. Phillips's postmodern Freud is a darker and more troubling figure than we see in Gay's biography. Just as Gay's dual allegiance to history and psychoanalysis can be seen in nearly all of his books, Phillips's dual allegiance to literature and psychoanalysis is strikingly evident, especially his Wildean wit. Phillips delights in defamiliarizing Freud, as in the following startling statement: "the fact that Freud invented psychoanalysis mostly out of conversations with men but through the treatment mostly of women—that psychoanalysis was a homosexual artifact—can tell us something about Freud's homosexual and heterosexual desire, what he wanted men and women for; our desires inform our facts and our fact-finding" (4). In a koanlike sentence, Phillips remarks that "Freud discovered psychoanalysis in his sleep" (126). After psychoanalysis, Phillips maintains, all our narratives of the past, including Freud's, are suspect. We see throughout Phillips's biography a paradoxical Freud whose most dogmatic quality is skepticism. Whereas Gay views Freud as Freud viewed himself, the man who solved the riddle of the Sphinx, Phillips sees Freud as sphinxlike, the thinker who raises questions about himself but never answers them. The only commonality between the two biographers is their recognition of Freud's greatness as a writer. "Freud would become," in Phillips's words, "the most literary of psychoanalysts" (78).

Peter J. Swales

Gay's voluminous scholarship is evident in the forty-page bibliographical essay at the end of the biography, where he surveys the massive research on Freud studies. It's likely that Gay wrote the bibliographical essay after he completed the biography, for many of the authors' names do not appear in the index, including that of Peter J. Swales, whom Gay describes as "offering confident conjectures" that Freud had a sexual relationship with his sister-in-law Minna Bernays. Another of Swales's confident conjectures was the claim that Freud tried to murder Fliess during their last meeting in 1900. Gay astutely describes Swales's—and, as we shall see, Frederick Crews's—method of reading: "When a statement that Freud makes concerning someone else may well apply to himself, Swales accepts it as evidence; when a statement fails to fit, he accuses Freud of disguising the material, or of brazen deception" (753). Nevertheless, Gay accepts the possibility that Freud may have had an affair with his sister-in-law and praises Swales's sleuthing. In the biography's acknowledgments, Gay thanks Swales for "liberally" supplying him with photocopies of his writings and other hard-to-get materials despite Swales's knowledge of Gay's "quizzical attitude" toward his biographical speculations and reconstructions. Swales, by contrast, does not try to be even-handed in his review of Gay's biography published in the *Los Angeles Times*. Swales ends the churlish review by sarcastically recommending the book "for those who enjoy an easy read and care little whether what they are reading is particularly well-informed or true—in other words, for those who like their food for the mind conveniently processed and prepackaged."

Swales believed, as he recklessly confided to Janet Malcolm in her 1984 exposé *In the Freud Archives*, that he was the "only person who has ever really understood Freud." The reason behind Swales's claim, he continued, was because they were dark doubles. "And in taking on Freud," Swales boasted to Malcolm, "I was taking on the monster that existed in myself." In Swales's view, "all people are devious and sinister. . . . For me, the world is full of shit"

(118). Given this scatological worldview, Swales never doubts that Freud was like himself, deceitful, manipulative, and hypocritical. One recalls the seventeenth-century French writer François de La Rochefoucauld's quip: "If we had no faults of our own, we would not take so much pleasure in noticing those of others."

Swales made a number of noteworthy scholarly discoveries. In his first and most influential psychoanalytic publication, "Freud, Minna Bernays, and the Conquest of Rome" (1982), Swales calls attention to what has become known as the *aliquis* episode in *The Psychopathology of Everyday Life* (1901). Swales shows persuasively that the person Freud encounters on a holiday trip in the summer of 1889, a young man of academic background who was familiar with Freud's writings, and who had forgotten the word aliquis, the indefinite Latin pronoun for "someone," was Freud himself. In his 1986 essay "Freud, His Teacher, and the Birth of Psychoanalysis," Swales discovered the identity of Freud's early patient "Frau Cäcilie M.," tracing her to the wealthy Viennese poetess Anna von Lieben. In "Freud, Katharina, and the First 'Wild Analysis'" (1988), Swales identifies Freud's patient as Aurelia Kronich, the daughter of Julius and Gertrude Kronich. These discoveries have deepened our understanding of Freud, but Swales, who described himself as a Welsh "guerilla historian" of psychoanalysis, became a Schadenfreudian, maintaining, as he wrote in "A Fascination with Witches" (1982), that Freud was a "witch-torturer reincarnate, exploiting the arts of persuasion" (155, n.47).

Swales died in 2022 at age seventy-three. In his *New York Times* obituary, Neil Genzlinger referred to him as a "self-taught scholar who shook up the cloistered world of Freudian studies." No other scholar has rocked the psychoanalytic world as did Swales. It is for this reason that Gay devotes so much attention to Swales in the bibliographical essay. His scholarship reveals an ongoing war with Freud; Swales takes a scorched-earth approach to psychoanalysis, destroying everything in its way. Swales's writings betray, as one of the anonymous reviewers of my book pointed out, a "symptomatic, scatological, self-referential assessment of Freud." Gay tried, and often succeeded, in taking a more balanced approach toward Freud, rising above the fray. Yet in his bibliographical essay, one can see his pained disillusionment with Freudian scholarship, as when he declares that an "astonishing share" of it is "malicious or downright absurd" (741). The rational Gay calls Paul Roazen's scholarship a "maddening mixture of hard digging, extensive interviewing, snap judgments, and uncertain tone" (744). Victor Tausk's suicide, Gay asserts, "has been the subject of envenomed controversy" (769), a metaphor that suggests he, too, has been severely stung.

Dying in Harness

Gay ends his biography with a heartfelt discussion of Freud's final days when, in irremediable pain, he reminded his physician, Max Schur, of their agreement to give him a fatal dose of morphine to end his suffering. Most of the material about Freud's physician-assisted suicide comes from Max Schur's *Freud: Living and Dying* (1972), but Gay provides new information gleaned from Schur's unpublished writings. Noting that Schur wrote six drafts of a lecture he gave in 1964 called "The Problem of Death in Freud's Writings," Gay remarks that "Schur seems to have agonized over these pages as he had not agonized over anything else all his life" (739). Gay recalls the letter Freud had written to the Swiss pastor Oskar Pfister nearly four decades earlier: "Let us die in harness, as King Macbeth says." The last sentence in Gay's *Freud* could not be more in character for an Enlightenment thinker—or an Enlightenment biographer. "The old stoic had kept control of his life to the end" (651).

Reading Freud—and Possibly Himself

Gay observes in *A Godless Jew* that it seems "only fair to psychoanalyze the first psychoanalyst" (58). Is it appropriate, then, to psychoanalyze Freud's psychobiographer—or at least speculate when the psychobiographer uses the veil of fiction to analyze himself? The question arises in Gay's last major psychoanalytic study, *Reading Freud: Explorations & Entertainments*, published in 1990, which contains an intriguing seven-page case study about the hidden psychological forces that sometimes lead to paralyzing indecision. In this "invented but plausible" vignette, Gay describes a professor of acoustical engineering, admired by his colleagues, and generally well paid with sufficient time for his passion, research into loudspeakers. The engineer lives in the Midwest and receives an enticing offer from a southern California company noted for its innovative sound systems. The unsolicited offer "seductively promises him not only life in the sun but a still higher salary and even more time for his 'own' work than his university has been willing to allow him." He is "tempted" by the offer, and his wife, with whom he has discussed the situation, appears to be "neutral." The California firm has given him a month to accept or reject the offer.

The engineering professor has informed his department chair about the attractive offer and has "shrewdly" negotiated for better working conditions. He appears to be in a win-win situation: regardless of the decision he makes, he will be better off professionally. Yet he is torn, deeply conflicted, uncharacteristically indecisive. "He wants to go and he wants to stay." He methodically dictates two letters to his secretary, one accepting, the other rejecting the offer. He makes his decision on the twenty-ninth day: he will remain at the university. His friends give him a party, and his department chair informs him privately that he can expect a substantial raise.

The engineering professor remains shaken, however, for he has not anticipated that the situation would produce a psychological crisis in him. "'I swear,' he told a friend later, 'that half an hour before I directed my secretary which letter to send, I had no idea which way I would jump.'" As Gay examines the situation, he discloses that unconscious psychological forces played a greater role than the engineering professor realizes. "His father, a practical man of business, had long disdained his academic post as unworthy of his talents, a fact of his life that had not entered into the engineer's conscious calculations at all." The fraught father–son relationship contributes to the engineering professor's psychological dilemma. "Two aspects of his unresolved oedipal problems, powerful if repressed ambivalent feelings toward his father, struggled for supremacy in him without his being aware of that conflict at all." Other submerged conflicts enter the story. "Among these were his overprotective impulses toward his wife (who, he correctly sensed, for all her strenuous neutrality, was sending him subtly pleading messages to remain in the region in which she had grown up), impulses competing with resentment against her soft dictatorship."

Gay then complicates the story. Suppose the California firm, knowing the engineering professor better than he knows himself, gives him a whole year or two to decide. Appalled by his psychological vacillation and bouts of anxiety, he decides to enter psychoanalysis, where he begins to confront some of the conflicts that have long bedeviled him: "his haunting oedipal mixed feelings—an unconscious identification with his father battling an equally unconscious rebelliousness against him—as well as his complex attitudes toward his wife." Psychoanalysis proves valuable, allowing him to respond more rationally to his confusing emotions. "He can now, as the analysts would say, test reality with a fair measure of success. Is he free now to move or to stay, or at least freer than before? Freud would say that he is" (*Reading Freud* 87–90). And so would Gay.

Was Gay writing about himself in this extended vignette? It's possible he was describing his own conflicted feelings about leaving Columbia in 1969 to join Yale, a move that would have required his wife, who grew up in New York City, to leave the region in which she was born. Entering psychoanalysis years later, Gay would have been able to dissect his agonizing career decision. Apart from the disguise of writing about an engineering professor, one can easily imagine the situation of an eminent history professor, passionately committed to scholarship, receiving an offer from another university—a dream job that would raise his salary and give him more time to write. (There is never any doubt that the engineering professor has acted ethically, not opportunistically: he has not, like others in his profession, cynically applied to another university simply to receive a salary increase at his own institution.) One can also imagine the engineering professor's father resembling Gay's father, a practical man of business. Gay never mentions in *My German Question* how his father felt about having an academic for a son, but we remember Gay's cruel words to him as a graduate student. But what about the engineering professor's relationship with his wife? Did Gay feel overprotective toward his own wife while at the same time resenting her control over him?

Possibly. In her 1996 *Unfinished People: Eastern European Jews Encounter America*, which won the National Jewish Book Award for nonfiction, Ruth Gay offers a fascinating cultural study that includes her own life growing up in the Bronx. Writing as a septuagenarian, she vividly dramatizes the conflict between two worlds, Eastern European Orthodox Judaism and American Reform Judaism. She recalls how her father, living to the age of ninety-eight, growing up in Poland, always referred to her sister and her as his "two disappointments" because they were not sons—an "offense to his manhood" (205). She conveys her father's test for finding a good-tempered wife:

> The prospective bride was given a basket of knotted yarns and asked to untangle them. As she worked, she was closely observed and her response to this difficult and maddening task became one of the measures of her acceptability. Although I remained prudently silent as I listened, I simmered with outrage as much at the story itself as at my father's smiling acceptance of it with its implication that women were created humbly and cheerfully to serve men. My feelings were relieved only by my thankfulness that I had been born in the Bronx and not in Bialystok. (209)

Based on this piquant passage and others, one may infer that Ruth Gay was an ardent feminist, from which one can conclude, to return to Peter Gay's vignette about the engineering professor, that she was an independent, strong-willed woman capable of soft dictatorship. If Gay's vignette is about himself, his wife must have chuckled, for each read closely the other's work: Ruth Gay dedicated *Unfinished People* to her husband.

If Gay was writing about himself in disguised form, then he was not only following in Freud's footsteps but also offering an example of his own gift for fiction, as he had done in the imaginary "review" he had "discovered," published in a fictitious German-sounding medical journal, of *The Interpretation of Dreams*. He recalls in *Reading Freud* the flap over an article in the *New York Times* written by Daniel Goleman in 1988 under the title "A Freud Spoof Is Slipped Past Many Scholars." Goleman's article highlights Gay's counterfeit review, published in 1981, which purportedly was an early evaluation of *The Interpretation of Dreams*. Unable to see its humor, some readers of Gay's satirical review (which is reprinted in *Reading Freud)*, such as Peter Swales, took it at face value, exposing their gullibility. Swales was so outraged by the review, which he regarded as intellectual fraud, that he wrote an open letter to Benno Schmidt, Yale's president, in which he called Gay a "consummate villain" and demanded, as Robert S. Boynton reported, that he be fired. Notwithstanding Gay's annoyance over the brouhaha, his gift for a fantastic rereading of early psychoanalytic history enabled him, if I am correct, to fictionalize his own case study without detection.

Regardless of whether he was writing about himself in this vignette, Gay's interest in the rational Freud is apparent. To make the unconscious conscious was not only Freud's credo but Gay's as well. The Enlightenment belief in knowledge as power was true for both men. "One may reasonably argue, and a psychoanalyst is bound to argue, that it is better to know realities than not to know them, and those realities certainly include the boundaries to one's freedom" (*Reading Freud* 90). Gay ends his vignette with an Enlightenment insight that informs his biography of Freud: "To be free is to wield the weapon of reason against the blandishments and the terror of illusions" (94).

Part II

Schadenfreudians

5

D. H. Lawrence

Evil Freud

There's no evidence that D. H. Lawrence read Freud, but he admired him briefly, as we learn from the editor and literary critic John Middleton Murry. In 1914, Murry had a conversation with Lawrence and the psychoanalyst David Eder, who had praised Lawrence's 1913 novel *Sons and Lovers* for its keen Freudian insights. Murry was bewildered by the fraught "life or death" discussion between Lawrence and Eder, who had translated into English *The Interpretation of Dreams* and was, as Freud acknowledged in his Foreword to a book about him, the first analyst in England. Murry confessed his ignorance when Lawrence asked him in Eder's presence whether he was familiar with Freud's writings. After Eder left, Lawrence berated Murry for his indifference and skepticism. "I felt that I was being indicted, rather unreasonably, for not taking SEX seriously," Murry complains to his readers, implying that he had no need for psychoanalysis because, unlike Lawrence, he was not tortured by sexuality. Murry and his wife, the New Zealand short story writer Katherine Mansfield, could not fathom Lawrence's fondness for psychoanalysis, and when the married couple made fun of Freud, "it only confirmed Lawrence in his suspicion that we were flippant about the Holy of Holies" (Nehls, vol. 1, 231–2).

Lawrence's faith in the Holy of Holies was short-lived. He soon detested psychoanalysis enough to write two major works on the subject, *Psychoanalysis and the Unconscious* and *Fantasia of the Unconscious*, published in 1921 and 1922, respectively. Lawrence did not understand psychoanalysis, but he assumed that the talking cure was antithetical to everything in which he fervently believed. The "great disaster of our civilization is the morbid hatred of sex," he thundered in "Sex versus Loveliness" in 1928, for which he held Freud responsible. "What, for example, could show a more poisoned hatred of sex than Freudian psychoanalysis?" (*Phoenix* II 528). Despite Lawrence's misunderstanding of Freud, many of his writings were strikingly psychoanalytic. Moreover, Lawrence anticipated some of the major developments in psychoanalysis that Freud himself missed. The story of Lawrence's vexed relationship to psychoanalysis is fascinating, illustrating the novelist's most famous critical injunction, expressed in *Studies in Classic American Literature*: "Never trust the artist. Trust the tale" (2).

Against Analysis

To judge from Lawrence's correspondence—he wrote over 5,700 letters, constituting eight volumes in the Cambridge University Press edition—Freud was responsible for all the evils of contemporary life. "I never did read Freud," he confided to an admirer in 1913, "but I have heard about him since I was in Germany" (*Letters*, vol. II, 80). He disliked most of what he heard, for his few references to Freud are negative. "The longer I live the less I like psychoanalysis," he admitted to the British psychoanalyst Barbara Low in 1916. "Depart from evil and do good—I think analysis is evil" (*Letters*, vol. III, 42). In Lawrence's view, analysands were guilty of blindly submitting to a process that robbed them of their spontaneity, vitality, and agency. "I rather hate therapy altogether," he railed in 1921: "doctors, healers, and all the rest. I believe that a real neurotic is a half devil, but a cured neurotic is a perfect devil. They assume perfect conscious and automatic control when they're cured: and it is just this conscious-automatic control that I find loathsome. . . . I would prefer that the neurotics died" (*Letters*, vol. IV, 142). Neurotics could not be cured, Lawrence contended, because self-reflection only deepens neurosis. "Thinking a lot about oneself is the beginning of neurosis," he opined in 1929, one year before his death at age forty-four (*Letters*, vol. VII, 551). Nor did Lawrence have any use for Jung, whom he described in 1926 as "very interesting in his own sort of fat muddled mystical way. Although he may be an initiate and a thrice-sealed adept, he's soft somewhere" (*Letters*, vol. V, 540). Psychoanalysis was a monolithic theory for Lawrence, and he made no distinction between Freud and the early dissidents, such as Jung and Alfred Adler.

Why did Lawrence maintain that psychoanalysis resulted in perfect conscious and automatic self-control? Not even Freud's most ardent supporters made this extreme claim. Lawrence envisioned verbal therapy as leading to automatons and zombies, men and women alienated from the world of instinct. To avoid this catastrophe, Lawrence insisted that one should follow one's blood consciousness, which he believed is unerringly true. Opposing blood consciousness was mental consciousness, associated with the (self-)destructive will. Anything that encouraged the expansion of mental consciousness, whether it was Platonic dualism, Christian ideology, or Freudian psychoanalysis, was inimical to creative existence.

Sons and Lovers

Lawrence's early masterpiece *Sons and Lovers* reveals one of the most powerful depictions of the Oedipus complex in literature. In a letter to Edward Garnett written in 1912, Lawrence summarizes the "split" in the novel's *Bildungsroman* hero, Paul Morel, who cannot free himself from his all-consuming desire for his mother to commit himself to either the spiritual Miriam Leivers or the sensual Clara Dawes:

> It follows this idea: a woman of character and refinement goes into the lower class, and has no satisfaction in her own life. She has had a passion for her husband, so the children are born of passion, and have heaps of vitality. But as her sons grow up she selects them as lovers—first the eldest, then the second. These sons are *urged* into life by their reciprocal love of their mother—urged on and on. But when they come to manhood, they can't love, because their mother is the strongest power in their lives, and holds them.—It's rather like Goethe and his mother and Frau von Stein and Christiana—As soon as the young men come into contact with women, there's a split. William gives his sex to a fribble, and his mother holds his soul. But the split kills him, because he doesn't know where he is. The next son gets a woman who fights for his soul—fights his mother. The son loves the mother—all the sons hate and are jealous of the father. The battle goes on between the mother and the girl, with the son as object. The mother gradually proves stronger, because of the tie of blood. The son decides to leave his soul in his mother's hands, and, like his elder brother, go for passion. He gets passion. Then the split begins to tell again. But, almost unconsciously, the mother realises what is the matter, and begins to die. The son casts off his mistress, attends to his mother dying. He is left in the end naked of everything, with the drift towards death. (*Letters*, vol. I, 476–7)

Two of Lawrence's authorial intentions are not apparent from the novel itself: the belief that the death of Paul's older brother, William, is caused by the conflict between spiritual and sexual love rather than by physical illness; and the implication that Paul is similarly doomed at the end. Despite the title of the novel's last chapter, "Derelict," Paul's situation is not hopeless, as the lyrical final sentences suggest: "But no, he would not give in. Turning sharply, he walked towards the city's gold phosphorescence. His fists were shut, his mouth set fast. He would not take that direction, to the darkness, to follow her. He walked towards the faintly humming, glowing town, quickly" (*Sons and Lovers* 420).

Nevertheless, there is no question about the accuracy of Lawrence's Oedipal interpretation of his fictional alter ego. Lawrence's close identification with Paul is apparent from other letters, as when he claims that the bond with his mother resembled that between a husband and his wife, one that has been "rather terrible, and has made me, in some respects, abnormal" (*Letters*, vol. I, 190). But Paul's psychological conflict lies deeper than the Oedipus complex. Freud largely ignored pre-Oedipal issues, the child's struggle to separate from the mother to form healthy boundaries between self and other, a process that Lawrence intuited. "I think this peculiar fusion of soul," he wrote in 1910, "never comes twice in a life-time—it doesn't seem natural" (*Letters*, vol. I, 190).

Sons and Lovers quickly caught the attention of psychoanalysts. Alfred Booth Kuttner's early review appeared in a 1916 issue of *The Psychoanalytic Review*. Kuttner highlighted the psychosexual conflicts surrounding Paul's Oedipal love. Some of Kuttner's assumptions are outdated, such as his conviction that psychoanalysis forms the basis for the "scientific study of human motives" (295). Additionally, like many of the early psychoanalysts, Kuttner pathologized fictional characters, as when he describes Paul as bearing "so many ear-marks of degeneracy and abnormal impulse" (307). Kuttner is too self-confident in his descriptions of the "normal evolution of love," too judgmental in his dismissal of the importance of Paul's painting, too narrow-minded in his characterization of Paul as "effeminate." Moreover, Kuttner follows Freud in appreciating literature not for its own sake but mainly as a confirmation of psychoanalytic theory. Literature becomes an "invaluable accessory to the psychologist," Kuttner declares in the beginning of his discussion (295), not realizing what psychoanalysis can learn from literature.

Despite these limitations, and without having read Lawrence's authorial explanation of the novel, Kuttner offers several insights into the novel, including a largely similar Oedipal interpretation of *Sons and Lovers*, especially Mrs. Morel's role in Paul's early fixation. "Her unappeased love, which can no longer go out towards her husband, turns to Paul for consolation; she *makes* him love her too well" (312). Without speculating on Lawrence's biography, Kuttner shows how similar psychosexual conflicts pervade his earlier writings, including the novel *The White Peacock* and the play *The Widowing of Mrs Holroyd*. "In each there is a deadly father or husband hate, a poignant sense of death, and a picture of marriage or love that does not satisfy" (315). Perhaps most significantly, Kuttner affirms the writing cure. In dramatizing his fictional characters' conflicts, Kuttner suggests, Lawrence frees himself from the conflicts that torment his characters:

> For Mr. Lawrence has escaped the destructive fate that dogs the hapless Paul by the grace of expression: out of the dark struggles of his own soul he has emerged as a triumphant artist. In every epoch the soul of the artist is sick with the problems of his generation. He cures himself by expression in his art. And by producing a catharsis in the spectator through the enjoyment of his art he also heals his fellow beings. His artistic stature is measured by the universality of the problem which his art has transfigured. (317)

In light of Kuttner's generally sympathetic review of *Sons and Lovers*, why did it offend Lawrence? "I hated the Psychoanalysis [*sic*] Review of *Sons and Lovers*," he protested bitterly to Barbara Low in 1916. "You know I think 'complexes' are vicious half-statements of the Freudians: sort of can't see wood for trees. When you've said Mutter-complex, you've said nothing—no more than if you called hysteria a nervous disease." In Lawrence's view, the Freudian critic had destroyed the beauty of the novel. "My poor book: it was, as art, a fairly complete truth: so they carve a half lie out of it, and say 'Voilà.' Swine!" (*Letters*, vol. II, 655).

Tellingly, Kuttner never claimed that he was revealing the full truth of *Sons and Lovers*, nor had Lawrence himself when he was explaining his authorial intentions. All interpretations, no matter how persuasive, are partial truths. We murder to dissect, Wordsworth realized, and Lawrence distrusted any analysis of literature which, however nuanced, fails to convey the aesthetic experience. Perhaps Lawrence objected to Kuttner's clinical language. Lawrence maintained that psychoanalytic "complexes" are a "myth" and do not exist, as he stated in 1922 (*Letters*, vol. IV, 279). Yet in his correspondence, Lawrence sometimes used psychoanalytic language himself, without irony or sarcasm. He warned Katherine Mansfield in a 1918 letter, which contained a copy of a book by Jung that he had recently read, to avoid making the same errors in her marriage to John Middleton Murry that Lawrence himself made with his wife, Frieda:

> Beware of it—this Mother-incest idea can become an obsession. But it seems to me there is this much truth in it: that at certain periods the man has a desire and a tendency to return unto the woman, make her his goal and end, find his justification in her. In this way he casts himself as it were into her womb, and she, the Magna Mater, receives him with gratification. This is a kind of incest. It seems to me it is what Jack does to you, and what repels and fascinates you. I have done it, and now struggle all my might to get out. In a way, Frieda is the devouring mother. (*Letters*, vol. III, 301–2)

Why, then, did Lawrence hate Kuttner's review? One suspects that Lawrence rejected Kuttner's interpretation partly because its truth was threateningly accurate. Kuttner highlighted Lawrence's conflicts that the novelist sought to portray more subtly—and ambiguously. Novelists conceal their identity through the veil of fiction; by contrast, literary critics, especially those who are psychoanalytically oriented, strive to look through the veil, thus exposing the writer's vulnerability.

A History of Psychoanalytic Literary Criticism

With the exception of *Hamlet*, *Sons and Lovers* has probably received more intense psychoanalytic scrutiny than any other literary text. Indeed, the history of psychoanalytic criticism of *Sons and Lovers* is a history of psychoanalytic literary criticism itself, from classical drive theory to Kohut's self psychology to relational and intersubjective psychoanalysis. Daniel Weiss's 1962 study *Oedipus in Nottingham* offered a detailed analysis of the rivalry between the father and son for the same woman. Lawrence's insight into the "devouring mother," the title of Judith Ruderman's 1984 book, anticipated a turning point in the history of Lawrence scholarship. Ruderman shows how the child's desire to fuse or merge with the mother awakens the fear of dependency and identity loss. To counteract this fear, Lawrence came to believe, as he conceded in the 1918 letter to Mansfield, that women must "yield some sort of precedence," by which he meant submission to male domination. "I do think men must go ahead absolutely in front of their women, without turning round to ask for permission or approval from their women. Consequently the women must follow as it were unquestioning. I can't help it, I believe this. Frieda doesn't. Hence our fight" (*Letters*, vol. III, 302). In my 1990 study *Narcissism and the Novel*, I explore Paul Morel's narcissistic conflicts, including the extent to which his need to be martyred in love unites him with his mother, both of whom see themselves as long-suffering, self-sacrificing, and misunderstood. The psychoanalytic literary critic James C. Cowan has authored two books, *D.H. Lawrence and the Trembling Balance* (1990), in which he calls *Sons and Lovers* the "first great psychoanalytic novel in English" (258), and *D.H. Lawrence: Self and Sexuality* (2002); both books show how Lawrence's characters suffer from narcissistic deficits rather than Oedipal conflicts. In her two books *Literature and the Relational Self* (1993) and *D.H. Lawrence and the Paradoxes of Psychic Life* (1999), Barbara Schapiro uses relational theory, as developed by Stephen A. Mitchell, to analyze issues of shame and envy.

Lawrence rewrote *Sons and Lovers* three times, the final version being the most Freudian. Frieda Lawrence influenced the final revision, as Frederick J. Hoffman points out in *Freudianism and the Literary Mind* (1957):

> "Yes. Lawrence knew about Freud before he wrote the final draft of *Sons and Lovers*," Frieda tells me in a letter of November 21, 1942. "I don't remember whether he had read Freud or heard of him before we met in 1912. But I was a great Freud admirer; we had long arguments and Lawrence's conclusion was more or less that Freud looked on sex too much from the doctor's point of view, that Freud's 'sex' and 'libido' were too limited and mechanical and that the root was deeper." (154)

In an irony that Lawrence did not appreciate, during his visit to the United States in 1924, when he and Frieda were staying in Taos, New Mexico, with Mabel Dodge Luhan, a patroness of the arts, she suffered a nervous breakdown and was treated by the Freudian psychoanalyst A. A. Brill. According to the biographer John Worthen (314), Luhan paid his bill by giving him the manuscript of *Sons and Lovers*, incurring the Lawrences' anger.

Psychoanalysis and the Unconscious

Lawrence's literary reputation rests primarily on four novels—*Sons and Lovers*, *The Rainbow*, *Women in Love*, and *Lady Chatterley's Lover*—short fiction, and poetry, but he was also a brilliant literary, social, and psychological critic. Today he might be called a "public intellectual," though he detested intellectuality. In his nonfictional writings he comes across as fiercely polemical, adopting a scorched-earth rhetorical strategy that not merely defeats his opponents but annihilates them from existence. Nowhere is Lawrence's satire more militantly aggressive than in *Psychoanalysis and the Unconscious*. Witness the opening paragraph in the first chapter, "Psychoanalysis *v.* Morality":

> Psychoanalysis has sprung many surprises on us, performed more than one volte-face before our indignant eyes. No sooner had we got used to the psychiatric quack who vehemently demonstrated the serpent of sex coiled round the root of all our actions, no sooner had we begun to feel honestly uneasy about our lurking complexes, than lo and behold the psychoanalytic gentleman reappeared on the stage with a theory of pure psychology. The medical faculty, which was on hot bricks over the therapeutic innovations, heaved a sigh of relief as it watched the ground warming under the feet of the professional psychologists. (3)

No matter that Freud was not a psychiatrist and that Lawrence was himself expert in abrupt and complete about faces and reversals. Nor does it matter that Lawrence's criticism of Freud, seeing sex everywhere, was precisely the complaint hurled at Lawrence himself by his many detractors. It does not even matter that Lawrence knew little about the man he sought to demolish. What matters, a century after Lawrence penned the two books that he hoped would put the final nail on his antagonist's coffin, ringing the death-knell of psychoanalysis, is that one can hardly find a livelier valediction, one in which, as Philip Rieff noted in his introduction to the 1960 Viking edition, Lawrence casts Freud in the role of the Judas of the unconscious while he portrays himself as the true disciple. Lawrence's misreading of Freud is an example of what Harold Bloom calls the anxiety of influence, in which a strong writer misunderstands a precursor to achieve greatness. Had he not generatively misread Freud, Lawrence might never have written his studies of psychoanalysis, depriving us of two provocative books. It's possible that Lawrence deliberately chose not to read Freud to avoid being influenced by him—the same reason Freud avoided certain authors, as he admitted to his confidant Wilhelm Fliess in 1895: "I do not want to read anything, because it plunges me into too many thoughts and stunts my gratification in discovery" (Masson 141).

Reading *Psychoanalysis and the Unconscious* for the first (or even second) time, one is struck by its strangeness. Lawrence conjures up a taxonomy of the physical and psychic forces constituting consciousness and unconsciousness. To give only one example, he argues that the center of primary consciousness lies in the solar plexus, and then, foreseeing our question, "how do you know this," he replies, "We feel it, as we feel hunger or love or hate" (20), an answer that is defiantly antiscientific.

It is easy to identify Lawrence's major misconception of Freudian theory, the belief that it dispenses with morality. "Psychoanalysis is out, under a therapeutic disguise, to do away entirely with the moral faculty in man" (4). But as Freud made clear in his 1908 essay "'Civilized' Sexual Morality and Modern Nervous Illness," although he traced neurotic illnesses to sexual repression, he never urged sexual promiscuity. Nor did he recommend acting out incestuous cravings, as Lawrence suggests in *Psychoanalysis and the Unconscious*. "Once, however, you accept the incest-craving as part of the normal sexuality of man, you must remove all repression of incest itself. In fact, you must admit incest as you now admit sexual marriage, as a duty even" (7). Freud never suggested that all sexual inhibitions be removed, only those that were psychologically unhealthy. Nor did Freud advocate the opposite extreme, sexual abstinence. "Experience shows that the majority of the people who make up our society are constitutionally unfit to face the task of abstinence" (*SE*, vol. 9, 193).

Having demonized Freud in the opening chapter of *Psychoanalysis and the Unconscious*, Lawrence devotes the second chapter, "The Incest Motive and Idealism," to a discussion of a young man who, as a result of his "profound love for his mother," finds it "impossible to realize himself in marriage," a dilemma that he writes about from painful experience. The young man's conundrum must remain secret until it is "either worn away or persuaded away" (11). The conflict will disappear, however, Lawrence maintains, if one rejects the Freudian unconscious, a "shadow cast from the mind," and instead embraces the "true unconscious," based on the "spontaneous life-motive in every organism" (13). This true unconscious, identified with the soul, is the "causeless created nature of the individual being" (15). Lawrence's vision of the unconscious, as Hoffman pointed out, was much more positive than Freud's, which helps to explain his faith in spontaneity and blood consciousness.

In the next two chapters, "The Birth of Consciousness" and "The Child and His Mother," Lawrence offers his own vision of the child's efforts to separate from the mother. Decades before the psychoanalyst Margaret Mahler studied the various phases of the separation-individuation process, Lawrence grasped the child's daunting challenges in forging identity. No psychoanalyst has described this conflict more vividly than Lawrence, who uses words like "rupture," "severances," and "cataclysm" to evoke the violence of maternal separation. Lawrence doesn't use the word *ambivalence* to evoke the child's fear of and desire for maternal separation, but he implies this in expressions like the "polarity of the dynamic consciousness" (24) that exists from the beginning of life. Nothing must alter this polarity, and if one pole is disturbed, so will be the other pole. Lawrence insists on the child's right to be left alone, a right for privacy, independence, and otherness that Paul strives to achieve in *Sons and Lovers*. Significantly, Lawrence neglects any discussion of the father's role in the child's development, an omission he seeks to correct in *Fantasia of the Unconscious*.

The key word in the penultimate chapter of *Psychoanalysis and the Unconscious*, "The Lover and the Beloved," is *gulf*, which he precedes with words like "irreparable," "unsurpassable," "far," "eternal," and "insuperable." However one may wish to overcome the distance between self and other, to merge mystically with another person, the gulf must be maintained: this is the singular challenge confronting Lawrence's authorial characters. Lawrence sympathizes with the mystics who rhapsodize over attaining the Infinite, but he always draws back, unwilling to sacrifice the uniqueness of the individual self.

In the final chapter, "Human Relations and the Unconscious," Lawrence returns to his central theme: anything that interferes with the dynamic circuit of the unconscious, such as the attempt to form an intellectual idea or ideal, is harmful, once again highlighting his objection to psychoanalysis. We can escape neurosis not through the false psychoanalytic notion of the unconscious but through an understanding of the true unconscious, with its vital polarity of energy. The paradox of writing and reading *Psychoanalysis and the Unconscious* is that it inevitably heightens our mental consciousness, which awakens Lawrence's deepest hostility.

Trigant Burrow

Lawrence referred briefly to Trigant Burrow in *Psychoanalysis and the Unconscious*, and in 1927 he reviewed *The Social Basis of Consciousness*, which had been published years earlier in *The Journal of Nervous and Mental Disease* and *The Psychoanalytic Review*. Given Lawrence's hatred of Freudian psychoanalysis, his enthusiastic review of Burrow's book is surprising. Burrow was a notable figure in the early history of psychoanalysis, though today he is largely forgotten. Born in Virginia in 1875, he studied literature at Fordham University, medicine at the University of Virginia, and experimental psychology at Johns Hopkins. He traveled to Europe to study psychoanalysis with Freud and Jung—the first American, according to Malcolm Pines, to study psychoanalysis from where it originated. Burrow was analyzed by Jung for one year in Zurich and was influenced by the Swiss analyst's theory of the collective unconscious. Returning to the United States, Burrow was twice elected president of the American Psychoanalytic Association, which he helped to found. Burrow was also one of the founders of group analysis and for a time practiced "mutual analysis," in which the analyst and patient shared self-disclosures with each other. The author of seven books and seventy articles, Burrow frequently criticized Freudian theory, resulting in his expulsion from the American Psychoanalytic Association, but his heretical views earned Lawrence's respect. Burrow's anti-authoritarianism, his willingness to be as critical of himself as he was of others, also appealed to Lawrence.

Lawrence begins his review of *The Social Basis of Consciousness* by praising Burrow's honesty—a rare quality among analysts, he reminds us. He lauds Burrow's willingness to change his mind about the Freudian unconscious. Lawrence concedes that the incest complex may be an accurate description of our psychological condition, but he believes that once the term is applied to human behavior, it becomes mechanistic and destructive. Lawrence characterizes the Freudian unconscious as "vicious," an adjective he uses three times in his six-page review. Lawrence apparently assumes that the Freudian unconscious and the incest complex are one and the same; he never mentions other aspects of psychoanalytic theory, such as defense mechanisms (projection, identification, regression, denial, displacement, reaction formation, or identification with the aggressor), transference, or clinical resistance. Lawrence never remarks that the Freudian unconscious contains repressed aggressive as well as sexual drives. Nor does Lawrence emphasize the momentous shift in psychoanalysis from drive theory to ego psychology. In his review, Lawrence makes a distinction between "sex," a positive word, and "sexuality," a negative word that implies for him a blind, self-seeking quality. The distinction between the two words remains unclear, however, and Lawrence links sexuality to concepts that he doesn't discuss in the review, such as homosexuality and narcissism. Lawrence was opposed to individual analysis because he believed that it exacerbated a patient's loneliness, isolation, and disconnection, resulting in what he calls the "idolatry of self." "What must be broken is the egocentric absolute of the individual" ("Review of *The Social Basis of Consciousness*," *Phoenix* 379). By contrast, he embraces Burrow's group analysis, which strengthens, in Lawrence's view, community, commonality, and connection.

Reading *The Social Basis of* Consciousness, one can see why Lawrence commended the book. Burrow was not a graceful writer—Lawrence compared some of his sentences to Laocoön snakes: "one never knows where the head is, nor the tail"—but his occasional epigrams enliven his prose. "The theory of psychoanalysis sets out with a premise; life does not. Psychoanalysis offers a solution; life is its own solution" (17). Burrow calls attention to the limits of his own profession. "The psychopathologist has offered interesting formulations regarding delusions of persecution, but none whatever regarding delusions that persecute" (223). Other times Burrow quotes Nietzsche: "May there not be—a question for alienists—neuroses of health?" (23). And Oscar Wilde: "There are in the world two tragedies. One is not getting what one wants and the other is getting it" (78). Unlike Freud, who was reluctant to write about the analyst's countertransference, fearing that it would damage the public image of the analyst's objectivity, Burrow readily acknowledges his own subjective bias, adding a human dimension to his observations. Freud believed, following Bleuler, who coined the word, that ambivalence characterizes both normal and neurotic behavior. Burrow expands ambivalence to the social unconscious. Ambivalence, which corresponds to Lawrence's word "polarity," based on opposed affective valences, conveys simultaneous love and hate, attraction and repulsion, desire and fear, a theory of dualism that can be seen throughout Lawrence's writings.

Burrow is less sanguine than Freud about the possibility of self-knowledge. "In our present mode of personalism and unconsciousness the attainment of consciousness is of its nature an impossible task" (*The Social Basis of Consciousness* 111). Sexual consciousness raises a red flag to him. "Our sexual self-consciousness is the perennial fig-leaf of early tradition foliating anew in our critical Twentieth Century," Burrow warns, sounding like Lawrence himself. "It is the division of the self of behaviour from the self of spontaneity, of the self as disparate entity from the self as an integral element in our common organic life that is the meaning of the incest-awe as of the neurosis, in its social as well as in its individual expression" (147–8). Burrow would not avoid the attempt to make the unconscious conscious, as Lawrence would, but he discerns the limits of self-knowledge. A dream cannot be taken alive, Burrow avers. "One may no more behold his *real* self in the mirror of the dream than in any other reflecting surface" (184).

Lawrence's distinction between sex and sexuality echoes Burrow's discussion in his chapter "Sexuality and Sex." Instead of dividing sexuality into different clinical or theoretical types and components, as Freud did, such as oral, anal, phallic, latent, and genital, Burrow admits that he now believes these distinctions are harmful.

> In the beginning of my analytic work I fully believed with other psychoanalysts that there was a condition of neurotic or "unconscious homosexuality" distinguishable from what I then believed to exist conversely as "heterosexuality." I was too theoretical, habituative, academic, too limited in the freedom of unsystematized observation to recognize that sexuality, as it now exists socially, is everywhere of one cloth. (210)

Lawrence must have found this passage reassuring, for as we shall see, his most autobiographical fictional characters not only suffered from intense Oedipal conflicts but also from homoerotic desires that could not be directly expressed in his novels and essays because of censorship laws and the threat of imprisonment.

Burrow values self-disclosure in *The Social Basis of Consciousness*, but he is not particularly self-disclosing except for one intriguing footnote:

> While a student of Jung's in the early days of psychoanalysis, at the time when Jung was the very organ of Freud's genius, the clear emanation of his spirit, I remarked to him one day that I had come to the conclusion that the neurotic individual

> inevitably married his mother. Jung's reply, alert as a flash, was characteristic of his brilliant, inclusive scope of vision. "I have come to the conclusion," he said, "that *every* individual inevitably marries his mother." (204–5)

Lawrence does not single out this footnote in his review of *The Social Basis of Consciousness*, but he agrees with it in *Fantasia of the Unconscious*.

Lawrence and Burrow corresponded with each other in the mid-1920s. They both felt that their writings were ignored or misunderstood by the reading public, and they genuinely appreciated each other's work. Indeed, Burrow was one of the few analysts who valued Lawrence's writings on psychoanalysis. In a letter written at the end of 1926, Lawrence praised Burrow for not "bullying" his readers and then asked a question that might be perceived as "rude"—Burrow's racial nationality: "England? Wales? surely not Jewish at all (that's not prejudice—only the psychology isn[']t Jewish," to which Burrow responded: "No, I am not a Jew. I like them and they like me, but racially I am not one of them" (*Letters*, vol. V, 612). Their exchange helps us understand Freud's hope that his would-be successor, Carl Jung, the son of a pastor, would change the public's conception of psychoanalysis, which had been dismissed by its critics as a "Jewish science."

In a letter written to Burrow in July 1927, Lawrence stated his belief that societal instinct was deeper than sex instinct—"and societal repression much more devastating." In his last letter to Burrow, written one month later, Lawrence confessed to suffering from being "cut-off" from everyone, along with being in despair over declining physical health from bronchial hemorrhages. Lawrence then invited Burrow to visit him in Europe (although they never did meet). "I should like to meet you. I love the way you pull the loose legs out of the tripods of the p-a-ytical pythonesses" (*Letters*, vol. VI, 99). Lawrence offered one criticism of *The Social Basis of Consciousness* that does not appear in his review:

> I didn't like your last chapter. One should never bow to one[']s audience. As for "forgiving," I never know what it means. *To forgive all is to understand all.* Whatever do you mean? There is no such *animal*—Can one "forgive" the social unconscious?—in oneself or outside? What's the point?—But you have some special meaning for forgive.—Only that last chapter has a bit of a humble christian apology sound—and the rest was so brave. (*Letters*, vol. VI, 113)

Burrow responded sympathetically to Lawrence's letter, offering perceptive analytic advice: "it is not you who are cut-off, but the image you have of 'you.'" The problem, Burrow explains, is a social one, caused by a "primitive fear-ridden society." In the spirit of mutual analysis, Burrow concurred with Lawrence's criticism of the final chapter in *The Social Basis of Consciousness*. "You are right—one cannot forgive. All our forgiveness is spiritual snobbery," adding, however, that if one is stupid enough to blame oneself, one should be stupid enough to forgive oneself (*Letters*, vol. VI, 115). Burrow esteemed Lawrence, but after his death, the psychoanalyst wrote a letter suggesting that Lawrence was responsible for some of his own psychological difficulties: "Lawrence had his part in the very persecutions that destroyed him. He was an equal element in the forces that isolated him, for all his outcries and protestations" (*A Search for Man's Sanity* 230).

Fantasia of the Unconscious

"I really don't want to convince anybody," Lawrence writes disingenuously in the foreword to *Fantasia of the Unconscious* (53), a continuation of *Psychoanalysis of the Unconscious*. The tendentious tone belies his words. He writes combatively about the development of the child's consciousness, offering a counterblast to Freudian psychoanalysis. Without calling attention to his own conflicted childhood, he offers recommendations that he hopes will produce healthy children. *Fantasia of the Unconscious* is hardly an early version of Dr. Benjamin Spock's bestselling books on baby and child care, but Lawrence believed that his recommendations would change his readers' lives. In offering his own version of child analysis, Lawrence plays many roles throughout the book: child psychologist, radical educator, social revolutionary, and oracle of love. A firebrand and agent provocateur, he writes for the elect, the limited few who have the patience and fortitude to read his ambitious agenda for far-reaching change. Readers may find themselves talking to themselves in exasperation as he alternately cajoles, seduces, and bullies them into submission—rereading my tattered edition of the book I used as an undergraduate, I notice my incredulous marginalia comments such as "he's nuts!" Nuts, perhaps, but never boring. He directs some of his satire against himself, referring self-mockingly to the "pseudo-philosophy" of the present book, adding that his "pollyanalytics" may be deduced from his novels and poems. He thus encourages us to read *Fantasia of the Unconscious* as disguised autobiography. Indeed, of all his nonfictional books, *Fantasia of the Unconscious* reveals—and conceals—the most private secrets of his life.

Fantasia of the Unconscious is an early example of performative art. Lawrence interrupts himself frequently to address his readers, hoping they will be kinder than the critics who savaged *Psychoanalysis and the Unconscious*, to which he refers, either seriously or tongue-in-cheek, as his "small but naturally immortal book" (67). He chooses a circuitous journey in his argument. "There is no straight path between you and me, dear reader, so don't blame me if my words fly like dust into your eyes and grit between your teeth, instead of like music into your ears" (66). David J. Gordon's observation about Lawrence's style in his literary criticism is equally true of his style in his two works of psychoanalysis: "Lawrence sometimes expresses whatever part of the truth he happens to be discussing with such positiveness and finality that he implies an absolute truth where he intends a negative one. In short, he overstates, and he must retract a little if he would make his meaning clear" (11).

Freud remains the antagonist in *Fantasia of the Unconscious*, the bogey man who must be ritualistically slain. Some of Lawrence's statements about psychoanalysis are correct albeit in need of qualification: "Freud is wrong in attributing a sexual motive to all human activity" (145). This was true in the beginning of Freud's career, but with the publication of *The Ego and the Id* in 1923, he abandoned libido theory in favor of ego psychology, his structural id-ego-superego model of the mind that emphasizes the study of defense mechanisms in normal and neurotic behavior. Throughout *Psychoanalysis and the Unconscious* and *Fantasia of the Unconscious*, Lawrence engages in binary thinking, valuing "Be thyself" over "Know thyself." Other familiar Lawrentian dichotomies include organic vs. mechanical, instinct vs. reason, experience vs. theory. Freud is always on the wrong side of the polar oppositions. Yet sometimes Lawrence comes close to Freud's revisions of psychoanalytic theory. Lawrence rejects Freud's interpretation of dreams as wish fulfillments, arguing instead that the meaning of "distress dreams" is invariably the "*reverse* of the soul's desire" (198). This resembles Freud's position in *Beyond the Pleasure Principle* (1920), where he theorizes the repetition-compulsion principle, the need to relive and master traumatic injury.

Lawrence's example of a lingering, haunting dream is noteworthy, an adolescent boy who develops a "profound and passionate love" for his mother. The Freudians, Lawrence remarks, would see the dream as evidence of a repressed incestuous dream, but this explanation is too simple. "The truth is," he explains, that "every man has, the moment he awakes, a hatred of his dream, and a great desire to be free of the dream, free of the persistent mother-image or sister-image of the dream" (197). Precisely, a Freudian would assert, especially when incestuous love becomes oppressive, as it did with Lawrence. Nearly all of Lawrence's comments about mother–son love are portentous. Geniuses mostly have great mothers, he warns us: "They mostly have sad fates" (159).

Sons and Lovers remains the spectral shadow text behind *Fantasia of the Unconscious*, which may be read as an annotation of Paul Morel's plight. It is "criminal to make a child too loving. No child should be induced to love too much" (97). Nor should children be implicated in their parents' battles. "It is despicable for any one parent to accept a child's sympathy against the other parent. And the one who *received* the sympathy is always more contemptible than the one who is hated" (131). We can understand our life only backward, but we must live it forward: Kierkegaard's insight is especially true of *Fantasia of the Unconscious*, where Lawrence's revised understanding of his family dynamics casts additional light on his hero's conflicts.

In cautioning against the danger of mother–son incest, Lawrence does not explicitly mention himself. Instead, he writes about the late nineteenth-century art critic John Ruskin. "When Mrs. Ruskin said that John Ruskin should have married his mother she spoke the truth. He *was* married to his mother" (153–4). A few pages later Lawrence writes, in French: "*On revient toujours a son premier amour*"—"one always goes back to one's first love"—and then cynically adds, "*On ne revient jamais a son premier amour*": "One never goes back to one's first love" (157). Frieda Lawrence made a similar observation about her husband in her 1934 memoir "*Not I, But the Wind . . .*":

> He was then rewriting his "Sons and Lovers," the first book he wrote with me, and I lived and suffered that book, and wrote bits of it when he would ask me: "What do you think my mother felt like then?" I had to go deeply into the character of Miriam and all the others; when he wrote his mother's death he was ill and his grief made me ill too, and he said: "If my mother had lived I could never have loved you, she wouldn't have let me go." But I think he got over it; only, this fierce and overpowerful love had harmed the boy who was not strong enough to bear it. In after years he said: "I would write a different 'Sons and Lovers' now; my mother was wrong, and I thought she was absolutely right." (56)

Jessie Chambers, the model for Miriam, similarly called attention to Lawrence's bondage to his mother. "In *Sons and Lovers* Lawrence handed his mother the laurels of victory" (202). Lawrence came to realize, belatedly, that he had been unfair to his father and wished he could have rewritten *Sons and Lovers* to convey a more positive image of him (Nehls, vol. 2, 126). It is likely, as Mark Spilka suggested, that Paul suffers from a greater problem than his mother's absorbing love: an emotional deficit caused by his absent father (39).

Unlike in *Sons and Lovers*, where Lawrence *always* sides with the mother, in *Fantasia of the Unconscious* he privileges the father's role in the son's development.

He has little to say about the daughter's development. He doesn't use the expression *father hunger* to describe a child who grows up with a father who is an absent presence; instead, he tells us that the father is necessary for the child's "life circuit" to be complete. The father supplies the "roughness, the sternness" (87) that offsets excessive maternal love. As Cowan notes in *D.H. Lawrence: Self and Sexuality*, he sounds moralistic throughout *Fantasia of the Unconscious*, appearing like an "omniscient Old Testament God" in his pronouncements (99). The key rule for boys is "proud, harsh manly rule" (123). Lawrence's flirtation with authoritarian male leaders in his leadership novels would seem to be an effort to create a positive masculine power that was lacking in his own life. He even favors corporal punishment, as long as the father retains a "wise, warm relationship" with the child.

Many scholars have pointed out Lawrence's "feminine" side: his delicacy, sensitivity, and attunement to emotional issues. Yet throughout *Fantasia of the Unconscious* he proclaims that a child is "either male or female" (131) and that men must not have female qualities. "The great thing is to keep the sexes pure"—"pure maleness in a man, pure femaleness in a woman" (215). By demanding purity, Lawrence rejected the "female" within him, as the British psychoanalyst Marion Milner pointed out as early as 1936: He "hated and despised" his female side because he was "afraid of it" (16; she made the same observation about herself, filling her life with "artificial male purposes" to conform to a patriarchal society). "Manliness" thus becomes a repudiation of what Lawrence perceives as unmanly softness.

Lawrence refers fleetingly to "phallic power" in *Fantasia of the Unconscious*, remarking on a bull's phallic horns and a woman's admiration of the "slender, abstracted bull loins" (200), an image perhaps of Lawrence's own slim body. His description of trees evokes phallic power. He worships the power of trees and would like to be one himself, with their "great lust of roots" and their towering strength and looming height: "great full-blooded trees, with strange tree-blood in them, soundlessly drumming" (82–3). Connie Chatterley feels her sexuality reawakening when she sits next to a young pine tree, the "erect, alive thing, with its top in the sun!" (*Lady Chatterley's Lover* 129). The lovemaking between Connie and the gamekeeper Oliver Mellors takes place in Wragby Wood, Lawrence's symbol for sexual fecundity in his last novel.

Male–Male Love

Like probably all novelists, Lawrence felt more freedom in baring hidden fears and desires in his fictional rather than nonfictional writings. He does not extol male–male love in his letters, *Psychoanalysis and the Unconscious*, or *Fantasia of the Unconscious*, but he does in his 1920 novel *Women in Love*, which would be more accurately titled *Men in Love*. The naked wrestling scene in the chapter called "Gladiatorial" between Lawrence's alter ego, Rupert Birkin, and Gerald Crich, based on John Middleton Murry, dramatizes the novelist's belief in *Blutbrüderschaft*, blood brotherhood. The impassioned description conjures up Birkin's homoerotic desire, which is far more convincing, aesthetically and psychologically, than the heterosexual desire between Birkin and the woman he marries, Ursula Brangwen. Moreover, Lawrence glorifies the male physique throughout the novel, largely ignoring the female body. The intense homoeroticism in *Women in Love* appears along with homophobia, as can be seen in the two gay German companions, Loerke and Leitner, who feel only contempt for each other. Yet despite homophobic passages in Lawrence's writings, *Women in Love* remains groundbreaking in its depiction of homosexual love. Lawrence penned a two-page foreword that appears in *Women in Love*, but he also wrote a seventeen-page prologue that he suppressed because of the rigid laws against homosexuality at the time. The prologue, published posthumously in *Phoenix II*, leaves little doubt about Birkin's—and presumably Lawrence's—homoerotic desire, though according to John Worthen, there is no evidence that Lawrence had any homosexual relationships. Perhaps not, but H.D. (Hilda Doolittle) asserts in *Tribute to Freud*, an account of being in analysis in 1933, that Frieda Lawrence once told her, "Lawrence does not really care for women. He only cares for men. Hilda, *you have no idea of what he is like*" (xiv).

Birkin tortures himself because he feels no sexual desire for Hermione, a woman who combines the worst features of Miriam in *Sons and Lovers*. Lawrence perceives Miriam and Hermione as spiritual vampires, trying to suck the blood out of Paul and Birkin, respectively. Both women, potential smother-mothers, embody the Magna Mater and, in Hermione's case, the Mater Dolorosa. "By her very suffering and humility she bound her son with chains, she held him her everlasting prisoner" (*Women in Love* 192). Birkin experiences the same split between spiritual and sexual love that Paul feels, a conflict that becomes "like a monomania." To save himself, Lawrence writes about Birkin in the prologue, "he must unite the two halves of himself, spiritual and sensual. And this is what no man can do at once, deliberately. It must happen to him" (102). As Cowan observes in *D.H. Lawrence: Self and Sexuality* (46), Birkin's psychic split in the presence of Hermione illustrates Freud's 1912 essay "On the Universal Tendency to Debasement in the Sphere of Love," where he writes about men who cannot feel both affectionate and sensual love for the same woman. "Where they love they do not desire," Freud observes, in one of his most aphoristic sentences, "and where they desire they cannot love" (*SE*, vol 11, 183). In *Fiction and the Unconscious* (1957), Simon O. Lesser was one of the first literary critics to note the parallels between Freud's essay and Lawrence's fictional characters. Lesser points out that while Freud's essay may make readers "squirm" (178), Lawrence's readers do not because the novelist avoids the psychoanalyst's intellectual discourse.

Birkin cannot will himself to feel passion for Hermione, nor can he prevent himself from feeling passion for men, a "desire to know this man, to have him, as it were to eat him, to take the very substance of him" (*Phoenix II* 106). The desire fills him with self-loathing. "It was a deep misery to him. And it would seem as if he had always loved men, always and only loved men. And this was the greatest suffering to him" (107). Few novelists have portrayed more evocatively the inseparability of sexual desires and fears, the longing and dread of sexual union, ecstasy and agony inescapably intertwined. *Women in Love* hints at the nature of Birkin's lovemaking with Ursula. He had taken her, the novelist writes, where she had never before been taken, "at the roots of her darkness and shame"; afterward, she became "quite happy" (296). Birkin and Ursula discover the "darkest, deepest strangest life-source of the human body, at the back and base of the loins" (306). Early Lawrence scholars did not remark on these cryptic references to anal intercourse. Near the end of *Lady Chatterley's Lover*, the indignant Clifford repeats a rumor that Mellors and Connie had been having sex, "as Benvenuto Cellini says, 'in the Italian way'" (335), another reference to anal intercourse.

The authorial Mellors writes about dreading intercourse with his estranged wife, Bertha Coutts. "She sort of got harder and harder to bring off," he confesses to Connie, and "she'd sort of tear at me down there, as if it was a beak tearing me" (261). Mellors's horror of her "beakishness" evokes the image of vagina dentate (Latin for "toothed vagina"), which the Viennese-born psychoanalyst Otto Fenichel conjectured in *The Psychoanalytic Theory of Neurosis* (1945) is not only a castration fear but also a "retaliatory fear for oral-sadistic impulses" (79). Mellors makes no attempt to conceal his hatred of female homosexuality. "When I'm with a woman who's really Lesbian," he confesses to Connie, "I fairly howl in my soul, wanting to kill her" (262–3).

Another male sexual fear appears in *Lady Chatterley's Lover*: the belief that women delay sexual orgasm to gain power over men. "For she only had to hold herself back in sexual intercourse, and let him finish and expend himself without herself coming to the crisis: and then she could prolong the connection and achieve her orgasm and her crisis while he was merely her tool" (40). The

Irish playwright Michaelis, who has a brief affair with Connie, becomes furious when she fails to have an orgasm at the same time he does, unleashing a torrent of misogynistic criticisms of all women: "Either they don't go off at all, as if they were dead in there . . . or else they wait till a chap's really done, and then they start in to bring themselves off, and a chap's got to hang on. I never had a woman yet who went off just at the same moment as I did" (94; ellipsis in original).

Despite his sympathetic insights into many of his female characters, Lawrence apparently did not know about the "orgasm gap" between the sexes, including the fact that women usually take longer to achieve orgasm than men. A foe of idealization, Lawrence nevertheless idealizes Mellors's astounding orgasms, which are entirely mindless and mystical, transporting Connie into a rapturous new world, healing her fractured soul. Curiously, in his rejection of mental consciousness, Lawrence eliminates the role of fantasy in lovemaking. In his 2000 memoir *Iris and Her Friends*, John Bayley recounts a story about a sleepy wife who tells her husband, "Oh, do get on with it, George," to which her husband responds ruefully, "Sorry, dear, I can't think of anyone at the moment" (206).

"Another Volume Up My Sleeve"

John Middleton Murry claimed that *Fantasia of the Unconscious* was Lawrence's "greatest book" (171); he also concluded that Lawrence was "neither a great novelist nor a great poet" (174). Both claims now strike us as bizarre. Neither *Psychoanalysis and the Unconscious* nor *Fantasia of the Unconscious* is read much today, but Lawrence's two polemics against Freud remain witty and beguiling, exuberant Schadenfreudian jeremiads that gave Lawrence pleasure in writing and offer pleasure to his readers. In the epilogue to *Fantasia of the Unconscious*, he promises us that the show is not over: "I've got another volume up my sleeve" (222). That volume never appeared, probably because Lawrence had nothing further to say about his adversary.

Almost a Freudian

In imagining his fictional protagonists' sexual desires and fears, Lawrence sought to deepen our understanding of what it means to be human. He was fiercely anti-psychoanalytic, yet paradoxically, many of his beliefs coincided with Freud's.

Some of these commonalities were unfortunate. Both men shared the patriarchal bias of their age, believing that women were different from and inferior to men. In *Fantasia of the Unconscious*, Lawrence falls back on the age-old binary that men are logical and women emotional, lamenting the modern reversal of "natural" roles where women are now active, men passive. Freud similarly devalued women, referring to the sexual life of adult women as psychology's "dark continent"; questioning, "What does a woman want?"; and believing that they have a less independent and mature superego than men. Yet some of Lawrence's greatest characters are female, such as Ursula Brangwen and Connie Chatterley, just as some of the most influential early psychoanalysts were women, including Anna Freud, Melanie Klein, Helene Deutsch, and Karen Horney.

Both Lawrence and Freud warned of the dangers of masturbation. "Instead of being a comparatively pure and harmless vice," Lawrence cautioned in "Pornography and Obscenity," "masturbation is certainly the most dangerous sexual vice that a society can be afflicted with, in the long run" (*Phoenix* 179). It's likely that Lawrence was thinking about masturbation when in *Fantasia of the Unconscious* he issues a mysterious fatherly warning to teenage boys to leave themselves alone, admitting that he speaks from personal experience. "You've got to go through these years, before you find a woman you want to marry, and whom you can marry. I went through them myself, and got myself worked up a good deal more than was good for me. Try to contain yourself" (146). Freud concurred, believing that masturbation is a source of neurasthenia. Noting that Freud never wrote about the pleasures of masturbation, Adam Phillips informs us in a footnote to *Winnicott* (1988). "The idea of developing a capacity for satisfying masturbatory experience has never, for some reason, found a place in psychoanalytic theory" (167, n.30). Phillips corrects that omission in *Monogamy* (1996). "Masturbation is traditionally taboo not because it damages your health—it is not only safe sex, it is safe incest—or because it is against the law, but because we fear it may be the truth about sex: that sex is something we do on our own" (101).

Both Lawrence and Freud struggled to come to terms with their own bisexuality, Lawrence in his search for *Blutbrüderschaft* relationships, Freud in his conviction, derived from his close friend Wilhelm Fliess, that all people are in varying degrees bisexual. "[B]isexuality!" Freud exclaimed to Fliess in an 1899 letter, "You are certainly right about it. I am accustoming myself to regarding every sexual act as a process in which four individuals are involved" (Masson 364)—implying two sets of male-and-female selves in every sexual act. Freud fainted twice in the presence of Jung, an event the founder of psychoanalysis interpreted as "some piece of unruly homosexual feeling at the root of the matter" (Jones, vol. 1, 317). In *Becoming Freud* (2014), Adam Phillips refers to psychoanalysis hyperbolically as a "homosexual artifact," an allusion to Freud's overheated relationship with Fliess (4).

Homosexuality remained a vexed problem for Lawrence and Freud. Lawrence avoided the topic in his letters, realizing that he needed the safety of fiction to explore homoerotic love. Freud believed that "passive homosexuality" was characteristic of all men. In *My Analysis with Freud* (1977), an account of his treatment from 1921 to 1922, Abram Kardiner writes about comparing notes with other analysands and discovering that unconscious homosexuality was a standard element of everyone's analysis. "Freud was convinced that the passive homosexuality constellation was practically universal among all men and remained fixed in the character of the individual, who could do nothing but reconcile himself to it" (99). Kardiner, one of the founders of the New York Psychoanalytic Society, the oldest in the country, believed that the experience of analysis with Freud was valuable, but he never accepted the concept of unconscious homosexuality. "It makes the patient address himself to a nonexistent state of affairs and augments his sense of helplessness, thereby confirming his feeling that he cannot direct his own life" (99).

Lawrence and Freud had different conceptions of the unconscious, but they were drawn to the netherworld of human existence, undertaking heroic journeys to the underworld that endangered their physical and psychological health. Both devoted their lives to writing about sex, for which they were reviled, ridiculed, and misunderstood, incurring the wrath of church and state. Accused of immorality, pornography, and, in Lawrence's case, treason and sedition during the Great War, both men authored books that were banned and burned, but they were silenced only by death, after which their reputations only grew.

Both sought to overcome the shame, stigma, and secrecy surrounding sex, viewing themselves as sexual liberators. "[Y]ou mustn't think I advocate perpetual sex," Lawrence instructed Lady Ottoline Morrell. "Far from it. Nothing nauseates me more than perpetual sex in and out of season. But I want, with *Lady C.*, to make an *adjustment in consciousness* to the basic physical realities" (*Lady Chatterley's Lover* 34). Freud sought a similar adjustment in consciousness. "I stand for an infinitely freer sex life," Freud wrote to James T. Putnam in 1915, "although I myself have made very little use of such freedom. Only so far as I considered myself entitled to" (*Letters of Sigmund Freud* 303). Lawrence took on the additional challenge of trying to transform shame over bodily functions into acceptance, even celebration. "An if tha shits an' if tha pisses," Mellors tells

Connie near the end of the story, using working-class vernacular that Lawrence identified with his collier-father's speech, "I'm glad. I don't want a woman as couldna shit nor piss" (284). Moments like this affirm the early title of the novel: *Tenderness*. Freud doesn't go as far as Lawrence does in exalting bodily functions, but in *Fragment of an Analysis of a Case of Hysteria* (1905), the story of Dora, he claims the rights of the gynecologist in speaking "with all possible frankness" about the organs and functions of sexual life, avoiding "perverse prurience" (*SE*, vol. 7, 9).

Both Lawrence and Freud returned repeatedly to the subject of love. Lawrence believed that the word was overused, as he states in *Fantasia of the Unconscious*: "It is time to drop the word love, and more than time to drop the ideal of love" (155). Nevertheless, three of his greatest novels have *love* in the title, and Harry T. Moore titled his 1974 biography *The Priest of Love*. Freud believed that insight, not love, leads to therapeutic cure, but he placed love at the center of psychological health. Both Lawrence and Freud defined health as the ability to love and work.

The Dionysian Lawrence and Apollonian Freud were products of different traditions and ages, the former influenced by late Romanticism, the latter a child of the Enlightenment, but both attempted to change the world through their writings. They had little love for humankind, and less for democracy. Many of their letters abound in misanthropic outbursts. "I have found little that is 'good' about human beings on the whole," Freud wrote to Oskar Pfister in 1918. "In my experience most of them are trash, no matter whether they publicly subscribe to this or that ethical doctrine or to none at all. That is something that you cannot say aloud, or perhaps even think" (Meng and E. Freud 61–2). Both men expected betrayal, which sometimes they unconsciously encouraged through intolerant words and deeds. Yet both would have been surprised by the monumental impact of their writings. Both sought a better world, and, one can argue, did much to improve it.

Both were consummate prose stylists, among the twentieth century's greatest writers. Lawrence did not experiment with stream-of-consciousness prose, as did James Joyce and Virginia Woolf, but he pioneered indirect free discourse, which enabled him to convey his characters' unspoken thoughts. Ironically, Freud was not pleased when he was nominated for the Nobel Prize in Literature rather than in Medicine. Nor was Freud entirely happy with the readability of his case studies, which he feared read like short stories. Lawrence never wanted to become an analyst, but surprisingly, Freud wanted to become a novelist, as Wilhelm Stekel reported in his *Autobiography*. "In my mind," Freud confided to him as they hiked through the forests of Berchtesgaden, "I always construct novels, using my experiences as a psychoanalyst; my wish is to become a novelist—but not yet; perhaps in the later years of my life" (Stekel 66). Freud never became a novelist—except to Schadenfreudians, who accused him of fabricating fictions.

Both believed in the therapeutic power of writing. "One sheds one[']s sicknesses in books," Lawrence declared in a 1913 letter about his experience creating *Sons and Lovers*, "repeats and presents again one[']s emotions, to be master of them" (*Letters*, vol. II, 90). Freud made a similar observation to Joan Riviere. He said, "Write it, write it, put it down in black and white; that's the way to deal with it; you get it out of your system!" (637). Lawrence and Freud knew from personal experience that writing does not magically release one from physical or psychological illness, but it is often a form of problem-solving, enabling the writer to chart a direction toward health.

Neither Lawrence nor Freud read the other's writings, although, according to H.D in *Tribute to Freud*, the analyst admired the ending of one of Lawrence's novels (144), but their followers did, resulting in a vast commentary on Freudians writing about Lawrentians and Lawrentians writing about Freudians. Lawrence and Freud did everything they could to champion healthy sexuality in an age when that goal seemed impossible. Both were unsurpassed in exploring ambivalence in all its forms: emotional, sexual, and interpersonal. Both understood the Wordsworthian insight that the child is father of the man and the Blakean truth that without contraries there is no progression. Both often contradicted themselves, without acknowledgment or apology, agreeing with Emerson that a foolish consistency is the hobgoblin of small minds, and with Whitman that one embraces multitudes. Both were devoted, in their own ways, to creating a balance between mind and body. Though one was committed to "being thyself" while the other was committed to "knowing thyself," they would agree that the two principles were both necessary for a healthy life. Work was the driving force in their lives, their lifeline and life's blood; they wrote to the end. And both pursued their visions of truth with monomaniacal intensity. It would be misleading to call Lawrence a Freudian, but in the end he was less of a Schadenfreudian than he imagined.

6

Vladimir Nabokov

Voodoo Freud

. . . all my books should be stamped Freudians, Keep Out.

—Introduction, *Bend Sinister*, xii

My books are not only blessed by a total lack of social significance, but are also mythproof: Freudians flutter around them avidly, approach with itching oviducts, stop, sniff, and recoil.

—Foreword, *The Eye*

No novelist waged a more relentless campaign against the talking cure than Vladimir Nabokov. Unlike D. H. Lawrence, who briefly flirted with psychoanalysis, Nabokov hated Freud from the beginning of his career. In novel after novel, he attacked the "Viennese witch doctor," as he sardonically calls Freud. Of the many types of people Nabokov satirizes, none evokes the foolishness and evil of the psychoanalyst, who embodies the qualities of sham and shaman, satan and charlatan, simpleton and stereotyper. In his tireless battle with Freud, Nabokov created a new art form, psychiatry baiting, and elevated the parody of the psychiatric case study to new heights in his masterpiece, *Lolita* (1955). Tormenting and heckling Nabokov's best characters, sadistic psychotherapists (a redundancy) conjure up ludicrous Oedipal complexes and primal scenes in the cruel attempt to explain away the inconsolable suffering Adam Krug, Pnin, Humbert, and the other solitary heroes must quietly endure.

Evil Incarnate

In almost every foreword to the English-language editions of his works, Nabokov continued his long-standing assault on Freud, an unprecedented war against psychoanalysis. The Foreword to *The Defense* (1930) reveals his typically sarcastic tone and the comic exaggeration of Freudianism:

> In the Prefaces I have been writing of late for the English-language editions of my Russians novels (and there are more to come) I have made it a rule to address a few words of encouragement to the Viennese delegation. The present Foreword shall not be an exception. Analysts and analyzed will enjoy, I hope, certain details of the treatment Luzhin is subjected to after his breakdown (such as the curative insinuation that a chess player sees Mom in his Queen and Pop in his opponents' King), and the little Freudian who mistakes a Pix-lok set for the key to a novel will no doubt continue to identify my characters with his comic-book notion of my parents, sweethearts and serial selves. (10–11)

Nabokov's strategy is always the same. First, he belittles the little Freudians (or their paid agents in American university departments of English), then he challenges them to analyze or anal-ize his works, warning them, however, of the dangerous traps he has set. Thus, the Foreword to *The Waltz Invention* (1938): "After the dreadful frustrations Freudians have experienced with my other books, I am sure they will refrain from inflicting upon *Waltz* a sublimation of the push-button power-feeling such as the manipulation of an elevator, up (erection!) and down (revenge suicide!)" (no page number). And *Despair* (1965): "The attractively shaped object or Wiener-schnitzel dream that the eager Freudian may think he distinguishes in the remoteness of my wastes will turn out to be on closer inspection a derisive mirage organized by my agents" (8). The Foreword to *King, Queen, Knave* (1928) is different only in the rare concession that not all his friends share his animus toward Freud. "As usual, I wish to observe that, as usual (and as usual several sensitive people I like will look huffy), the Viennese delegation has not been invited. If, however, a resolute Freudian manages to slip in, he or she should be warned that a number of cruel traps have been set here and there in the novel" (x). The evocation of a departed psychoanalytic ghost appears in the introduction to the uncompleted novel *Ultima Thule*. "Freudians are no longer around, I understand, so I do not need to warn them not to touch my circles with their symbols" (*A Russian Beauty and Other Stories* [1973] 148).

Even when Nabokov believes Freud is safely dead and buried, he cannot resist a parting shot, as he does in the Foreword to *Glory* (1932). Only through overkill will the enemy vanish forever. "Nowadays, when Freudism is discredited, the author recalls with a whistle of wonder that not so long ago—say before 1959 (*i.e.*, before the publication of the first of the seven forewords to his Englished novels)—a child's personality was supposed to split automatically in sympathetic consequence of parental divorce" (xiii). To seal tightly the Freudian coffin, Nabokov writes a letter in 1967 to the editor of *Encounter* to welcome Freud's book on Woodrow Wilson "not only because of its comic appeal, which is great, but because that surely must be the last rusty nail in the Viennese Quack's coffin" (*Strong Opinions* [1973] 215). And to make sure that naïve undergraduates do not resurrect the ghost of Freud, Nabokov condemns psychoanalytic literary criticism in *Lectures on Literature* (1980). Rejecting the belief that *The Metamorphosis* reveals Kafka's ambivalent relationship to his father, and that the image of Gregor as an insect resembles the son's feelings of worthlessness to his parents, Nabokov sternly warns his students: "I am interested here in bugs, not in humbugs, and I reject this nonsense" (256).

Nabokov's virulence is astonishing and unsoftened by time. The invective is bitter, savagely mirthful, and unprecedented. It is as if Freud is the central figure in Nabokov's life, always shadowing the novelist. Freud's name appears as early as the third paragraph in the autobiographical *Speak, Memory* (1951). In discussing his lifelong rebellion against darkness, Nabokov singles out the most sinister threat to the imagination.

> I have ransacked my oldest dreams for keys and clues—and let me say at once that I reject completely the vulgar, shabby, fundamentally medieval world of Freud, with its crankish quest for sexual symbols (something like searching for Baconian acrostics in Shakespeare's works), and its bitter little embryos spying, from their natural nooks, upon the love life of their parents. (20)

In addition to associating Freud with antiquated medievalism, Nabokov links him to literary and political repression. At the end of *Speak, Memory*, he bids an unfond farewell to Freud, leaving him and his fellow travelers "to jog on, in their third-class carriage of thought, through the police state of sexual myth (incidentally, what a great mistake on the part of dictators to ignore psychoanalysis—a whole generation might be so easily corrupted that way!" (300–1).

It could be argued, of course, that by insisting in his prefaces that Freudians must keep out, Nabokov invites them to enter and that, if Freud had not existed, Nabokov would have had to invent him. Indeed, one senses that Freud is Nabokov's alter ego, a hated part of the self that the novelist had to defeat again and again. To borrow Richard Curle's vivid description of Joseph Conrad's equally well-known detestation of Dostoevsky, "He did not despise him as one despises a nonentity, he hated him as one might hate Lucifer and the forces of darkness" (26).

Although critics have long recognized Nabokov's animosity, few have been disturbed by it. In fact, many if not most Nabokov scholars have appeared to share his assumption that Freudians adhere to monolithic dogma, that psychoanalysis never developed beyond the stage of drive psychology, and that Freud never revised his theories nor admitted to intellectual skepticism. "Nabokov appears to object to Freudianism as a kind of internal Marxism proceeding upon the assumption that the common is of greater import than the individual," Andrew Field notes in *Nabokov: His Life in Art* (1967), adding that "in the late 1960's one can already clearly see that the corner has been turned regarding Freudianism in literature, and there are fewer and fewer important writers and critics who slavishly accept and practice the Freudian prescription" (264). At no time have important writers and critics "slavishly" accepted the Freudian "prescription." Even when Field tries to be more dispassionate than Nabokov, his language gives him away. Alfred Appel, Jr., the editor of the indispensable *The Annotated Lolita* (1970), does not try to be impartial. He accepts all of Nabokov's judgments of psychoanalysis, including disdain of the "clinical-minded." Arguing that the analyst's reductive interpretation of *Lolita* justifies Nabokov's parody (not surprisingly, there have been few psychoanalytic studies of the novel), Appel assumes there can be only one Freudian approach—unenlightened. "By creating a surface that is rich in 'psychological' clues, but which finally resists and then openly mocks the interpretations of depth psychology, Nabokov is able to dispatch any Freudians who choose to 'play' in the blitzkrieg game that is the novel's first sixty-or-so pages" (lxi–lxii).

A more thoughtful discussion of Nabokov's quarrel with Freud comes from Page Stegner in *The Portable Nabokov* (1973). "Psychotherapy is constantly under attack in Nabokov's fiction, and it becomes a kind of outstanding symbol for the clinical, sterile stereotyping mind that perceives its surroundings in hackneyed and rigid terms" (xxi). Yet, in *Escape into Aesthetics* (1966), Stegner concludes his discussion of Nabokov's anti-Freudianism with a statement that is more generous than the truth allows: "his satire of depth psychology, intended or not, emerges really as criticism of the debasement of Freud's work by a passively adaptive, unimaginative, leisured society—most emphatically, though not exclusively, American" (43). It is not the debasement of Freud's work but Freud's debasing vision to which Nabokov continually returns in his writings. Freud is, quite simply, evil incarnate to him. There are bad artists in Nabokov's world but no good psychotherapists.

In his interviews, Nabokov gave many reasons for his rejection of the talking cure. He objects both to the absurdity of Freudian theory and to the gullibility of people who succumb to therapy. Psychoanalysis strikes him as farcical, especially the Oedipus complex. "Let the credulous and the vulgar continue to believe that all mental woes can be cured by a daily application of old Greek myths to their private parts" (*Strong Opinions* 66). A more serious objection to psychoanalysis is the threat it poses to morality and individual freedom. Like Doris Lessing and, as we shall see, Thomas Szasz, Nabokov believed that society is moving toward what James Robitscher has called a "psychiatrocracy," a "state in which psychiatry has expanded to fill the roles of police, judges, educators, social workers, and eventually politicians" (473). In Nabokov's words, "The Freudian faith leads to dangerous ethical consequences, such as when a filthy murderer with the brain of a tapeworm is given a lighter sentence because his mother spanked him too much or too little—it works both ways" (*Strong Opinions* 116). Yet, unlike Lessing, Nabokov rejects the social or utilitarian view of art, and he would dismiss the idea that his novels are intended directly or indirectly to illuminate the dangers of totalitarianism or the therapeutic state. He spurned the idea that his contempt for psychoanalysis arose from personal experience with therapy. When asked by an interviewer whether he had been in analysis, he expressed horror, indignant at the idea. "Bookish familiarity only," he dryly answered. He ritualistically proceeded to bury his adversary.

> The ordeal itself is much too silly and disgusting to be contemplated even as a joke. Freudism and all it has tainted with its grotesque implications and methods appears to me to be one of the vilest deceits practiced by people on themselves and on others. I reject it utterly, along with a few other medieval items still adored by the ignorant, the conventional, or the very sick. (*Strong Opinions* 23–4)

In another interview in *Strong Opinions*, he expanded upon his aversion to psychiatry, revealing the extent to which Freud occupies his everyday life:

> I cannot conceive how anybody in his right mind should go to a psychoanalyst, but of course if one's mind is deranged one might try anything; after all, quacks and cranks, shamans and holy men, kings and hypnotists have cured people—especially hysterical people. Our grandsons no doubt will regard today's psychoanalysts with the same amused contempt as we do astrology and phrenology. One of the greatest pieces of charlatanic, and satanic, nonsense imposed on a gullible public is the Freudian interpretation of dreams. I take gleeful pleasure every morning in refuting the Viennese quack by recalling and explaining the details of my dreams without using one single reference to sexual symbols or mythical complexes. I urge my potential patients to do likewise. (47)

Freud's name is likely to appear anywhere in Nabokov's universe, sometimes in the least flattering places. In *Bend Sinister* (1947), Adam Krug, who lives in a repressive Marxist state, gazes down into the bottom of a toilet bowl. What does he see? "At the bottom of the bowl a safety razor envelope with Dr. S. Freud's face and signature flouted" (85). The image is appropriately anal. In *Speak, Memory* Nabokov recalled how underneath the windows of his Biarritz apartment a "huge custard-colored balloon was being inflated by Sigismond Lejoyeux, a local aeronaut" (156). (Freud's name in German means "joy.") In *Ada, or Ardor* (1969), there is a "Dr. Sig Heiler" and a "Dr. Froid . . . who may have been an émigré brother with a passport-changed name of the Dr. Froit of Signy-Mondieu-Mondieu" (27). Although Van is a psychiatrist, he comes to realize that the "mistake—the lewd, ludicrous and vulgar mistake of the Signy-Mondieu analysts consists in their regarding a real object, a pompon, say, or a pumpkin (actually seen in a dream by the patient) as a significant abstraction of the real object, as a bumpkin's bonbon or one-half of the bust" (363). Often, Nabokov does not mention Freud by name, referring to him instead by the city in which he resided. "Viennese quack," "Viennese witch doctor, "Viennese wizard."

Nabokov's quarrel with Freud dates back to the beginning of his career as a writer. His earliest parody of Freud appears in a 1931 Paris weekly. Titled "What Everybody Must Know," the article—written under the pseudonym Sirin—contains a naïve first-person narrator, obviously a convert to the Freudian faith, who delivers a sales pitch for his newly patented product *Freudism for All* (qtd. by Field, *Nabokov: His Life in Art* 263). Nabokov employs his favorite weapon against psychoanalysis, *reductio ad absurdum*, to undermine the Freudian stages of psychosexual development. There is the "Tantalus complex," the "penal servitude complex," and the "happy marriage complex." *Freudism for All* contains all the familiar psychoanalytic themes Nabokov satirizes for the remaining forty-five years of his writing career: the Oedipus complex, unconscious motivation, dream interpretation, biological drives. Nabokov's antipsychiatry predates Lessing's, though it lacks her introspective analysis in *The Golden Notebook* (1962). Long before most writers began warning of the therapeutic state, Nabokov ridiculed the cult of psychotherapy and progressive education. The gentle Pnin is embarrassed by the "psihooslinie ('psychoasinine')" interests of his former wife, a psychiatrist. Her husband, also a psychiatrist, evolves the ingenious idea of applying the theories of group therapy to marriage counseling. The procedure involves a "tension-releasing" circle modeled along the lines of a quilting bee, where young women share "with absolute frankness" their marital problems with each other. Later the husbands are similarly interviewed by doctors, and cigars as well as "anatomic charts" are passed around. Nabokov condemns the goal of tension reduction in group psychotherapy because it represents to him a contemptible effort to eliminate the inevitable suffering every sensitive person must endure. Pnin affirms his creator's views when he calls psychotherapy "nothing but a kind of microcosmos of communism—all that psychiatry. . . . Why not leave their private sorrows to people? Is sorrow not, one asks, the only thing in the world people really possess?" (52).

Implicit in Nabokov's rejection of Freud is the link between psychoanalysis and Marxism. Viewing "cure" as a form of manipulation, mind control, and enslavement, Nabokov cannot imagine therapy that is not collusive and conspiratorial. *Bend Sinister*, Nabokov's first novel in English, is a parable of the therapeutic state in which psychiatry promotes adaptation to an insane political system. Professor Adam Krug, a philosopher, refuses to submit to the party line of Paduk, dictator (and Krug's former classmate) of the young Soviet type of state. Pervading the country is the Marxist-sounding ideology of Ekwilism, a "violent and virulent political doctrine." Allied to Ekwilism is the grim Institute for Abnormal Children where, through a mix-up of identities characteristic of the collectivist state, Krug's young son David is sent. Operating according to the tension-reduction principle of group psychotherapy as practiced in *Pnin*, the institute serves as a euphemistic "release instrument" for hardened criminals. The psychological theory combines cathartic release with orgiastic violence:

> if once a week the really difficult patients could enjoy the possibility of venting in full their repressed yearnings (the exaggerated urge to hurt, destroy, etc.) upon some little human creature of no value to the community, then, by degrees, the evil in them would be allowed to escape, would be, so to say, "effundated," and eventually they would become good citizens. (218)

Mistaken for one of their unfortunate victims, David is fatally beaten up in one of the most gruesome scenes found anywhere in Nabokov's blood-bespattered universe. Invoking the language of the psychotherapist and sociologist, Nabokov mimics the detached objectivity of the social scientist. The brutes at first keep their distance from the little person, but then a transformation begins as the "community spirit (positive) was conquering the individual whims (negative)." They become "*organized*." The female psychiatrist Doktor Amalia von Wytwyl refers to the "wonderful moment" in which, to use her technical language, "'the ego,' he goes 'ouf' (out) and the pure 'egg' (common extract of egos) 'remains'" (219). Less clinically, the bloodthirsty group literally tears apart the helpless victim.

What's in a Name?

Why does Nabokov place psychoanalysis among the ranks of communism, fascism, and other forms of totalitarian control? Thomas R. Frosch has argued that "Ultimately, we have to understand Nabokov's anti-Freudianism in the context of a hatred for allegory and symbolism in general" (175). It is certainly true that Nabokov disapproved of allegory and symbolism, believing they impinged upon the artist's freedom, but this hardly seems sufficient to explain the virulence of his attack against Freud. It seems more probable that biographical reasons still unknown to us influenced his thinking. Nabokov's contempt for Freud was part of a larger reaction against despised elements of Russian and German autocracy that he blamed for the destruction of his family and his exile to Western Europe and the United States. Most of his fictional psychiatrists have German names: Doktor Frau Amalia von Wytwyl née Bachofen and Dr. Hammecke in *Bend Sinister*; Dr. Eric Wind (a German) and his Russian psychiatrist wife Liza Bogolepov in *Pnin*; Dr. Blanche Schwartzmann and Melanie Weiss in *Lolita*, whose names mean "White Blackman" and "Black White," respectively, because, as Appel notes in *The Annotated Lolita*, "to Nabokov, Freudians figuratively see no colors other than black and white" (326); Dr. Sig Heiler and Dr. Froit of Signy-Mondieu-Mondieu in *Ada*; and so on. These psychiatrists conform to the stereotype of the vicious German. There are, it is true, non-German psychiatrists. There is an Italian named Dr. Bonomini in *Ultima Thule* and the Anglo-Saxon clinical psychologist John Ray in *Lolita*, both of whom are typically inane but not insane or malevolent. Hovering over all these therapists is their spiritual father, the Viennese witch doctor, whose German-speaking background remains felt. As Douglas Fowler has observed, "Germany is always a part of the Nabokovian code for evil, and psychiatrists are its high priests" (196).

Yet why does Nabokov endorse these ugly stereotypes, especially when the object of his scorn was also victimized by the same forces the novelist detested? If anything, one might expect Nabokov to feel a degree of sympathy for Freud. Nowhere among Nabokov's savage criticisms of Freud is the recognition that the psychoanalyst was a member of a persecuted minority group that remained outside of German and Viennese society. The Nazis' persecution of the Freud family was as severe as the Bolshevists' persecution of the Nabokov family. Nabokov's brother died in a German concentration camp in 1945, and his father was shot and killed at a political meeting in 1922 while shielding a speaker from two Russian assassins. Although Freud and his immediate family were allowed to flee Vienna, four of his elderly sisters were less fortunate; they were murdered in German concentration camps. Freud cherished freedom of expression and thought as much as Nabokov did. Both men were repelled by the brutality they witnessed and did everything they could to oppose cruelty and injustice.

Moreover, in viewing Freud as a German victimizer instead of as a Jewish victim, Nabokov contradicts the impassioned discussion of racial prejudice that appears in *Pale Fire* (1962). Kinbote tells us that more than anything on earth John Shade loathed vulgarity and brutality, particularly when they were united in racial prejudice. As a man of letters, Shade

> could not help preferring "is a Jew" to "is Jewish" and "is a Negro" to "is colored"; but immediately added that this way of alluding to two kinds of bias in one breath was a good example of careless, or demagogic, lumping (much exploited by Left-Wingers) since it erased the distinction between two historical hells: diabolical persecution and the barbarous traditions of slavery. (217)

Nabokov married a Jewish woman, and he was always sensitive to anti-Semitism. Yet, in rendering Freudianism into Nazism, he seems guilty of his own diabolical persecution.

Nabokov's blind spot to psychoanalysis, then, amounts to an obsession, as G. M. Hyde notes. "It would be wrong to assume that Nabokov has *in fact* repudiated Freud just because of his frequent anti-Freudian quips," adding that Nabokov's objections to Freud often seem themselves obsessive (96–7, n.24).

At what point does a master parodist unconsciously begin to parody himself? Jack Cockerell's heartless impersonations of the eccentric hero of *Pnin* compel the narrator to observe that "the whole thing grew to be such a bore that I fell wondering if by some poetical vengeance this Pnin business had not become with Cockerell the kind of fatal obsession which substitutes its own victim for that of the initial ridicule" (189). Has Nabokov similarly fallen victim to a fatal obsession?

"Acute Nervous Exhaustion"

There's little evidence that Nabokov suffered from psychological illness or entered psychotherapy—except for one puzzling biographical event upon which no one, to my knowledge, has commented. *The Nabokov-Wilson Letters* (1979) contains a veiled reference to Nabokov's "acute nervous exhaustion" in June 1946, shortly after completing *Bend Sinister*. Nabokov wrote a letter to Edmund Wilson, who was at the time a close friend and confidant (they later became bitter enemies in what was one of the century's most notorious literary feuds):

> With the feeling I had 1. some serious heart trouble, 2. ulcers, 3. cancer in the gullet and 4. stones everywhere, I had myself thoroughly examined at a good hospital. The doctor (a Prof. Siegfried Tannhäuser) found that I was constitutionally in fine shape but was suffering from acute nervous exhaustion due to the entomology-Wellesley-novel combination, and suggested my taking a two months vacation. (170)

In the next letter to Wilson, July 18, 1946, Nabokov added: "I am 'recuperating' (from what was practically a 'nervous breakdown') in New Hampshire." Nabokov's use of quotation marks in the second letter suggests a greater degree of ironic self-detachment than in the first letter, where the tone, apart from the contrived Wagnerian name of the doctor, is more serious. If he was indeed approaching a mental breakdown, it seems unlikely that he would have consulted a much-hated psychotherapist. Andrew Field makes no mention of this in *Nabokov: His Life in Part* (1977), though he does say that "throughout his life Nabokov has suffered from recurrent headaches, which no pills have helped enough" (251). Apart from this event, Nabokov's hatred of Freud remains a biographical mystery. Indeed, we know little about Nabokov the man and, as Phyllis A. Roth concluded in 1982, many questions about Nabokov the artist will remain unanswered "until we constitute Nabokov the man behind the mystification" (58).

Until then, we can try to demystify Nabokov's curious attitude toward Freud from the scattered clues in his fiction and his references to historical psychoanalysts. We may be surprised, in fact, by the degree to which Nabokov's writings reflect psychological theory, apart from the numerous traps he sets to ambush the Freudian critic. Despite his contempt for psychology as a discipline, Nabokov was a psychological novelist, whether or not he was parodying the subject. And he was well acquainted with books on abnormal psychology and case study material. Andrew Field points out that the library of Nabokov's father contained such titles as *The Sexual Instinct and Its Morbid Manifestations* and a good collection of the works of Havelock Ellis (*Nabokov: His Life in Part* 96). We also know that Nabokov's fictional characters have been reading actual psychoanalytic studies. In *Pale Fire*, Kinbote recalls how he once tried to read certain tidbits from a learned book on psychoanalysis he had filched from a classroom, a book widely used in American colleges. (English professors in American universities, he says, are soaked in Freudian fancies.) Kinbote cites two psychoanalytic texts and gives appropriate quotations from each book. He also helpfully provides us with precise bibliographical information to locate both books:

> By picking the nose in spite of all commands to the contrary, or when a youth is all the time sticking his finger through his button-hole . . . the analytic teacher knows that the appetite of the lustful one knows no limit in his phantasies. (Quoted by Prof C. from Dr. Oskar Pfister, *The Psychoanalytical Method*, 1917, NY, 79)
>
> The little cap of red velvet in the German version of Little Red Riding Hood is a symbol of menstruation. (Quoted by Prof. C. from Eric Fromm, *The Forgotten Language*, 1951, NY, 240)

Kinbote allows the quotations to speak for themselves, though he cannot resist one caustic rhetorical question: "Do these clowns really *believe* what they teach?" (*Pale Fire* 271).

Kinbote has no difficulty demolishing Prof. C.'s Freudian approach to literature, and few critics, literary or psychoanalytic, would probably care to defend the quoted passages. Alfred Appel, for example, endorses Kinbote's attack, agreeing that "no parodist could improve on" Fromm's realization or Pfister's "felicitously expressed thought" (*The Annotated Lolita* 327). If one takes the trouble to read *The Psychoanalytic Method* (Nabokov slightly misquotes the title) and *The Forgotten Language*, however, the quoted passages appear less ludicrous. Pfister, for instance, who was a pastor and seminary teacher in Zurich, discusses the dynamics of symptomatology in the quoted passage. In the cited case study, he shows how an apparently meaningless gesture may reveal a complicated symbolism. He talks about a fifteen-year-old pupil who was accustomed to making a peculiar and offensive grimace with his nose and finger. The analyst traces back the obsession to an internal conflict involving the youth's ambivalence toward masturbation, which both attracted and repelled him. Since symptoms are overdetermined, there may be additional meanings to the teenager's compulsive act that Pfister perhaps missed. However, this interpretation is at least plausible. And his major thesis is sound: "He who engages for a long time in the analysis of apparently meaningless gestures, which constantly recur, gradually becomes able to read intimate secrets with certainty from these stereotyped habits" (*The Psychoanalytic Method* 78). Incidentally, one of Nabokov's most celebrated characters, lost in his own masturbatory reverie, would agree with the "analytic teacher" that "the appetite of the lustful knows no limit in his phantasies."

Kinbote's allusion to Erich Fromm's *The Forgotten Language*, a National Book Award finalist, also has interest to Nabokov's readers. Fromm's interpretation of

Little Red Riding Hood (more precisely, Little Red-Cap, the Brothers Grimm version of the story) offers several insights into the famous children's fairy tale and, as we shall see, a famous twentieth-century novel that is in its own way a supreme fairy tale. In his discussion of the tale, Fromm makes the sound observation that the command not to stray into the menacing forest hints at a warning against the loss of innocence. The little girl, approaching womanhood, is now confronted with the problem of sex. There is nothing outlandish about Fromm's interpretation of the color red as suggestive of passion and menstruation. Indeed, Nabokov is notorious for his complete rejection of symbolism, sexual and otherwise. The wolf in the fairy tale symbolizes a ruthless and cunning man eager to devour the little girl, an act filled with sexual implications. Fromm argues that the wolf's attempt to usurp the grandmother's role becomes an ironic commentary on the male's inability to bear children, an interpretation that is only slightly more difficult to accept. At the end of the story, the wolf, who has swallowed the little girl, is made ridiculous by the attempt to play the role of a pregnant woman with a living being in his belly. The girl puts stones into his stomach, and he dies. "His deed, according to the primitive law of retaliation, is punished according to his crime: he is killed by the stones, the symbol of sterility, which mock his usurpation of the pregnant woman's role." In Fromm's view, the fairy tale dramatizes the male–female conflict. "It is a story of triumph by man-hating women, ending with their victory, exactly the opposite of the Oedipus myth, which lets the male emerge victorious from this battle" (241). Paradoxically, Little Red Riding Hood's rites of passage experience has intriguing relevance to Nabokov's parodic masterpiece, a novel about a poetical wolf man who, in ravishing the little girl, grows heavy with child and eventually gives birth to one of the great literary creations of the century.

Lolita

With its false scents, clever ambushes, and multiedged ironies, *Lolita* is the supreme parody of the psychiatric case study. The novel brilliantly puts into practice Nabokov's strategy in the forewords to his other stories: it lures in unsuspecting Freudians and then springs the trap upon them. *Lolita* mocks the psychopathological approach to literature and taunts the reader to solve the mystery of Humbert's obsession with his nymphet. As Elizabeth Phillips remarked in 1960, "Nabokov's ironic version of the 'psychopathological' case history ridicules both the method and the content of the formula by which the inspiration of art has been Freudianized" (101). The intensity of the novel's attack on the talking cure is unrivaled in literature. Calling himself "King Sigmund the Second," Humbert belittles Freud at every opportunity, daring anyone to tell him something about himself he does not already know. At times it seems that Freud, not Quilty, is the secret antagonist in *Lolita*. In this novel, the Viennese witch doctor is revealed for what he is, less a mad doctor than Nabokov's white whale, a shadowy symbol of satanic proportions who must be killed again and again lest the universe go awry. Nothing less than the purity of literature and the survival of the imagination are at stake in *Lolita* and, if both Humbert and his maker become monomaniacal in their pursuit of evil, that is incidental to the outcome. The battle lines are drawn.

The irony begins with the mock Foreword to *Lolita* by John Ray, Jr., PhD, whose training in clinical psychology qualifies him as a Fraudian. In his role as editor of Hubert's confessional manuscript, Ray confirms Nabokov's belief that the difference between the rapist and therapist is a matter of spacing. Ray's introduction to Humbert's story lends the appearance of clinical authenticity, which is precisely what Nabokov parodies. Ray asserts that literature should elevate and inculcate, that human nature can be improved, that art functions as a warning of the dangers of abnormalcy and perversion. "[F]or in this poignant personal study there lurks a general lesson; the wayward child, the egotistic mother, the panting maniac—these are not only vivid characters in a unique story: they warn us of dangerous trends; they point out potent evils" (*The Annotated Lolita* 7–8). Ray assumes, furthermore, that Humbert is a pervert, that his case study should alert us to future Humberts lusting for our daughters, that the chief value of literature lies not in aesthetic beauty but in social and ethical import, and that psychopathology menaces us to the same extent that communism does. Ray's language at the end of the introduction evokes the hysterical rhetoric of McCarthyism.

The irony, then, is that Ray edits a story whose literary meaning remains beyond his understanding. Nabokov introduces the novel to us through an unreliable narrator and then proceeds to wrest *Lolita* out of Ray's clinical grasp. Oddly enough, Ray is not without a degree of insight into Humbert's story. He wisely refrains from editing or altering the manuscript apart from the correction of "obvious solecisms." He preserves the author's anonymity by telling us that "its author's bizarre cognomen is his own invention." The psychologist surprisingly rejects the charge of pornography, arguing that what is "offensive" in a story is frequently a synonym for "unusual." A great work of art, he realizes, is always original and shocking. Although he remains horrified by the author, he can appreciate the power of the manuscript. "But how magically his singing violin can conjure up a tendresse, a compassion for Lolita that makes us entranced with the book while abhorring its author!" (Which author is Ray referring to here—Humbert or Nabokov? If the latter, then Nabokov is poking fun at Ray even as the psychologist is disparaging the novelist!) Ray also concedes a point that Nabokov's other therapists would have missed: "that had our demented diarist gone, in the fatal summer of 1947, to a competent psycho-pathologist, there would have been no disaster; but then, neither would there have been this book" (7). In short, there is a ray of truth in the psychologist's introduction, although Nabokov would remind us that a "competent psychopathologist" is a contradiction in terms.

One must wonder, however, whether Dr. Ray is aware of Humbert's sadistic pleasure in foiling his psychiatrists. Given Nabokov's delight in deception, Humbert maintains a poker face in analyzing his "symptomatology" and bouts of insanity. In his contempt of Freud, Humbert is Nabokov's faithful son. "At first, I planned to take a degree in psychiatry as many *manqué* talents do; but I was even more *manqué* than that" (17). Wooed by psychoanalysts with their "pseudoliberations of pseudolibidoes," Humbert claims to have suffered several major psychological breakdowns that have caused him to be hospitalized in expensive sanatoriums where he perfects his maker's art: psychiatry baiting:

> I discovered there was an endless source of robust enjoyment in trifling with psychiatrists: cunningly leading them on; never letting them see that you know all the tricks of the trade; inventing for them elaborate dreams, pure classics in style (which make *them*, the dream-extortionists, dream and wake up shrieking); teasing them with fake "primal scenes"; and never allowing them the slightest glimpse of one's real sexual predicament. By bribing a nurse I won access to some files and discovered, with glee, cards calling me "potentially homosexual" and "totally impotent." The sport was so excellent, its results—in *my* case—so ruddy that I stayed on for a whole month after I was quite well (sleeping admirably and eating like a schoolgirl). And then I added another week just for the pleasure of taking on a powerful newcomer, a displaced (and, surely, deranged) celebrity, known for his knack of making patients believe they had witnessed their own conception. (36–7)

Not for a moment does Nabokov consider Humbert's anti-Freudianism an example of clinical resistance to therapy. Questions of transference and countertransference seem as alien to Nabokov as they would to B. F. Skinner, the American psychologist regarded as the founder of Behaviorism. Humbert's criticisms of psychoanalysis coincide exactly with Nabokov's position, and both use the identical parodic attack to demolish the foe. The reader cannot take seriously Humbert's declarations of past insanity, and there is nothing that threatens his lucidity or verbal power. The psychiatrists fail to uncover his deception. "I love to fool doctors," he confides merrily. In his role of "Jean-Jacques Humbert," he fabricates the most histrionic Rousseauvian confession. He can play the role of analyst or patient. "The child therapist in me (a fake, as most of them are—but no matter) regurgitated neo-Freudian hash and conjured up a dreaming and exaggerating Dolly in the 'latency' period of childhood" (126). Never deviating from his anti-Freudianism, he expects the reader to share his point of view. "Mid-twentieth century ideas concerning child-parent relationships have been considerably tainted by the scholastic rigmarole and standardized symbols of the psychoanalytic racket, but I hope I am addressing myself to unbiased readers" (287).

How much psychoanalytic theory has Humbert—and Nabokov—mastered? The question is difficult to answer, if only because the novelist may be assimilating more Freudian theory than he cares to parody. Humbert's mocking allusions to the "dream-extortionists," and Van's equally contemptuous reference in *Ada* to "Sig's epoch-making confession," suggest that *The Interpretation of Dreams* (1900) forms the cornerstone of Nabokov's understanding or misunderstanding of psychoanalytic theory. Nearly all of the parodist's comments focus on early libido theory, which represents historically the beginning of psychoanalysis, the emphasis on biological drives. Nabokov strongly objects to the biologizing of psychology, especially the Oedipus complex. He also attacks the "theatrical" side of psychoanalysis: the primal scene, the death wish, the birth trauma. Nabokov's fictional psychiatrists undertake the most preposterous research, with predictable conclusions. In *Ultima Thule*, Dr. Bonomini studies the "dynamics of the psyche," seeking to demonstrate that "all psychic disorders could be explained by subliminal memories of calamities that befell the patient's forbears" (*A Russian Beauty and Other Stories* 161). If a patient was suffering from megalomania, for example, it would be necessary to determine which of his great-grandfathers was a power-hungry failure. In *Pale Fire*, an old psychiatrist warns the Prince of Zembla that his vices had subconsciously killed his mother and would continue to kill the mother in him until he renounced sodomy. Otto Rank's theory of birth trauma also comes under attack. The narrator of *Pnin* refers to a "phenomenon of suffocation that a veteran psychoanalyst, whose name escapes me, has explained as being the subconsciously evoked shock of one's baptism which causes an explosion of intervening recollections between the first immersion and the last" (21). Pnin refers disapprovingly to Dr. Halp's "theory of birth being an act of suicide on the part of the infant."

A list of the books written by Nabokov's psychiatric researchers reveals a world gone mad over the mind-curing industry. Psychiatry, progressive education, the self-help business, how-to books, and psychobabble are exposed as the shams of shamans. Once again, Nabokov attacks the biologizing of psychology and the comic nature of psychoanalytic theory. Betty Bliss, one of Pnin's former graduate students, writes a paper on "Dostoevski and Gestalt Psychology," which nicely expresses Nabokov's deprecation of his nineteenth-century Russian predecessor. Before her marriage to Eric Wind, Liza Bogolepov works at the Meudon sanatorium directed by a destructive psychiatrist called Dr. Rosetta Stone. Psychotherapy, implies Nabokov, generates arcane hieroglyphics. The Winds' delightful son Victor proves to be a "problem child" because of his disturbing lack of pathology. The boy contradicts his parents' deeply held belief that "every male child had an ardent desire to castrate his father and a nostalgic urge to enter his mother's body." The father is so alarmed by his son's normalcy that he has him tested by the leading prognosticators of psychological health: the Godunov Drawing-of-an-Animal test, the Fairview Adult Test, the Kent–Rosanoff Absolutely Free Association Test, and the Augusta Angst Abstract Test. Unfortunately, Victor's interpretation of Rorschach ink blots proves of little interest to the psychologists, and the poor boy is finally left to struggle through life on his own. His parents, though, remain committed to their professional training and collaborate to write an essay on "Group Psychotherapy Applied to Marriage Counseling" for a psychiatric journal. In *Ultima Thule*, Dr. Bonomini writes a book called *The Heroics of Insanity*. In *Lolita*, John Ray receives the Poling Prize for a modest work titled "Do the Senses Make Sense?" in which certain morbid states and perversions are discussed. Nabokov has the last word, however, to this proliferating psychological literature. Near the end of *Ada*, Van grows disgusted with the "Sig" school of psychiatry and writes a paper called *The Farce of Group Therapy in Sexual Maladjustment*. The epigraph to the study contains a passage from Sig's epoch-making confession: "In my student days I became a *deflowerer* because I failed to pass my botany examination" (577). Van's paper proves to be devastating to the psychiatric establishment. "The Union of Marital Counselors and Catharticians at first wanted to sue but then preferred to detumify."

Van's reference to becoming a deflowerer warrants additional commentary, for it enables us to see Nabokov's indebtedness to Freud. In Freud's correspondence to his confidant Wilhelm Fliess, he refers to a friend's dreams in which he is a "deflowerer" of every person he sees. "And why was it," Freud rhetorically asks Fliess, "that at Interlaken, when he was fourteen, he masturbated in such a peculiar attitude in the W.C.? It was so that he could get a good view of the Jungfrau [literally, 'maiden']" (Masson 345). Nabokov was so amused by Freud's letter that after returning home from a trip to the Rockies, he wrote a letter to Edmund Wilson in August 1956 in which he observes: "Incidentally, in one of his letters to Fliess the Viennese Sage mentions a young patient who masturbated in the w.c. of an Interlaken hotel in a special contracted position so as to be able to glimpse (now comes the Viennese Sage's curative explanation) the Jungfrau" (Karlinsky 300). In *Lolita*, there is a three-page account of Humbert's ecstatic masturbation in the presence of his "Jungfrau," the maiden Dolly Haze—an example of how the novelist transmuted Freud's words into the stuff of art.

Nabokov demonstrates that he can out-psychologize the most orthodox Freudian; Humbert is less interested in proving the psychoanalyst incorrect than in casting him into hell. Both novelist and narrator ransack the psychoanalytic canon and then load their own cannon or torpedoes with enough explosives to sink the deepest depth reading. Humbert would have us believe that his tragic passion for Lolita springs from an unhappy love affair with Annabel Leigh, a lovely child of thirteen who is only a few months younger than he. Humbert falls madly in love with her, and they meet surreptitiously to carry out their youthful romance. Fate intervenes, and within a few months she dies of typhus, their love unconsummated. Humbert remains convinced that "in a certain magic and fateful way Lolita began with Annabel." The physical similarities between the two girls seem to support his statement. He emphasizes the Poesque quality of the doomed love, and he is highly conscious—self-conscious—of the parallels between Annabel Leigh and Annabel Lee. Humbert marries Charlotte Haze to be near her daughter, just as Poe marries his girl-cousin to be near his beloved aunt. But the parallel to Poe is misleading, as Andrew Field points out.

> The historian of literature knows, however, that Poe married his child bride primarily to tighten his rather strange and neurotic ties to her guardian aunt. If *Lolita* were indeed modeled on the life of Poe (as at least one article [by Elizabeth Phillips] has tried to maintain), Humbert would marry Lolita in order to be closer to her mother Charlotte! (*Nabokov: His Life in Art* 338)

The possibility that Humbert's love for Lolita is a repetition of his thwarted love for another nymphet, Annabel Leigh, thus turns out to be a dead end.

Another psychiatric dead end is the "Daddy's Girl" theme. Just as Humbert never tires of referring to Lolita as his daughter, so does Nabokov exploit all the ironies implicit in the apparently incestuous relationship. "Be a father to my little girl" (70), Charlotte writes to Humbert, and he proceeds to carry out her wish. He marries the detestable mother only to be near her desirable daughter whom he is happy to help raise. "Lolita, with an incestuous thrill, I had grown to regard as *my* child" (82), he adds parenthetically. After Charlotte's death, he informs Lolita that "For all practical purposes I am your father" (121). This is the relationship he announces to others, particularly to motel owners. His lecture on the history of incest is truly impressive: no one can question his devotion to research. When he finally catches up with Quilty, he introduces himself as Lolita's father and insists that the playwright stole his child. Quilty denies the kidnapping, maintaining that he rescued the girl from a "beastly pervert." The reader's response to this Oedipal play is that Humbert protests too much. There are simply too many Freudian "clues" for us to take seriously and, like Philip Roth's Portnoy, Humbert is too comfortable in his posture of lying on the analytic couch. Nabokov endows Humbert with the classic symptoms of an Oedipus complex, L. R. Hiatt remarked in 1967, but then hides this secret from public gaze. "It is a strange game for an author to play. If he wins, the reader loses the point of the book" (370). It is possible, of course, that there are Oedipal implications of Humbert's relationship to Lolita, but not the interpretation he deceptively offers.

Similarly, Nabokov parodies the subjects of homosexuality and impotence. Humbert refers gleefully to the psychiatrist's diagnosis of him as "potentially homosexual" and "totally impotent." He recalls a dream that seems to be culled from *The Interpretation of Dreams*.

> Sometimes I attempt to kill in my dreams. But do you know what happens? For instance I hold a gun. For instance I aim at a bland, quietly interested enemy. Oh, I press the trigger all right, but one bullet after another feebly drops on the floor from the sheepish muzzle. In those dreams, my only thought is to conceal the fiasco from my foe, who is slowly growing annoyed. (49)

The limpness of the unmanly bullets foreshadows the comic killing of Claire Quilty, Humbert's "evil double." Lest we miss the deep symbolism of the shooting, Humbert pointedly tells us that "we must remember that a pistol is the Freudian symbol of the Ur-father's central forelimb" (218). Fingering his gun in the presence of the man who has married Lolita, Dick Schiller, Humbert imagines shooting his sexual rival. But one wonders whether murder or detumescence is Humbert's goal. He conjures up a scene in which he "pulled the pistol's foreskin back, and then enjoyed the orgasm of the crushed finger: I was always a good little follower of the Viennese medicine man" (276). On another occasion, Humbert psychoanalyzes the symbolism of the fountain pen, the anatomical relative of the pistol. The fact that Quilty does not use a fountain pen indicates, "as any psychoanalyst will tell you," that the patient was a "repressed undinist" (252). Quilty obligingly admits that he had no fun with Dolly because he is "practically impotent," and then he implores Humbert to postpone the killing so that he can nurse his impotence. The shooting of Quilty parodies the ineffectuality of Humbert's bullets and the incomplete sexual gratification of the act. As the phallic bullets penetrate Quilty, his face twitches in an absurd clownish manner, and he emits a "feminine 'ah!'" as if the bullets were tickling him.

Nabokov parodies the Daddy's Girl theme and the impotence motif in *Lolita*, but he remains more serious about traumatic loss. In the beginning, Humbert discloses cryptically that his mother died in a freak accident—"picnic, lightning"—when he was three years old. He returns to the theme of maternal loss near the end of the story, telling us that "in retrospect no yearnings of the accepted kind could I ever graft upon any moment of my youth, no matter how savagely psychotherapists heckled me in my later periods of depression" (289). Apart from the question why sadistic therapists would want to heckle him, Humbert fears a similarly tragic death awaiting Lolita. Nabokov leaves us with the names of Quilty's plays, such as *The Lady Who Loved Lightning*. Lolita does not die from lightning but during childbirth, as does Humbert's first wife, Valeria. Is there a link between pregnancy and death? A significance to the premature deaths of Humbert's women: His mother, Annabel Leigh, Valeria, Lolita? Is Nabokov parodying the theme of traumatic loss, or is he using parody to conceal the overwhelming pain of death?

In other words, to what extent does Nabokov's use of parody invalidate a psychological interpretation of *Lolita*? If parody is viewed as a protective shield, against what is the novelist defending? No writer poses a greater threat or challenge to psychoanalytic criticism than Nabokov, who is not only the century's most virulently anti-Freudian novelist but also one of the greatest literary figures of our time, unquestionably a genius—and a genius at deception. His duplicity, as James R. Rambeau has observed, places his readers in a defensive position; "they must first prove they understand what Nabokov is *doing* before they can judge the final effects of his fiction" (30). Most readers have concluded that Nabokov's fiction is psychoanalytically impenetrable. Curiously, Nabokov's condemnation of psychoanalysis derives from his belief that it perpetrates a cruel hoax or deception on an unsuspecting public. "Freudism and all it has tainted with its grotesque implications and methods appears to me to be one of the vilest deceits practiced by people on themselves and others" (*Strong Opinions* 23–4). One would assume that Nabokov is irrevocably opposed to deception and that everything deceptive is evil. Not true. He consistently affirms the quality of deception in art and nature. "I discovered in nature the nonutilitarian delights that I sought in art. Both were a form of magic, both were a game of intricate enchantment and deception" (*Speak, Memory* 125). And in *Strong Opinions* he reveals that "all art is deception and so is nature; all is deception in that good cheat, from the insect that mimics a leaf to the popular enticements of procreation" (11). How, then, does the psychoanalyst's deception differ from the artist's? Cannot the analyst be a good cheat, as the insect and artist are, inventing strategies that unlock hidden truths?

Obviously not, for Nabokov. He praises the artist as an encoder of fictional reality, while he condemns the analyst as a false decoder of psychic reality. The issue for Nabokov is not the question of deep reality—his novels are as multilayered as onions and as difficult to peel—but the principle of freedom and control. Anything that impinges upon the artist's ability to create a self-enclosed and self-determined world becomes a threat to his autonomy. And the major threat lies in the Freudian assertion that one is neither fully aware nor in control of one's fears and desires. The artist generates and sustains Nabokov's reality, not the reality unlocked by the analyst. Nothing could be further from Nabokov's assumptions than a world in which dreams follow psychic, as opposed to artistic, laws and which contain meanings discoverable through the tools of psychoanalysis. Nabokov insists that only the artist can create magical reality; only the artist can lie truthfully. In *Pale Fire*, Kinbote mentions that "'reality' is neither the subject nor the object of true art which creates its own special reality having nothing to do with the average 'reality' perceived by the communal eye" (130). The artist's deceptions lead to freedom and independence; the psychoanalyst's deceptions lead to slavery. For Nabokov, the artist is married to creation, the analyst wedded to destruction.

Behind Nabokov's explicit rejection of psychology lies an implicit psychology of art: the belief that art and psychoanalysis exist at opposite poles of the imagination; the conviction that art, not analysis, is the last defense against suffering and injustice; the affirmation of the artist's autonomy amid deterministic forces. Art and psychoanalysis represent good and evil, respectively, in Nabokov's world. Thus, Humbert begins his story in a psychopathic ward and drives his doctors crazy. The artist or writer remains at the center of Nabokov's universe but always hidden behind a mask. Art becomes a refuge or sanctuary, with the artist, not the therapist, as the real healer.

Rescue Fantasies

Contrary to Humbert's assertions, there is an implicit psychology underlying *Lolita*, and it involves Humbert, a lyrical writer, whose theme is the creation and preservation of his beloved nymphet as a delicately wrought object of art. Critics have noted the two Lolitas in the novel: the real Dolores Haze, whose coarse mannerisms and speech betray a satirical and often unflattering portrait of innocence and experience; and the symbolic or mythic Lolita, the creation of Humbert's imagination. There is an almost Platonic need to subordinate the real Dolly Haze to the alluring man-made fantasy of Lolita, to transmute fleshy reality into artistic purity. "What I had madly possessed was not she, but my own creation, another, fanciful Lolita—perhaps, more real than Lolita; overlapping, encasing her; floating between me and her, and having no will, no consciousness—indeed, no life of her own" (64). Humbert loves the gum-chewing, comic-book-reading, hardened bobby-soxer, juvenile clothes and all; but he is more enchanted with his own autoerotic creation, the product of his febrile imagination. He cannot stop rendering her into an object of art, a fictional love object in his own image. His imagination animates Lolita; without him, she cannot exist. Insofar as Lolita is created by Humbert, a diarist whose heroic faith in the power of language endows her with immortality, he becomes, like his own creator—Vladimir Nabokov—a rescuer and redeemer of beauty and truth.

It is Humbert's imagination, not his phallus, that is the vital energizing spirit behind his artistic creativity. "It is not the artistic aptitudes that are secondary sexual characters as some shams and shamans have said; it is the other way around: sex is but the ancilla of art" (261). Yet, whichever theory of creativity one accepts, the psychoanalyst's or novelist's, Humbert's devotion to Lolita resides less in her body or sex than in his imaginative recreation of her. "I am not concerned with the so-called 'sex' at all. Anybody can imagine those elements of animality. A greater endeavor lures me on: to fix once for all the perilous magic of nymphets" (136). Whether or not we take seriously his self-proclaimed nympholepsy, his fascination for girl-children arises from a paradoxical union of "tender dreamy childishness and a kind of eerie vulgarity," a fusion of chaste and profane love. For all its eroticism, *Lolita* remains curiously suspicious of the biological components of sexuality. Like Pygmalion, Humbert demonstrates that the artist can rival God as the creator of life; but unlike the Greek sculptor, Humbert remains more infatuated with the inner artistic vision, the Keatsian ravished bride of stillness whose flight and pursuit are forever frozen into marble immobility. Humbert inevitably loses Lolita, as all people must lose their loved ones; but through the creation of the manuscript, the writer preserves a merged relationship with her, a union that will never dissolve, not even after the deaths of Dolly Haze and Humbert Humbert. Artistic creation unites artist and subject in an ecstatic oneness suggestive of the mother–child relationship. Humbert's devotion to art may be seen as an attempt to master the inevitability of death and recreate a new reality that will defy the ravages of time. The artist thus pursues a rescue fantasy in which the nymphet's unformed beauty is given shape and preserved from change.

At the risk of succumbing to clinical black magic, we may briefly invoke the Viennese witch doctor's voodooism to explain Humbert's rescue fantasy. In "A Special Type of Choice of Object Made by Men" (1910), part of his contributions to the psychology of love, Freud discusses the phenomenon of rescue fantasies and the family romance. He lists four necessary preconditions for this type of object choice. First, there must be an injured third party, such as a husband, fiancé, or friend, who claims possession of the girl or woman in question. Second, the woman's fidelity or reliability must be open to question—either the faint hint of scandal attached to a married woman or the implication of an openly promiscuous way of life. This is often termed "love for a prostitute." This precondition is necessary, Freud says, because the man experiences jealousy toward the third party. "What is strange is that it is not the lawful possessor of the loved one who becomes the target of this jealousy, but strangers, making their appearance for the first time, in relation to whom the loved one can be brought under suspicion" (*SE*, vol. 11, 167). Third, instead of the woman's value being measured by her sexual integrity and correspondingly reduced by promiscuous behavior, as it is in "normal" love, the situation is reversed. A woman becomes more desirable as she approaches the behavior of a prostitute. The final precondition is that a man of this type expresses the need to rescue the woman he desires from ruin. "The man is convinced that she is in need of him, that without him she would lose all moral control and rapidly sink to a lamentable level" (*SE*, vol. 11, 168).

The psychical origins of this type of love derive from the infantile fixation of tender feelings for the mother, Freud conjectures, and represent a consequence of that fixation. The love objects usually turn out to be mother surrogates, and the object from which he is rescuing the mother surrogate usually is the father. "It is at once clear that for the child who is growing up in the family circle the fact of the mother belonging to the father becomes an inseparable part of the mother's essence, and that the injured third party is none other than the father himself" (*SE*, vol. 11, 169). To defend himself against the realization of incestuous attachment to the mother, the son divorces spiritual from sensual love. The split reveals the antithetical image of woman: the madonna and the whore. Freud links the rescue motif to the Oedipus complex (he uses the term for the first time in this essay), which he relates to the family romance he had discussed in the preface to Otto Rank's well-known book, *The Myth of the Birth of the Hero*, first published in German in 1909 and translated into English in 1959. In the family romance, the son exalts one or both of his parents in an effort to recreate the happy vanished days of his childhood when his parents seemed to be the noblest and dearest of all people. In one of his most daring imaginative leaps in "A Special Type of Choice of Object Made by Men," Freud asserts that the son's need to rescue his mother acquires the significance of giving her a child in his own image.

> His mother gave him a life—his own life—and in exchange he gives her another life, that of a child which has the greatest resemblance to himself. The son shows his gratitude by wishing to have by his mother a son who is like himself: in other words, in the rescue-phantasy he is completely identifying himself with his father. All his instincts, those of tenderness, gratitude, lustfulness, defiance and independence, find satisfaction in the single wish *to be his own father*. Even the element of danger has not been lost in the change of meaning; for the act of birth itself is the danger from which he was saved by his mother's efforts. (173)

Without presuming to illuminate the mystery of *Lolita*, we may suggest that Humbert's rescue fantasy affirms the refuge of art, the only immortality he can bequeath upon his beloved Dolly. Just as the rescue fantasy implies a splitting of the mother image into the sacred and profane, the well-known madonna/whore complex, so does Humbert see Lolita and all nymphets as a paradoxical fusion of tender dreamy childishness and eerie vulgarity. From a legal point of view, he kidnaps and corrupts an innocent adolescent; yet from the novelist's point of view, he attempts to rescue her from sordid reality and worship her to the point of Mariolatry. There are several ironies surrounding Lolita's identity and Humbert's treatment of her. The innocent girl turns out to be far more sexually experienced than Humbert imagined; *she* seduces him. Although Humbert does not know this in advance, her desirability to him only increases when she is stolen by Quilty, the "injured third party" and the object of Humbert's rage. Humbert is less guilty of sexually violating Lolita than of attempting to control omnipotently her life and smothering her independence. Gladys M. Clifton is correct when she argues that readers have tended to overvalue Humbert's perspective and undervalue Lolita's (164).

Ironically, although Humbert brutally thwarts Lolita's natural wishes for separation and independence, thus depriving her not only of her childhood but the right to choose her own adult life, he also unconsciously attempts to save her from the life experiences, particularly marriage and motherhood, that will eventually destroy her. The world of reality proves deadly to the doomed Lolita, not because Humbert is trying to extinguish her autonomy, but because the novel insists upon her premature death by time and the biological trap. Risking life and liberty for the pursuit of a cruel mistress, Humbert is the classic unrequited lover, betrayed by a woman who is unaware of his heroic sacrifice. This too is one of the preconditions Freud talks about in his analysis of the rescue fantasy. "By her propensity to be fickle and unfaithful the loved one brings herself into dangerous situations, and thus it is understandable that the lover should be at pains to protect her from these dangers by watching over her virtue and counteracting her bad inclinations" (*SE*, vol. 11, 172). This is what Humbert does: he is an all-controlling father.

The little we learn about his own father is inconclusive evidence on which to speculate Humbert's relationship to the family romance. Besides, Nabokov is probably setting another trap for the psychoanalytic reader who seeks a connection between father and son. Humbert insists he adored his father, a strong, virile man. It may be that Humbert's attraction to the tomboyish quality of nymphets contains a bisexual element related to his identification with his father. "The specific psychological quality of Humbert's perversion is very close to homosexuality," Andrew Field writes, emphasizing, however, that Humbert is not in fact homosexual *(Nabokov: His Life in Art* 339). By contrast, Quilty is homosexual and represents Humbert's perverse alter ego. Nabokov's parody of the double has been extensively studied. Psychoanalytically, the phenomenon of the double affirms the ability to split off part of the self to maintain a cohesive identity. Quilty may be interpreted in several different ways: a narcissistic extension of the self, a mirror image of Humbert's bad self, the human tendency toward duplication. Otto Rank's conclusion in his pioneering study, *The Double*, published in English in 1979, casts light on the Humbert–Quilty relationship. "So it happens that the double, who personifies narcissistic self-love, becomes an unequivocal rival in sexual love; or else, originally created as a wish-defense against a dreaded eternal destruction, he reappears in superstition as the messenger of death" (86). Compared to perverted Quilty, Humbert seems wondrously normal. Humbert refers to Quilty as his brother, but he may also be the bad father in his unloving treatment of Lolita. Hence Humbert's need to murder him. Both men are artists, one an enormously prolific playwright, the other a lyrical-confessional novelist. Significantly, neither Quilty nor Humbert is procreative.

Lolita is a novel of passion but not procreation. The distinction is worth pursuing. The link among love, pregnancy, and death identifies the novel with fatal passion, destructive to the childbearing mother and aborted offspring. Lolita's death seems to be a punishment for her illicit love, illicit not from society's point of view but from Humbert's, the broken-hearted lover. The deaths of his first wife, Valeria, and eternal wife, Lolita, highlight a sterility associated with reality that sharply contrasts the fecundity of the artist's imagination. Lolita's creativity turns out to be literally a figment of the artist's imagination. Feeling her warm weight in his lap, he remarks that he was "always 'with Lolita,' as a woman is 'with child'" (109). As man and artist, Humbert embodies all the roles of the Freudian family romance. He is the loyal son devoted to the muse of invention; the mature lover or enchanted hunter in quest of his Mission Dolores; the spiritual father hovering over his child in an effort to protect her from inartistic lovers and from the mortal enemy of the nymphet, time; and the mother creator, always pregnant with Lolita, begetting and immortalizing her through the novelist's act of labor, the creation of art.

The Freudian interpretation of Humbert's rescue fantasy suggests an underlying Oedipal level of meaning, but, in light of more recent psychoanalytic research in the areas of ego psychology, identity formation, and separation-individuation, other meanings emerge from *Lolita*. Nabokov does not seem to be aware of ego psychology, the shift in emphasis away from instinctual drives to the defensive and adaptive functions of the autonomous ego. Humbert's commitment to art reveals an attempt to master fears of death and preserve forever Lolita's beauty. This agrees with Phyllis Roth's conclusion that "despite his asseverations to the contrary, Nabokov, like others, employed his art to master fears, anxieties, and unacceptable desires, transforming them into a transcendent fiction which is acceptably 'ascetic'" (44). Paradoxically, the fear of death leads to the strongest affirmation of immortality, thus demonstrating Nabokov's triumphant assertions of individuality and free will. One of the mysteries of the novel is how Humbert can continue to idealize Lolita even after she repeatedly rejects him. But Nabokov also shows how the creative process resolves the dualistic tension between unity and separation. Before Humbert writes the manuscript, he is separated from Lolita; yet he fuses with her during the creative act to achieve a new union. And insofar as his story is intended for others to read and participate in, Nabokov enacts once again the paradox of separation and oneness that defines all interactions. Humbert's merging with a higher ideal that will outlive him has an undeniably therapeutic effect on him. "I see nothing for the treatment of my misery but the melancholy and very local palliative of articulate art" (285). Humbert is the only therapist Nabokov celebrates, the creative artist who rescues life from death, form from chaos, triumph from defeat.

Lolita has intriguing implications for Heinz Kohut's self psychology. Although Humbert sees Lolita with painful clarity, he idealizes her and mirrors her self-love. The act of writing resembles the mirroring and idealizing transference relationship that Kohut speaks about in the treatment of narcissistic personality disorders, though it is not necessary to label Humbert in pathological terms. Kohut's self psychology, in fact, can be extended to normal personality development. Viewed from this perspective, the creation of the manuscript allows Humbert to restore his damaged self by transmuting the object (or in Kohutian terms the self-object) of his autoerotic love, Lolita, into a new internalization. Through art he achieves a restoration of the self.

Lolita, then, is not exempt from its own unique subterranean mythic system and psychology. Curiously, Nabokov's story is a reversal of the fairy tale of the wolf and Little Red Riding Hood that Kinbote dismisses in *Pale Fire*. Fromm's interpretation, we recall, suggests that the wolf is made ridiculous in the attempt to imitate a pregnant woman by having a living being in its belly. Humbert does not eat Lolita, although he would like to. "My only grudge against nature was that I could not turn my Lolita inside out and apply voracious lips to her young matrix, her unknown heart, her nacreous liver, the sea-grapes of her lungs, her comely twin kidneys" (167). Humbert first incorporates her into his imagination and then into the body of his art. Tellingly, in Nabokov's fairy tale, the roles of the huntsman and wolf are reversed. Instead of rescuing the innocent teenager, the huntsman marries her, impregnates her, and fills her belly with the living thing that will eventually destroy her. As lover and husband, Dick Schiller is the unenchanted hunter. Life without art is sterile and meaningless. By contrast, the poetical wolf is the good father in his attempt to rescue his beloved daughter from Quilty's maltreatment and Schiller's artificial insemination. Despite the wolf's tyrannical control over her, neither his voracious appetite nor his deceptive identity has harmed the little girl. Fromm's interpretation of the classic fairy tale highlights the man's defeat in the Oedipal battle, but in Nabokov's transformation, the wolf has the last word. He has swallowed the delicious girl and then given birth to a new Lolita who will outlive all the participants in the magical drama.

Given their differences over sex, love, psychoanalysis, and art, it is impossible to believe that Freud and Nabokov could agree on anything. No difference is more fundamental than this: for Freud, art is a substitute gratification for life; for Nabokov, life is a substitute gratification for art. Yet, in the final analysis, there are surprising similarities between them. The Viennese witch doctor's voodooism and black magic parallel the trickster-novelist's marvelous spells and wiles. In Nabokov's view, Freud is more of an artist, albeit a bad one, than a real scientist, and the novelist is always attempting to prove that his magic is more potent than the analyst's. Indeed, Nabokov's sorcery may be viewed as an elaborate "disappearing act" to cast the psychoanalyst into the void, yet in a curious way he needed to keep Freud alive, if only to make him appear upon command in his forewords and fictions. Nabokov's criticisms of Freud may also be turned against the novelist. Rejecting Freud's labyrinthine symbolism and mythology, "something like searching for Baconian acrostics in Shakespeare's works," Nabokov became, next to Joyce, the supreme fabulous artificer of twentieth-century literature. He devised a fictional system of Baconian acrostics that continues to confound generations of literary critics eager to decipher hidden patterns and wicked word puzzles in his writings. Moreover, both men adapted their obsessional personalities to creative purposes. Freud's quest for knowledge and faith in his intellectual powers were matched by Nabokov's complete mastery and omnipotent control of his fictional universe. Freud's case studies probably contain no greater assortment of mad and eccentric characters than those found in Nabokov's stories, which present a dazzling array of psychopaths, sadists, perverts, paranoids, and suicides. Freud wrote like a novelist (when his name was mentioned for the Nobel Prize, it was more often for literature than for medicine), and Nabokov had the insight of a shrewd clinician. Both geniuses changed their professions in ways we are only beginning to understand. Each was fascinated by the other's field but also deeply ambivalent toward it. Although Freud's admiration for artists is well known, he also disparaged them, reducing the man of letters to a neurotic or a narcissist, and claiming that unlike the scientist, which he considered himself to be, the artist is incapable of abstinence or renunciation. Nabokov reciprocated these feelings with a vengeance.

Finally, both men had strong prejudices and, in celebrating the autonomy of their separate disciplines, they erred in similar ways. Not only does Freud equate art with the pleasure principle and science with the reality principle, but he makes the astonishing statement in "Creative Writers and Day-Dreaming" that "We may lay it down that a happy person never phantasies, only an unsatisfied one" (*SE*, vol. 9, 146). The psychoanalyst can be guilty of outrageous pronouncements, as in this claim in *Introductory Lectures on Psycho-Analysis*: "The 'creative' imagination, indeed, is quite incapable of *inventing* anything; it can only combine components that are strange to one another" (*SE*, vol. 15, 172). The assertion is no less startling than Nabokov's insistence that the artist's fictional universe remains fiercely independent of reality. "Literature was born not the day when a boy crying wolf, wolf came running out of the Neanderthal valley with a big gray wolf at his heels; literature was born on the day when a boy came crying wolf, wolf and there was no wolf behind him" (*Lectures on Literature* 5). Future scholars will no doubt explore the extent to which Nabokov's celebrated Wolf-Man, Humbert Humbert, echoes the unheard cries of the young artist. Nor should this distress Nabokov's faithful readers. It is inconceivable that biographical knowledge will diminish the greatness of his achievement or the mystery of his art.

Unsolved Mystery

Since 1985, when I first wrote about Nabokov in *The Talking* Cure, we have learned much about the novelist's life, but nothing biographically explains his Freudian Schadenfreude. Nabokov's posthumous publications continue to document his obsession with Freud. The 2019 publication of *Think, Write, Speak*, composed of his uncollected essays, reviews, interviews, and letters to the editor, is 527 pages long. The index contains more bibliographic citations to Freud than to any other writer with the exception of Shakespeare and Alexander Pushkin, whose novel in verse *Eugene Onegin* Nabokov translated into English in 1965. All the citations to Freud are predictably vituperative.

Biographers remain fascinated by Nabokov and his wife, Véra, but they add no new information about the novelist's demonization of Freud. In *Vladimir Nabokov: The American Years* (1991), Brian Boyd quotes the novelist's letter about suffering from acute nervous exhaustion but offers no biographical commentary. Although never a clinical term, nervous exhaustion implies extreme mental or emotional stress and usually refers to serious anxiety or depression. Surely Boyd knew that Nabokov's mocking Wagnerian reference to "Prof. Siegfried Tannhäuser" implied a hated psychiatrist: one would think that Nabokov's nervous exhaustion would have piqued Boyd's biographical interest, but it did not. I hoped that Boyd's 2011 volume of essays, *Stalking Nabokov*, would provide further information about the novelist's pleasure in hating Freud, but there's only a cursory reference to the subject, supporting Nabokov's contempt of psychoanalysis. Despite another sensationalistic title, Andrea Pitzer's 2013 biography *The Secret History of Vladimir Nabokov* contains scarcely a word about the novelist's attitude toward psychoanalysis, nor does Stacy Schiff's 2000 biography *Véra (Mrs. Vladimir Nabokov)* shed new light on this subject.

I came across one essay, however, that helps explain Nabokov's complicated feelings about mental health. In an article published in the *Times Literary Supplement* in 2016, Galya Diment, a professor of Slavic languages and literature at the University of Washington, writes about being diagnosed with temporal lobe epilepsy and the possibility that Nabokov may have similarly suffered from a mild form of epilepsy. Ironically, the first time Diment experienced an epileptic seizure occurred at a 2012 Nabokov conference in New Zealand organized by Boyd. Diment presents compelling evidence, based on a close reading of Nabokov's memoir, novels, and letters, that he too suffered from some form of epilepsy. There was also a family history of epilepsy: his first cousin, the composer Nicolas Nabokov, suffered from it. The most famous example of a literary author with epilepsy was Dostoevsky, who experienced grand mal seizures, the symptoms of which he projected onto his fictional characters. Nabokov detested Dostoevsky, whom he considered a third-rate novelist. Diment ends her article with a wry irony: "For Vladimir Nabokov, there was, after all, no worse fate than being forever coupled with Fyodor Dostoevsky, except, perhaps being forever linked with Sigmund Freud." Lauren Slater also writes about temporal lobe epilepsy in *Lying: A Metaphorical Memoir* (2000), though one cannot tell in this trickster memoir whether the author is telling the truth, as I discuss in *Mad Muse* (2019).

Several psychoanalytic studies should be mentioned. In *Freud and Nabokov* (1988), Geoffrey Green agrees that Nabokov's disdain of Freud is the "grandest and most extravagant contempt for psychoanalysis known in modern literature" (1). Green cites one of Freud's most revealing observations about himself in *The Interpretation of Dreams*—"My emotional life has always insisted that I should have an intimate friend and a hated enemy" (*SE*, vol. 5, 483)—and then astutely makes the same observation about the novelist: "Nabokov had similar needs" (80). In *Contingency, Irony, and Solidarity* (1989), the American philosopher Richard Rorty invokes Harold Bloom's influential theory of the "anxiety of influence" to suggest that Nabokov's envy of Freud reflects his "resentment of the precursor who may have written all one's best lines" (154). The literary critic Leland de la Durantaye points out in an article published in *American Imago* in 2005 that it is likely Nabokov had encountered Freud's study of the Wolf-Man who was, like the novelist himself, a Russian rendered destitute and homeless by the Russian Revolution. De la Durantaye concludes that it is "neither possible nor necessary to judge—as so many of Nabokov's critics and defenders have endeavored to do—whether Nabokov's resistance to Freud was determined or overdetermined by factors or feelings of which he was not aware" (68). And in *Nabokov's Mimicry of Freud* (2017), the Korean literary scholar Teckyoung Kwon argues persuasively that the novelist's antipathy toward the psychoanalyst betrays an attitude of aggressive imitation. Kwon, who translated *Lolita* into Korean in 1997, shows the many aspects of this mimicry, including resemblance with a difference, contingency, the double, transgression, and metamorphosis.

Nabokov died in 1977 at the age of seventy-eight. It is unlikely that we will discover a biographical smoking gun to explain his Schadenfreude toward his dark double. Their relationship will always be uncanny, inviting us to see each of them through the other's eyes as well as through our own.

7

Thomas Szasz

Duplicitous Freud

The *duplicity* of nature and art was for Nabokov an honorific word, though not the duplicity of psychoanalysis. For Thomas Szasz, psychiatry was by its nature duplicitous, and he derived grim pleasure from attacking the mental health profession. In the beginning of his career, Szasz implied that Freud was, or should have been, a libertarian, like himself, though Szasz would have been the first to acknowledge that "libertarian Freud" is an oxymoron. Libertarian Freud soon gave way to duplicitous Freud, whom Szasz accused in his later writings of being a "base rhetorician." Szasz rarely said a good word about Freud or psychoanalysis, but he was harsher in his denunciations of psychiatry. The leader of the American "antipsychiatry" movement, a term he categorically rejected, Szasz coined the expression the "myth of mental illness," the title of his most famous or infamous 1961 book, as well as "the therapeutic state" and "pharmacracy," titles of later books. Szasz was the most polarizing psychiatrist of his age, and while many of his criticisms were prescient, his solutions to psychiatric problems remain extreme.

Szasz was born to Jewish parents in Budapest, Hungary, in 1920, moved to the United States in 1938 to escape the Nazis, and received both his undergraduate and medical degrees at the University of Cincinnati. He studied at the Chicago Institute for Psychoanalysis, where he later taught, and in 1956 he became a professor of psychiatry at the State University of New York College of Medicine, in Syracuse, New York, now called SUNY Upstate Medical University, retiring in 1990. The author of thirty-five books and over six hundred articles and reviews, Szasz wrote two books on psychoanalysis with strikingly different titles and themes: *The Ethics of Psychoanalysis: The Theory and Method of Autonomous Psychotherapy* (1965) and *Karl Kraus and the Soul-Doctors: A Pioneer Critic and His Criticism of Psychiatry and Psychoanalysis* (1976). The title of another book, *The Medicalization of Everyday Life: Selected Essays* (2007), contains an allusion to

Freud's *The Psychopathology of Everyday Life* (1901). Three of Szasz's books were on suicide, including *Fatal Freedom: The Ethics and Politics of Suicide* (1999), *"My Madness Saved Me": The Madness and Marriage of Virginia Woolf* (2006), and *Suicide Prohibition: The Shame of Medicine* (2011). Nor was his preoccupation with suicide solely a scholarly concern: his former wife, Rosine Loshkazian Szasz, committed suicide in 1971, at age forty-four, and he ended his own life in 2012 at age ninety-two after suffering a fall that resulted in a broken vertebrae in his spine.

In the beginning, Szasz wrote respectfully about Freud the man even when he disagreed with Freudian theory, and for this reason it would be misleading to call his early books anti-Freudian. He remained throughout his life a member of both the American Psychoanalytic Association and the American Psychiatric Association. Yet Szasz became contemptuous of psychiatry and psychoanalysis, as can be seen in his aphoristic *Words to the Wise: A Medical-Philosophical Dictionary* (2004), where he states that "Psychiatry is lynching by means of a diagnosis" (25). Psychiatry became for Szasz "the sewer into which modern societies discharge their insoluble moral and social problems" (159). Generalizations like these pervade Szasz's writings, conjuring the image of a Schadenfreudian. Demonizing psychiatry became an art form to Szasz, as it did for Nabokov, albeit for different reasons. The latter vilified the Viennese witch doctor mainly for aesthetic reasons, regarding psychoanalysis as an affront to the beauty and complexity of art; the former reviled psychiatry for crimes against humanity.

The Myth of Mental Illness

One must understand Szasz's critique of psychiatry before one can evaluate its strengths and weaknesses. To begin with, Szasz argues that insofar as disease or illness affects only the body, not the mind, there is no mental illness. To believe in mental illness, as nearly all mental health professionals do, is to believe in a myth—and, according to Szasz, though not to students of mythology, all myths are false. Mental illness remains for Szasz a metaphor for problems in living. Those who appear to be mentally ill, whether they realize it or not, are engaged in "malingering," that is, impersonating socially legitimized roles of illness. If there is no mental illness, there is no hospitalization, treatment, or cure for it. Eliminating the concept of mental illness, according to Szasz, eliminates the stigma surrounding it. Banishing mental illness also means banishing the insanity plea.

Szasz cannot be faulted for trying to make psychiatry as noncoercive as possible, nor for believing that psychotherapy can increase patients' freedom and responsibility. By calling attention to psychiatry's historically paternalistic attitude, Szasz seeks to replace it with a more enlightened egalitarian relationship between therapist and patient. The many awards and honors he received—a partial list includes the Martin Buber Award (1974), Humanist Laureate Award (1995), and American Psychological Association Rollo May Award (1998)—testify to his humanitarian efforts. Near the end of *The Myth of Mental Illness*, he urges everyone, including mental health professionals and the general public, to keep an open mind about psychiatric interventions. He concedes in the appendix that special occasions justify involuntary psychiatric interventions for people who are declared to be legally incompetent, though this qualification is generally absent from his later books.

Szasz offers one example in *The Myth of Mental Illness* of how genuine psychoanalysis might occur, though he grants that his example rarely happens. "Tell me more!" a "devout psychoanalyst" says to a "hysterical" patient:

> To be sure, the analyst, if he is worth his salt, implies more than this; what he usually implies is something of this sort: "I believe that you believe that you are sick (in the sense that your body is ailing). Your belief, however, is probably false. Indeed, you probably believe that you are sick—and want me to believe it—so that we should not have to deal with your real troubles—which are personal, not physical." (116)

One can imagine the patient's surprise hearing the analyst's unnerving comment, along with her defensiveness, but there is something heartening about "Tell me more!" The patient may fail to understand that she is not sick, as she believed, but the analyst emboldens her to find out why she feels—and acts—this way. One can see how Szasz encourages dialogue between therapist and patient, rejecting one type of explanatory system, the medical model, in favor of another type, a communications and linguistic model. The patient may not grasp at first the distinction between her personal and physical problems, but with her therapist's help, she can benefit from the talking cure.

What happens, however, if, for whatever reason, the patient cannot speak? If she is so distraught that she stares mutely at the analyst—or cannot or will not attend a therapy session? Or if she begins threatening to harm herself or others? Or if she cannot afford psychotherapy? Szasz refused to participate in the patient's "extra-analytic life," meaning that he did not accept reimbursements from the patient's health insurance provider; as a libertarian, he was philosophically opposed to health insurance regardless of whether it is public or private. Szasz does not raise these questions.

Szasz's critique of the alliance between psychiatry and the state did not mean he was antipsychiatry, a word he associated with R. D. Laing, the author of the influential book *The Divided Self* (1960). Laing argued that mental illness, including schizophrenia, could lead to heightened creativity, and he encouraged his patients to journey through their "madness" to experience breakthroughs denied to those who did not make similar psychic voyages. "Antipsychiatry is a type of psychiatry," Szasz retorts; "the psychiatrist *qua* health-care professional is a fraud, and so too is the antipsychiatrist" (xxviii).

Criticisms of *The Myth of Mental Illness*

The publication of *The Myth of Mental Illness* evoked fierce criticism. In "Fifty Years After *The Myth of Mental Illness*" the preface to the 2010 Harper Perennial edition, Szasz contends that his "great, unforgivable sin" was "calling *public* attention to the linguistic pretensions of psychiatry and its preemptive rhetoric" (xii). He cites several scholars, ranging from linguists to medical historians, who enthusiastically praised the book. Szasz ignores, however, the major arguments of his detractors. Some forms of physical illness, like mental illness, are defined mainly in terms of syndrome, such as migraine, rather than in terms of morphological abnormality. Moreover, certain illnesses, such as schizophrenia and manic depression, have a strong genetic component, a fact Szasz does not adequately address. Other criticisms appear in *Thomas Szasz: Primary Values and Contentions*, edited by Richard E. Vatz and Lee Weinberg (1983). "[M]uch of the behavior by which the more extreme forms of mental illness are diagnosed remains unmotivated and hence nonrational," Michael S. Moore points out (185). C. G. Schoenfeld faults Szasz for failing to provide clinical evidence to support the claim that mental illness does not exist. "That is, he fails to offer his readers detailed descriptions, case histories, and the like of a representative cross section of persons whom psychiatrists usually judge to be neurotic or psychotic, but whom he has interviewed or examined as a psychiatrist, and whom he has demonstrated to be completely normal" (199).

Additional objections to *The Myth of Mental Illness* appear in *Szasz Under Fire: The Psychiatric Abolitionist Faces His Critics* (2004), edited by Jeffrey A. Schaler. In reading Szasz's responses to his critics, one sees that he rarely changes his mind or makes any concessions or apologies. Many medical historians not included in *Szasz Under Fire* have assailed *The Myth of Mental Illness*. Eliot S. Valenstein points out in *Blaming the Brain* (1998) that while there is merit in some of Szasz's arguments, "his criticism of the 'mental disease' label seems to throw out the baby with the bathwater" (150). In *Shrinks: The Untold Story of Psychiatry* (2015), Jeffrey A. Lieberman relates a comment Szasz expressed to him privately. "He made it pretty clear he understood that schizophrenia qualified as a true brain disease, but he was never going to say so publicly" (113). Lieberman reports a disturbing story told to him by Aaron Beck, the founder of cognitive therapy:

> I had been treating a potentially homicidal inpatient who made contact with Thomas Szasz, who then put direct pressure on the Pennsylvania Hospital to discharge the patient. After he was released, the patient was responsible for several murders and was only stopped when his wife, whom he threatened to kill, shot him. I think that the "myth of mental illness" promulgated by Szasz was not only absurd but also damaging to the patients themselves. (113)

Those who knew Szasz personally report that while he was highly ideological in his writings, he was less so in his private life. In *Thomas Szasz: An Appraisal of His Legacy* (2019), the psychiatrist Allen Frances asked Szasz the following question while they were having dinner together:

> I posed to him a hypothetical situation in which his son was having a transient psychotic episode, was hearing voices commanding that he kill himself, felt compelled to act on the commands, and refused any treatment or advice. I asked: "As a father, Tom, would you stand by your libertarian principles or would you feel compelled to protect your son from himself, even if this required a very temporary coercion?" Tom smiled ruefully and said: "I am a father first and protector of human rights second." (170)

Szasz values logical clarity and linguistic purity, but binary thinking characterizes his work. Implicit in Szasz's writings lies the conviction that there is an unequivocal right and wrong in psychiatry and psychoanalysis: those with differing views are dangerously in error. He insists in *The Myth of Mental Illness*, for example, that "mental hospitals are like prisons, not hospitals; that involuntary mental hospitalization is a type of imprisonment, not medical care; and that coercive psychiatrists function as judges and jailers, not healers" (xii). Like Nabokov's attitude toward mental health professionals, Szasz allows for no exceptions, no qualifications, no ambiguities. Nor does Szasz concede that other psychiatric researchers may be driven, as he is, by the desire for scientific knowledge and the wish to alleviate suffering. The "search for the biological and physical causes of so-called psychopathological phenomena is motivated more by the investigator's craving for prestige and power than by his desire for understanding and clarity" (77). Szasz makes other incendiary statements. How would his hysterical patient have reacted, we wonder, upon hearing him say that "patients with hysteria and with most so-called mental illnesses do not make 'appropriate' efforts to get well" (197)? How do you convince patients that they are malingering and do not wish to get well?

To his credit, Szasz's comments about Freud in *The Myth of Mental Illness* are accurate. He praises Freud for showing the child's need for and dependence on his or her parents, especially the mother or the mother surrogate. He singles out Freud's insight into the antithetical meaning of certain words that can simultaneously express opposite meanings. "This antithetical meaning of certain symbols is an important characteristic of dream psychology" (155)—though dream psychology is a subject that Szasz rarely discusses. He does not concur with Freud that the earliest years of childhood indelibly shape later adult behavior, but he concedes that the rules one learns early influence later life. He commends Freud for condemning the social and medical hypocrisies surrounding sex and money. Szasz's objections to Freud are also pertinent, including the misogynistic element in classical psychoanalytic theory. Szasz is balanced in his evaluation of Freud's work, but that will soon change.

One can hear pride in Szasz's voice when he asserts that after the publication of *The Myth of Mental Illness*, "psychiatry has not been the same since" (270). Yet he also confesses resentfully that he became a "nonperson" in American psychiatry" (271). Ironically, without realizing it, Szasz treated those psychiatrists who did not agree with him—nearly everyone—as nonpersons, lumping them all into the category of oppressive and coercive controllers of mass conformity.

The Ethics of Psychoanalysis

Writing *The Myth of Mental Illness*, Szasz admitted in the 1988 preface to his first book, *Pain and Pleasure* (1957), "freed me to be myself" (vii). It is an odd statement because Szasz continues to speak positively about Freud in his next book, *Law, Liberty, and Psychiatry* (1963), where he refers to Freud as the "greatest scientist of the mind who ever lived" (x), and in the book published two years later, *The Ethics of Psychoanalysis*. Freud's great contribution to psychotherapy, Szasz writes, "lies in having laid the foundations for a therapy that seeks to enlarge the patient's choices and hence his freedom and responsibility" (*The*

Ethics of Psychoanalysis 16). Szasz regards Freud as a "fearlessly honest man; he eschewed pretense and gimmickry" (35). Szasz's next sentence, however, is ominous. "But, as psychoanalysis became successful and socially respectable, it succumbed more and more to pseudoinstrumentalism." Freud would not have recognized Szasz's vision of psychoanalysis as primarily a "*moral exercise* or, if one wishes to put it that way, a *moral therapy*" (202). Nor does Szasz approve of Freud's insistence that patients in analysis remain in a state of "abstinence," denied the satisfaction of their desires until the end of treatment. "Here we see Freud advocating manipulating and coercing the patient, ostensibly in the interests of analysis. This is absurd" (186). No less absurd in Szasz's view is institutional psychoanalysis; he regarded psychoanalytic institutes as inimical to the core values of freedom and responsibility.

Sounding more like an attorney concerned with the drawing up of contracts and torts than like a psychoanalyst, Szasz introduces the idea of autonomous psychotherapy. Unlike the "heteronomous" therapist, Szasz's pejorative term for the therapist who is responsive to the needs of patients and their relatives, thus guilty, in effect, of infantilizing them, the "autonomous" therapist is "not for hire; neither with money nor with complaints and suffering can he be bought" (*The Ethics of Psychoanalysis* 44). In *Words to the Wise*, Szasz defines autonomy as the "paradigmatic heresy, the quintessential affront against authority" (8). Another Szaszian term for autonomous psychotherapy is "contractual psychotherapy," based on a mutually accepted set of promises and expectations. Szasz's aim is to transform psychoanalysis into a "*fully* contractual type of psychotherapy" (*The Ethics of Psychoanalysis* 113), by which he means spelling out explicitly the terms of the contract before a patient begins treatment. The Szaszian analyst makes two unique and, for nearly all mental health professionals, highly problematic promises to the patient: not to make the "therapeutic decision" to hospitalize the patient or protect him or her from committing suicide. The patient's sole responsibility is to pay his or her bill on time, including paying for missed sessions even if the patient is ill. Thus, the "hypochondriacal patient," who, according to Szasz, uses illness as a way to avoid responsibility, has a choice of paying for sessions canceled for "illness" or terminating therapy. Szasz ends *The Ethics of Psychoanalysis* with the central principle of autonomous psychotherapy: "You are not responsible for the patient, his health (mental or physical), or his conduct; for all this, the patient is responsible. But you are responsible for your conduct" (220).

In laying out the ethics of psychoanalysis, Szasz places little or no emphasis on the traditional aspects of the talking cure: the unconscious, dream interpretation, repression, infantile sexuality, defense mechanisms, transference, and countertransference. He believes in the analyst's role in listening to the patient's free associations, but he warns against the analyst playing an active role. "If we use transitive verbs to describe what goes on between therapist and patient, it is either an error or it is not autonomous psychotherapy" (*The Ethics of Psychoanalysis* 38). Sometimes Szasz sounds like a classical analyst, as when he says that attempts to shorten analytic sessions from the traditional fifty minutes are "deplorable" (166). Mostly, though, Szasz offers untraditional advice to the psychoanalyst, as he makes clear in the epilogue, where he urges psychiatrists not to let their medical training get in the way of therapy. Analysts must fulfill their contracts with patients, but as a libertarian Szasz spends more time describing what analysts should *not* do. They must avoid being coerced by their patients' "emergencies," avoid misconstruing their patients' feelings about them, and avoid taking notes. Analysts are finally responsible for their own rather than for their patients' conduct, a belief that sharply limits the analyst's emotional engagement with patients.

As a libertarian, does Szasz approve of sexual relations between a therapist and patient? I raise this question because in *Schizophrenia: The Sacred Symbol of Psychiatry* (1976), Szasz states that he is "not against voluntary psychiatry, or psychiatric relations between consenting adults" (49). The sentence is ambiguous: What does psychiatric relations between consenting adults mean? He appears to answer the question in *Coercion as Cure* (2007): "Consensual relations—religious, psychiatric, sexual—pose no special moral or political problems" (15). But every professional medical and psychological association has banned sexual relations between a therapist and patient, which are not only inappropriate but also illegal. As Paul Mosher and I show in volume 1 of *Off the Tracks*, "Sexual and Nonsexual Boundary Violations" (2019), this form of analyst misconduct almost always dooms therapy.

Karl Kraus and the Soul-Doctors

The original title of Szasz's 1976 book was *Karl Kraus and the Soul-Doctors: A Pioneer Critic and His Criticism of Psychiatry and Psychoanalysis*, but he changed the title in the reprinted 1990 edition to *Anti-Freud: Karl Kraus's Criticism of Psychoanalysis and Psychiatry*. The difference in titles is significant. Szasz admired the Viennese satirist and social critic because Kraus lambasted Freud and psychoanalysis. Indeed, none of Freud's many contemporary critics was more hostile than Kraus, who scornfully branded psychoanalysis as the disease it purports to cure. Although Szasz never admits his powerful overidentification, his explicit praise of Kraus reveals implicit self-praise. Kraus's writings "run against the grain of our contemporary intellectual mores" (xii), like Szasz's writings. Kraus was regarded as the "leading satirist and social critic in Vienna and in many parts of the German-speaking world" (16). Szasz, too, became the most outspoken psychiatric critic of his age. Kraus warned against the "psychiatric and psychoanalytic demagogues and destroyers of our words and our world" (18), like Szasz. Kraus was effective in "unmasking the great unmasker" (22), like Szasz. "Increasingly, Kraus saw psychoanalysis as an ideology destructive of individualism and personal responsibility, and the vigor of his condemnation of it increased apace" (30)—like Szasz. Unlike the "base rhetorician" Freud, an expression Szasz uses several times, Kraus was a noble rhetorician—as Szasz saw himself. "Kraus fully recognized Freud's 'genius'—just as he recognized Hitler's—but he regarded it as a genius for evil rather than good" (96). Szasz felt the same way. To the end of his life, Kraus was "still smiting the psychoanalysts with his satirical thunderbolts" (30)—again, like Szasz. Most literary critics and historians describe Kraus as an example of a self-hating Jew who converted to Catholicism, but Szasz rejects this view. Nevertheless, Szasz admits that Kraus's "Jewish-intellectual criterion for approval is based on the maxim, 'If you are not with us, you are against us'" (9). This was no less true of Szasz.

Words to the Wise

Szasz was careful at times to distinguish between psychiatrists and psychoanalysts, as he does in *Cruel Compassion* (1994), where the "psychiatrist controls and coerces, the psychoanalyst contracts and cooperates. The former wields power, the latter has authority" (157). But this distinction disappears in his later writings. Szasz's ideas did not change much, but his rhetoric did. He became more polemical, more vitriolic, more dismissive. Accusatory rhetoric mars his writing; one senses, from his book titles alone, that he was the grand inquisitor of psychiatry, rooting out evil wherever he saw it: everywhere. Nor does he direct his ruthless sarcasm against himself: humility was not one of his vices. By the time he wrote *Words to the Wise*, Szasz had become virulently anti-Freudian. He accuses Freud and Marx of using vivid metaphors "literally to enslave others" (66). Freud's "only discovery," he now opines, is the recognition that mental illness is a problem for the patient's family and society; for the patient, "mental illness is a solution" (107). Whereas Freud, anticipating a patient's objections to psychotherapy, wrote wryly, in the last paragraph of *Studies on Hysteria*, that "much will be gained if we succeed in transforming your hysterical illness into common unhappiness" (*SE*, vol. 2, 305), Szasz reduces this to "somatic treatments help the patient to exchange ordinary unhappiness for the miseries of psychiatric cures" (168).

Among the longest entries in *Words to the Wise* are "suicide," which Szasz philosophically supports as an inalienable human right, and "suicide prevention," to which he remains unalterably opposed. "Killing oneself is a choice and hence an expression of one's personal freedom. Forcibly interfering with that freedom is, *by definition*, a deprivation of liberty" (226). Szasz refers to three celebrities who were saved from suicide through the use of psychotropic drugs: Mike Wallace, William Styron, and Kay Redfield Jamison. Szasz calls them, disdainfully, "trophy patients," and likens their stories about how psychiatry saved them to "cures at Lourdes" (119). In doing so, Szasz does them an injustice.

Wallace, the legendary journalist who became famous cohosting *Sixty Minutes*, acknowledged publicly his long struggle with depression, which culminated in a suicide attempt, when he overdosed on sleeping pills. When his wife found him unconscious in bed, he was rushed to a hospital, where he had his stomach pumped. Psychotherapy and antidepressant medication aided his recovery. Wallace never doubted that he suffered from debilitating depression and unambiguously recommended psychiatry to others suffering from mood disorders. Bearing witness to mental illness was necessary for Wallace: he and his friend, the humorist Art Buchwald, disclosed on *Larry King Live* in 1997 their history of depression. Styron also needed to bear witness. He first wrote about depression in his iconic 1990 memoir *Darkness Visible*, his harrowing account of depression from its onset in October 1985 to its near-fatal ending two months later, when, unable to pen a suicide note because his words sounded melodramatic, he hospitalized himself and began the healing process. Styron was not helped by psychiatric medication, as Szasz incorrectly implies; rather, it was the safety of the hospital and the healing process of time that led to his recovery. Styron never wrote about his depression after the publication of *Darkness Visible*, when he became so agitated that he agreed reluctantly to receive electroconvulsive therapy, the treatment of last resort for the mood disorder. He was in such torment that he wrote a suicide letter to his readers apologizing for the decision to end his life. Styron died of natural causes in 2006, at age eighty-one, and despite the fact that his last years were grim, he worked tirelessly to destigmatize mental illness, a disease that remains "nearly incomprehensible to those who have not experienced it in its extreme mode" (*Darkness Visible* 7).

Neither Wallace nor Styron wrote about Szasz, but Jamison had much to say about him in *Night Falls Fast: Understanding Suicide* (1999). Jamison, a professor of psychiatry at Johns Hopkins University and recipient of a MacArthur "Genius Grant," chronicles in her riveting 1995 book *An Unquiet Mind: A Memoir of Moods and Madness* her lifelong struggle with manic depression and a near-fatal suicide attempt. For years she was terrified to admit publicly her illness, fearful that the admission would prevent her from practicing psychotherapy. In both *An Unquiet Mind* and *Night Falls Fast* she acknowledges her methodical efforts to kill herself and her gratitude that she was prevented from doing so. After disagreeing with Szasz's view that there is no connection between suicide and mental illness, a "belief," she adds, that is "supported neither by the clinical and scientific literature nor, indeed, by any data presented by Szasz himself," she discusses a 1994 malpractice suit in which his insurance company agreed to pay a large settlement to the widow of one of his patients, a physician, who suffered from manic-depressive illness and committed suicide:

> The legal complaint filed against Szasz charged that he instructed and advised his patient to stop taking lithium in June 1990; in December of the same year, the doctor, after beating himself in the head with a hammer and inflicting lacerations to his neck, hanged himself with battery cables. The complaint further charged that Szasz had failed to render "psychiatric medical care and treatment in conformity with the customary and accepted sound standards of medical care," "failed to properly diagnose and treat," "failed to provide proper therapy to treat manic depression," and "failed to keep adequate and proper medical records." Although Szasz's attorney maintained that the patient had stopped taking lithium of his own accord and Szasz himself did not concede he had committed malpractice, the court ruled that the widow was to receive $650,000 in settlement. Szasz, despite his distaste for the psychiatric establishment, was a member of the American Psychiatric Association, and it was the organization's malpractice insurance carrier that ended up paying the settlement. (*Night Falls Fast* 254–5)

Tellingly, Szasz does not mention this malpractice suit in *Words to the Wise* nor in any of his other writings. There is no need for him to do so—yet, in *Schizophrenia: The Sacred Symbol of Psychiatry*, he goes out of his way to discuss in detail how the prominent psychoanalyst John Rosen lost a malpractice suit in the late 1950s that was brought against him for abusing a patient in the guise of a new treatment for schizophrenia called "direct analysis." Szasz is rightly filled with indignation and disgust over this psychiatric abuse of power, yet there's not a word about the malpractice suit brought against him.

Stung by Jamison's comments, Szasz sought to undercut her credibility first in *"My Madness Saved Me": The Marriage and Madness of Virginia Woolf*, where he states that her career as a "manic-depressive, suicidal-exuberant mental patient does not provide her, popular opinion notwithstanding, with medical or genetic expertise" (99), and then in *Psychiatry: The Science of Lies* (2008), where he refers to her as a "self-defined manic depressive, and expert on 'bipolar disease' and its biological-coercive treatment" (90). The last three words are a cruel parody of the truth: Jamison states unequivocally that lithium has saved her life. Szasz makes another misleading statement about her. It's jarring when he refers to her "alleged illness and near-death experience" and then quotes a long passage from her website in which, after her disastrous decision to stop taking lithium, she began to experience a manic high that evoked the glorious feeling of flying past stars. Back on lithium, Jamison can only remember what that visionary feeling was like. "Long since that extended voyage of my mind and soul, Saturn and its icy rings took on an elegiacal beauty, and I don't see Saturn's image now without feeling an acute sadness at its being so far away from me, so unobtainable in so many ways" (100). Szasz implies that lithium deprived Jamison of this epiphanic experience, when, in fact, as Jamison repeatedly insists, without lithium, her intense manic highs would soon plunge her into unbearably low emotional states that lead inescapably to suicidal thoughts.

Fatal Freedom, *"My Madness Saved Me,"* and *Suicide Prohibition*

To what extent did Szasz's malpractice suit compel him to write three books in the next decade—*Fatal Freedom: The Ethics and Politics of Suicide*, *"My Madness Saved Me": The Madness and Marriage of Virginia Woolf*, and *Suicide Prohibition: The Shame of Medicine*—justifying a patient's right to commit suicide without a psychiatrist's intervention? The books contain a myriad of questionable charges, as when he claims that those who deny suicide is a logical, reasonable choice, such as psychiatrists, politicians, and lawyers, are engaged in self-serving motivation. Why does he always assume that those who disagree with him are guilty of base motivation? Throughout *Fatal Freedom: The Ethics and Politics of Suicide*, Szasz uses the Latin expression, *Cui Bono?*, informing us that the rhetorical question, popularized by Cicero, refers to disputants' hidden interests.

Szasz is unimpressed with Freud's belief that suicide is internalized aggression initially directed against another person, though there is much evidence to support the theory, especially when suicide survivors—those who are affected by a loved one's self-death—feel anger, as if part of themselves has also been killed, as well as grief.

In rejecting the claim that untreated mental illness leads to suicide, Szasz makes the opposite claim, for which there is little evidence: that the treatment of mental illness *causes* suicide. It's true that suicide may be experienced as a "liberation" by both the subject and his or her survivors, as Szasz avers, but suicide survivors' feeling of liberation is often accompanied by crushing guilt. It's also true, as Szasz states, that we cannot predict whether a parent, had he or she not committed suicide, would have had a beneficial or harmful influence on a child's life, thus rendering false any generalization about the effect of parental suicide on a child's life. Nevertheless, countless clinical and empirical studies show how a child is devastated by a parent's suicide—and how the child is at increased risk for suicide later in life. Nor are children alone at increased risk. The psychiatrist James L. Knoll IV, one of the coeditors of *Thomas Szasz: An Appraisal of His Legacy*, reports that losing a close relative to suicide increases a mourner's risk of suicide by threefold; losing a spouse to suicide increases the mourner's risk by ten to sixteenfold (110). Few would argue with Szasz's observation that the defeats that most damage a person's will to live involve the loss of a child, spouse, or lover, from which he draws the commonsensical conclusion that to avoid killing oneself, one must try to avoid feeling trapped; but he fails to acknowledge that those who feel trapped may sometimes need interventions by others. Szasz talks about suicide as if it is only a personal act, but it is also an interpersonal act. I believe, as many others do, that one has a right to commit suicide, but I also believe that others have a right, indeed, an obligation, to try to prevent suicide.

In the preface to "*My Madness Saved Me*": *The Madness and Marriage of Virginia Woolf*, Szasz attempts to convert a weakness of his scholarship into a strength, admitting that his denial of mental illness is not based on medical, psychiatric, or neuroscientific research but on critical thinking, which, he wants us to believe, cannot be falsified. I doubt any Virginia Woolf scholar would agree with his conclusion that she was a "victim of neither mental illness, nor psychiatry, nor her husband—the three ways she is regularly portrayed. Instead, she was an intelligent and self-assertive person, a moral agent who used mental illness, psychiatry, and her husband to fashion for herself a life of her own choosing." Szasz's study of Woolf betrays a startling lack of empathy, as when he alleges that she killed herself "to enhance her fame" (88).

Suicide Prohibition: The Shame of Medicine is Szasz's last book, published one year before his death, and thus demands special scrutiny. He cites in the preface Johann Wolfgang von Goethe, the author of the largely autobiographical epistolary novel *The Sorrows of Young Werther* (1774), but he doesn't mention the scores of copycat suicides the novel provoked, some readers holding a copy of the book and dressed in Werther's clothes, blue tailcoats, and yellow waistcoats, when they ended their lives. Nor does Szasz mention that in later life Goethe refused to reread the novel because of its dangerous romanticization of suicide. Szasz's generalization that "voluntary death is relatively infrequent in America" (4) is incorrect. Even before COVID-19, suicide had been increasing at an alarming rate, especially among the young and the old. Labeling the support for suicide prevention an affront to human dignity, personal responsibility, and individual liberty, Szasz rules out an effort on the part of university administrators to prevent students from killing themselves. After quoting the president of Cornell University, who urged students to ask for help if they were in crisis, Szasz insensitively responds: "The stupid know how to ask for help without going to college. The smart need to go to Cornell to learn to do so" (23).

Many of Szasz's statements in *Suicide Prohibition* are factually incorrect, including the assertion that there is no evidence suicide prevention programs work. In a 2019 study, Lewitzka and her associates demonstrate that the implementation of a national strategy is an effective tool to reduce suicide rates which, according to the World Health Organization, result in a million deaths each year. What's perhaps most disconcerting about *Suicide Prohibition* is a word that never appears in the book, *ambivalence*, a state of mind that characterizes many if not most people who attempt or succeed in killing themselves, wishing, simultaneously, and contradictorily, both to die and live. George Howe Colt remarks in *The Enigma of Suicide* (1992) that Szasz and other civil libertarians misunderstand the nature of suicidal thinking, which is based not on rational thinking and freedom of choice but on ambivalence and impulsiveness (341). Szasz was opposed to coercive psychiatry, but he never admitted that a coercive environment may cause or contribute to a person's suicide. Moreover, contrary to what Szasz implies, the overwhelming majority of people who survive a suicide attempt never attempt it again.

Cui Bono?

There is no biography of Szasz—not surprising because he was an intensely private man—and one can only speculate about how his vision of psychoanalysis and psychiatry was affected by his ex-wife's suicide. We know about the suicide only because Schaler mentions it in "Kaddish for Thomas Szasz." (None of the many obituaries of Szasz refers to this detail.) For many people, suicide is, literally, an unspeakable subject. Unspeakable but not forgettable. The eerie silence surrounding suicide condemns those who have taken their own lives to a spectral existence as skeletons in the closet, where they haunt the living.

Szasz *never* wrote about Rosine's death—nor has anyone who has written on Szasz, with the exception of Schaler, mentioned it. Astonishingly, Szasz never refers to his former wife or her suicide in his twenty-eight-page essay "An Autobiographical Sketch," appearing in *Szasz Under Fire*. He devotes pages to his parents; his childhood governess, Kisu; his beloved brother, George; and his many teachers. He mentions briefly his two daughters, but there is not a single word about his ex-wife or her death. Intent on demolishing one taboo after another in psychiatry, Szasz unwittingly confirms the major taboo associated with suicide: never talk or write about it.

Yet although Szasz never wrote directly about this event, there are comments in *Suicide Prohibition* that hint at the wrenching aftermath of the suicide. After asserting that suicide is a kind of emigration, where the suicide decides to "move from the land of the living to the land of the dead," choosing "to firmly separate himself from his family and friends," Szasz adds, "Every emigrant knows from personal experience that it is painful to leave one's home and exchange one's mother tongue for a 'foreign' language" (77). This was almost certainly true of Rosine Loshkazian Szasz, an Armenian emigrant who separated herself from her husband and two young daughters after nineteen years of marriage. A few pages later, Szasz adds a noteworthy parenthetical remark. After developing the metaphor of divorce as marital secession and suicide as personal secession, he writes: "The fact that not all those individuals personally affected may find the separation voluntary or peaceful—for example, children in a divorce—is important but does not affect the argument I am advancing" (80).

But what Szasz was unwilling to say publicly in his writings about the aftermath of suicide on a family he confessed in private. In an obituary written shortly after Szasz's death, his close friend and disciple Schaler remarks in "Kaddish for Thomas Szasz" that he was saddened but not surprised by the suicide.

> Tom and I both agreed that the right to life includes the right to death, and that the state has absolutely no business regulating either, so long as the pursuit of liberty did not injure others directly. Tom told me that he was concerned about the effect his suicide would have on his daughters, seeing that their mother, Rosine, had committed suicide, too, after she and Tom were divorced, many years ago.

The key word here is *directly*; neither Schaler nor Szasz explored suicide's devastating *indirect* impact on relatives and friends. Suicide, it has been mordantly said, is the gift that keeps on giving, an act that has lasting intergenerational implications.

In writing about suicide as an ethical rather than medical or psychological issue, Szasz ignores the shattering relational implications for the suicide survivor, particularly survivor guilt, a phenomenon Freud named. The creator of psychoanalysis emphasized the feelings of self-reproach that regularly accompany survivor guilt, and clinicians have confirmed that this self-reproach darkens the lives, often permanently, of most suicide survivors. As a psychoanalyst, Szasz was surely aware of this phenomenon. As the husband of a wife who committed suicide, he decided never to write about his former wife or the nature of her death. It's likely he believed that the suicide was private, no one's business except his own and, perhaps, his daughters; it's also likely that Szasz hoped that silence was the best way to deny the ongoing reality of suicide.

Indeed, it's significant that Szasz did not begin to write in detail about suicide until after his wife's death. His early books reveal almost nothing about suicide, while the books written after her death focus entirely or partly on suicide. Rereading *The Ethics of Psychoanalysis* in light of Rosine Szasz's suicide, one wonders about the extent to which the idea of strict autonomy, for both a therapist and a spouse, enabled Szasz to deny whatever feelings of grief, guilt, remorse, and anger he experienced at the time. Schaler, who created and manages Szasz's website, devotes only one sentence to the suicide, almost as if it were an afterthought, but he makes an outrageous claim, in words expressed in a long parenthesis, that may reveal an insight into Szasz's troubled marriage:

> (Tom often considered social workers among the worst members of the mental health profession, perhaps because they were such blatant servants of the therapeutic state, perhaps because, at least at the masters level, they seemed uniquely stupid, I just don't know. Very few seem to know much about thinking. Most are fluent when it comes to therapy gimmicks.) He and I once talked about what social workers did. He said, "they are the worst." I can see why.

Szasz's belief that social workers are the worst may be seen in his study of Virginia Woolf, where he quotes W. H. Auden's observation that writers can be guilty of every human conceit but one, the conceit of the social worker: "We are all here on earth to help others; what on earth the others are here for, I don't know" (21). Szasz then adds that while Leonard Woolf was a writer, he must have regarded himself as a social worker, deluded into thinking that he could help his wife. Szasz's contempt and snobbery become more troubling because his wife was a social worker. One can only imagine how she must have felt living with a man who ridiculed her own profession—and how this devaluation may have harmed her marriage, sabotaged her self-esteem, and aggravated her "problems in living," Szasz's euphemism for mental illness.

Given Szasz's divorce, one is struck by his bitter and cynical comments about marriage in the two books he wrote immediately after her suicide. "Marriage is a gift man gives to a woman," he jests in *The Second Sin* (1973), "for which she never forgives him," adding that "marriage now serves the bride to deceive the groom and vice versa: each thinks he or she will get the better of the bargain. Frequently, each soon concludes that he or she got the worst of it" (5–6). The same disillusionment appears in *Heresies* (1976). "Marriages are said to be made in heaven, which must be why they don't work here on earth" (15). There are no positive remarks about marriage in the two books, only negative ones, the most chilling of which is the following metaphor of the modern marriage: "two competent swimmers in the water, safe but solitary; they decide to play, one pretending to drown, the other pretending to rescue; grappling in this charade, they sink, panic, and drown together" (*Heresies* 16).

Szasz detested psychobiography, regarding the genre as a profanation and violation of an author's privacy. He despised Freud's 1910 study *Leonardo da Vinci and a Memory of His Childhood* because of the emphasis on the artist's homosexuality. Szasz would have been similarly outraged by my psychobiographical suggestion that his wife's suicide influenced the nature of his theorizings. And yet one need not be a psychoanalyst to recognize the conscious and unconscious forces that shape scholarship, particularly the impact of suicide on a writer's life. There are, almost always, personal agendas in a scholar's work, as Daniel Rancour-Laferriere points out in *Self-Analysis in Literary Study: Exploring Hidden Agendas* (1994). Szasz's future biographers will no doubt pursue these questions.

Late Writings

Except for early books like *The Ethics of Psychoanalysis*, one could not tell from Szasz's writings that he was a practicing psychoanalyst. He never seemed to wonder about the countertransferential implications of his assault against psychiatry. Szasz's colleagues and friends felt he was charming and friendly in person, but he didn't seem to realize that he treated his adversaries in print as if they were nonpersons, the way he believed he was treated himself. He was guarded about *compassion*, linking it to the word *cold*, the title of one of his books. He dismissed most psychiatric cures as *coercion* and implied that psychiatric liberation was *oppression*, words that appeared in two other book titles. And psychiatry was *The Science of Lies*, still another book title. Of his nearly three dozen books, only two early ones, *Law, Liberty, and Psychiatry* and *Psychiatric Justice* (1965), and one later one, *Faith in Freedom: Libertarian Principles and Psychiatric Practices* (2004), have titles heralding psychiatry's hopeful possibilities. Szasz's early message never changed, though it became shriller and more repetitive. It's likely that he regarded himself as a latter-day Karl Kraus, a tragic prophet who was trying to warn his countrymen to dangers they were not ready to hear. In the Syracuse *Post-Standard* obituary, Szasz was quoted as saying in 1992 that "I am probably the only psychiatrist in the world whose hands are clean. I have never committed anyone. I have never given electric shock. I have never, ever, ever given drugs to a mental patient." Szasz may have viewed himself as blameless—but most saints do not proclaim their own moral purity.

Though he would not appreciate the comparison, Szasz had much in common with Freud. Both men inspired ardent love from their supporters and vitriolic hate from their detractors. Both were prepared, partly as a result of being atheistic Jews, to remain in the opposition, members of what Freud called proudly the "compact minority," defiant to the end. Freud believed that as a result of his creation, psychoanalysis, he was ranked with Copernicus and Darwin, delivering scientific wounds to humankind's narcissism. Szasz similarly believed that his radical ideas had irrevocably changed psychiatry. Freud created a psychological approach to cure his patients' mental illness; Szasz created a counterapproach that denied the existence of mental illness. Both warned against *furor therapeuticus*—overzealous treatment. Both sought to separate psychoanalysis from medicine. Szasz was right that early psychoanalysis had much in common with religions and cults, requiring unquestioning faith from supporters, and excommunicating heretics. But Szasz was a cofounder of the "Citizens Commission for Human Rights," a front organization for the cult-like Church of Scientology which, like Szasz, did not believe in the existence of mental illness. L. Ron Hubbard, Scientology's founder, at first esteemed Freud, regarding him in *Handbook for Preclears* (1989) as the "grand old man of psychosomatic healing" (113), but later he became violently anti-Freudian, creating his own system of mental healing, Dianetics. Szasz was never a Scientologist, but he believed that the enemy of an enemy was a friend. Both Freud and Szasz, steeped in the humanities, turned to literature, philosophy, history, and art for confirmation of their theories. Both wrote to the end of their lives, never losing faith that their written words would eventually prove the validity of their ideas. History will judge Freud and Szasz differently, however; the former's Schadenfreudianism was largely limited to his unconscious ambivalence over being an Eastern European Jew, struggling to be accepted into mainstream Viennese culture; the latter's Schadenfreudianism extended to every aspect of his profession, including denying people the opportunity to save themselves from their worst fears about themselves.

8

Frederick Crews

Demonic Freud

Thomas Szasz's contempt for psychiatry parallels Frederick Crews's contempt for Freud. For decades, Crews has been the country's most infamous Schadenfreudian, authoring book after book claiming that psychoanalysis is nothing more than pseudoscience, a cult based on the false authority of its founder. Yet early in his career, Crews wrote a bold psychoanalytic study of Nathaniel Hawthorne, *The Sins of the Fathers* (1966), a title filled with prescient irony that later came back to haunt the author. Crews's trajectory from Freud idolater to Freud-basher is long and fascinating and discloses the dangers of idealization turning into virulent devaluation—and then demonization.

Idealization has a long and controversial history in psychoanalysis, as G. M. Berger noted in 1993. Is idealization, as Freud believed, an attempt to regain the lost equilibrium of a blissful state of merger, or, as Melanie Klein maintained, a defense against primary aggressive drives? The question remains unresolved, but there is general agreement that idealization is a natural developmental process in which a child invests magical power in another person, usually a parent. The idealized person embodies wisdom, power, and goodness, the ability to protect the child from harm. In time, idealization turns into inevitable disappointment and anger when the omnipotent parent becomes human, all too human. For most people, shattered idealization leads to a more realistic understanding of the formerly idealized parent. In some cases, however, idealization results in permanent devaluation: the once-admired person remains permanently reviled. Occasionally, as Crews's later writings demonstrate, the reviled person becomes the target of Schadenfreude.

Crews's early writings reveal his belief that Freud was a heroic figure who, single-handedly, created an explanatory system that was a master key to unlock all human knowledge. The image of Freud as a Faustian figure may be seen in *The Sins of the Fathers*, in which Crews uses psychoanalysis to cast light on the mysteries of Hawthorne. Only Freud, in Crews's view, could expose the meaning of Hawthorne's ambivalence toward his ancestors, ambivalence that appears in his most powerful stories. In the following years, however, as doubts began undermining his faith in psychoanalysis, Crews rejected other psychoanalytic scholars who in his view lacked Freud's keen imagination, and then, finally, reluctantly, inexorably, he rejected Freud himself. But Crews's rejection of Freud was total: he ultimately found *nothing* positive about the man he had once admired. One senses that Crews has never overcome the trauma of his early "seduction" by psychoanalysis, a narcissistic injury that motivates most of his scholarship.

Freud famously defined psychological health as the ability to love and work. According to this definition, Crews is a paragon of health. He has been married to the same woman, Elizabeth Crews, for nearly sixty years; in every book he warmly acknowledges his indebtedness to her. Born in 1933, Crews taught for thirty-six years at UC Berkeley, retiring in 1994 as chair of the English Department. He is a prolific author: he was eighty-four when *Freud: The Making of an Illusion* appeared in 2017. How would we define Crews's intellectual health? If we use F. Scott Fitzgerald's definition—"The test of a first-rate intelligence is the ability to hold two opposed ideas in the mind at the same time and still retain the ability to function" (69)—the answer is less clear. Crews has *not* been able to hold two opposed views of Freud in his mind; instead, he transforms Freud from an all-good to an all-bad figure, each extreme a distortion of the truth.

As is often the case, what's past is prologue, sometimes, a problematic prologue. To understand the meaning of Crews's vituperative assault on psychoanalysis, we need to grasp the intensity of his idealization of Freud in his early books. Many scholars have tried to explain Crews's long journey from first embracing and then rejecting psychoanalysis, but they have not looked closely at this pattern from the beginning of his career to the present. I don't wish to imply, nor do I believe, that disagreement with psychoanalytic theory betokens clinical "resistance." In lurching from one extreme view of psychoanalysis to the opposite extreme, Crews misses the nuanced insights of the murky middle, where most of the truth lies.

The Tragedy of Manners

Few literary scholars have their doctoral dissertations published, and only a handful have their *undergraduate* prize essays published. For this reason alone,

Crews's first book, *The Tragedy of Manners: Moral Drama in the Later Novels of Henry James*, published by Yale University Press in 1957, when he was only twenty-four, is unusual. There is no hint that Crews will devote himself to the sins of the fathers in a future book. He demonstrates exemplary filial gratitude, dedicating *The Tragedy of Manners* to his parents and thanking his mother for being the "indispensable typist" of the manuscript. He also expresses gratitude to the two professors who inspired and supervised the project.

Crews's approach throughout *The Tragedy of Manners* is cautious and restrained. Following in the tradition of the reigning critical approach in mid-twentieth-century American literary scholarship, New Criticism, Crews offers a close reading of James's novels, affirming irony, paradox, wit, and ambiguity. He displays in *The Tragedy of Manners* thoughtful humanistic criticism, focusing on the "dramatic opposition of certain moral and social values" in three late James novels. Some of Crews's literary pronouncements would later evoke disbelief in light of *The Sins of the Fathers*. "We can say, flatly, that every character in *The Wings of the Dove* is a product of his society, and is therefore to a certain extent innocent of his own thoughts" (62). Only twice does Crews use the word *ambivalence* that becomes a leitmotif in *The Sins of the Fathers*, though neither time does he use it psychoanalytically. Fanny Assingham in *The Golden Bowl* displays "comic ambivalence" between American simplicity and an "equally American desire to be sophisticated" (92). One page later he refers to another character's "ambivalence of motive," both selfish and idealistic. Occasionally Crews uses the expression "psychologically speaking," though what follows is not psychoanalytic, as when a character is caught between the upper and lower classes (20).

E.M. Forster: The Perils of Humanism

Only three brief references to Freud appear in Crews's second book, *E.M. Forster: The Perils of Humanism* (1962). Like his study of Henry James, the Forster book is not psychoanalytic, though Crews refers in passing to "Freud's great discovery" that time does not exist in the unconscious (157). In a footnote, Crews cites an admired passage from Ernest Jones's biography in which Freud asserts that he was neither a Fascist nor a Communist, neither black nor red. "'No,' he replied, one should be 'flesh coloured'" (23, n.3). Crews uses a memorable passage from Nietzsche's *Beyond Good and Evil* for one of the book's two epigraphs: "And if thou gaze too long into an abyss, the abyss will also gaze into thee"—a warning that assumes heightened irony in Crews's later writings when, in gazing at what he perceives to be the horror wrought by Freud, he reduces psychoanalysis to a grim Gothic nightmare. Crews later changed his mind about Nietzsche, calling him in *The Critics Bear It Away* (1992) one of the "thoroughgoing enemies of democracy" (xix).

The Sins of the Fathers

Most literary critics, psychoanalytic and nonpsychoanalytic alike, would be proud to author a book like *The Sins of the Fathers: Hawthorne's Psychological Themes*, published when Crews was thirty-three. Viewing *The Sins of the Fathers* from the vantage point of half a century later, one sees nothing wild or crude about his use of psychoanalytic theory, nothing that would make Crews wish to recant the book a few years later. It's true that one of his assertions betrays binary "either/or thinking" which, in retrospect, an author might have regretted, but Crews's thesis is persuasive: Hawthorne's deep ambivalence toward his Puritan ancestors shows up in his stories, which abound in patricidal themes. Freud popularized the word *ambivalence*, coined in 1910 by his Swiss colleague Eugen Bleuler, but one need not be a psychoanalyst to see how love and hate, fear and desire, attraction and repulsion are inseparably fused throughout Hawthorne's writings. How, then, can we explain Crews's ambivalence toward his own offspring, *The Sins of the Fathers*?

Crews announces his thesis early in *The Sins of the Fathers*. Once we have ceased trying to make the nineteenth-century writer into a source of "oracular wisdom," he asserts, "we perceive that Hawthorne's keynote was neither piety nor impiety, but ambivalence" (7). Crews is drawn to the self-divided, self-tormented Hawthorne who both embraces and retreats from dark truths. Crews rejects any "simplistic psychology that looks only at surfaces—an especially drastic weakness in approaching Hawthorne" (6). Behind Hawthorne's moralism, and "often directly contradicting it, lies a sure insight into everything that is terrible, uncontrollable, and therefore *demoralizing* in human nature" (8). Only those literary critics and biographers who approach Hawthorne from a "religious-didactic" viewpoint (5), the "moral critics," would wish to disagree with Crews's thesis. Crews doesn't identify himself in *The Sins of the Fathers* as the author of an earlier "moral study" of Henry James, though he declares that James was right in saying that Hawthorne "cared for the deeper psychology" (16).

Attracted to boldness, not faintheartedness, Crews hopes that the "timid little revolution" effected by the "symbolic approach" to Hawthorne has "now run its course" (5). He acknowledges that he cannot refrain from "chiding" scholars for their "normalization" of Hawthorne, which springs from a "failure of intuition" (5). No one can accuse Crews of a failure of intuition in *The Sins of the Fathers*. Most of his intuitions, however, are supported by convincing textual evidence. Crews deftly traces Hawthorne's filial ambivalence throughout his writings, including his relentless rejection of his Puritan ancestors for the sin of hypocrisy. "We would not go far wrong in saying that the finding and punishment of sin were *all* that he [Hawthorne] found noteworthy in the Puritan character" (33). Scarcely two decades later, we would not go far wrong in saying that the finding and punishment of pseudoscience were *all* that Crews found noteworthy in the Freudian character.

Crews offers an Oedipal reading of Hawthorne's fiction, focusing on the twin subjects of incest and murder, and ignoring pre-Oedipal readings that would become popular among psychoanalytic literary critics a few years later. Declaring that "ancestry is associated with incestry" (58), Crews identifies the sexual guilt of Hawthorne's characters. We murder to dissect, William Wordsworth observed, but Crews's dissection of Hawthorne's guilt-ridden characters, such as Arthur Dimmesdale and Roger Chillingworth (a "psychoanalyst *manqué*") in *The Scarlet Letter*, the eponymous Young Goodman Brown, and Robin in "My Kinsman, Major Molineux," makes them more human and relatable.

A voracious reader, Crews writes about psychoanalysis as an insider, someone who has studied systematically the entirety of Freud's work. He refers to Freud's essays on the psychology of love, written between 1910 and 1918; Freud's correspondence to Marie Bonaparte; *Fragment of an Analysis of a Case of Hysteria* ("Dora") (1905); *Notes Upon a Case of Obsessional Neurosis* ("The Rat Man") (1909); *From the History of an Infantile Neurosis* ("The Wolf-Man") (1918); "Medusa's Head" (1940); *Leonardo da Vinci and a Memory of His Childhood* (1910); *The Psychopathology of Everyday Life* (1901); "Some Character-Types Met with in Psycho-Analytic Work" (1916); and "Repression" (1915). Crews's references suggest that he is more interested in Freud's early and middle writings than in his later, openly more speculative writings, such as his controversial "death instinct" in *Beyond the Pleasure Principle* (1920).

The first phase of psychoanalysis, an emphasis on drive theory or "id psychology," dominates Crews's thinking, albeit he also uses the language of the second phase, ego psychology. He has no interest in the third phase, the psychology of the self. Throughout *The Sins of the Fathers*, he refers to the dynamics of the unconscious, including instinctual drives and sexual symbolism.

He is comfortable with the ideas of repression, projection, displacement, sado-masochism, castration, sublimation, and Freudian slips. Dimmesdale's blasphemous behavior toward his parishioners reflects a "return of the repressed, and in a form which Freud noted to be typical in severely holy persons" (146). Crews doesn't use projective identification, a term popularized by Melanie Klein, but he understands how it leads to psychological irony. Puritans, he avers, are the repressive side of Hawthorne himself: "the party or faculty of censorship inevitably gets attached to the impulses it is trying to extirpate" (31).

Crews accepts Freud's structural hypothesis of the mind, the interaction of id, superego, and ego, along with the repetition-compulsion principle. He welcomes the Freudian idea of the "omnipotence of thoughts," the belief that in the unconscious there is no distinction between the thought and the deed: one can feel guilt for murderous thoughts without having acted on them. Crews never doubts the existence of the unconscious or the role of fantasy in both health and illness. By contrast, he shows little interest, here or elsewhere, in narcissism theory, reader-response criticism, relational psychoanalysis, or in any of the Freudian "dissidents," such as Carl Jung or Alfred Adler. Nor does Crews express interest in feminist psychoanalytic literary criticism or "French Freud," Lacan or his followers.

Significantly, Crews never doubts the scientific basis of psychoanalysis, a question that will obsess him after writing *The Sins of the Fathers*. He accepts unquestioningly that psychoanalysis is the preeminent study of human subjectivity, a method to understand our waking and sleeping lives. Sometimes he seems so embarrassed by the obvious truth of his psychoanalytic statements that he feels obliged to add "of course," as when he declares, "For a Freudian, of course, there is nothing startling in the idea that fictional plots may gratify fantasies and strike subtle compromises with obsession" (154). That which is "offensive to moral logic," such as Dimmesdale's psychology of self-punishment, "perfectly observes the logic of psychoanalysis" (261).

Apart from Freud, Crew cites approvingly many of the early psychoanalysts, including Ernest Jones, Karl Abraham, Sandor Ferenczi, and Karl Menninger. He refers sympathetically to American literary critics who used psychoanalysis in their writings: Lionel Trilling, Leslie Fiedler, and Simon O. Lesser. Crews's detailed footnotes reveal the depth of his knowledge of psychoanalytic scholarship. In a footnote, he refers to Thomas Mann's essay "Freud and the Future" in which the German novelist elaborates upon Freud's understanding not only of the artist but of humankind in general. A footnote near the end of *The Sins of the Fathers* demonstrates Crews's familiarity with Erik Erikson's 1958 psychobiographical study *Young Man Luther*. "Luther's later career as Erikson expounds it—powerful identification with a father after a titanic rebellion—may cast some light on Hawthorne's ancestral researches in England and the last romances." The difference, in Crews's view, is that whereas Hawthorne's Oedipal antagonism remained unresolved, Luther in contrast "became the tyrant he had so boldly opposed" (248, n.11).

Given Crews's nuanced use of psychoanalysis, it's surprising to come across a statement implying an all-or-nothing approach to Freud's work. "Revolutionary as his influence has been, Freud did not alter human nature: either we are entitled to use Freudianism retroactively or we must say that it is false" (258–9). One cannot imagine *any* contemporary analyst endorsing this statement. Freudian theory has undergone continuous revision, first by Freud himself, then by his disciples, including those who remained loyal to Freud and those who broke away to form their own movements. Crews doesn't challenge some of the more dogmatic statements in psychoanalysis, such as his implicit endorsement of Ernest Jones's assertion that, in Crews's words, "an obsession with death always signifies an unconscious dread of impotence" (253). A few of Crews's conclusions are open to debate, as when he opines that Hawthorne's evocation of Puritan times "gave him *a guilty identity, which was better than none*" (38).

Freud's belief in knowledge as power runs throughout *The Sins of the Fathers*. If Hawthorne had a "moral ideal," Crews suggests, or rather an "ideal of normality," it is "simply the psychoanalytic ideal of being free from feelings of guilt." Mental health, Crews continues, "consists in weakening or pacifying the superego whose symbolic agent may be a real father but is more likely to be a surrogate figure," a "watchful Deity, a line of stern ancestors, or even the collective past itself" (265).

Throughout *The Sins of the Fathers*, Crews remains fascinated with the heroic Freud. Crews ends *The Sins of the Fathers* with one of Freud's most self-revealing and Promethean statements, from *Fragment of an Analysis of a Case of Hysteria*: "No one who, like me, conjures up the most evil of those half-tamed demons that inhabit the human breast, and seeks to wrestle with them, can expect to come through the struggle unscathed." Crews then adds, in the final sentence of *The Sins of the Fathers*, "Let that be our epitaph for a writer whose anguished brooding has given us an urgent, a subtle, and an emotionally profound fiction" (271). Had Crews wished to end his study of Hawthorne with a less herculean vision of Freud, he could have chosen a sentence that appears in the same paragraph as conjuring up half-tamed demons, when Freud writes, "I have always avoided acting a part, and have contented myself with practising the humbler arts of psychology" (*SE*, vol. 7, 109). These two quotations depict a more realistic view of Freud than either quote alone, a more flesh-colored Freud.

Given Crews's emphasis throughout *The Sins of the Fathers* on filial ambivalence and his later categorical rejection of Freud, an obvious father figure, the question inevitably arises: Are there *any* loving fathers in Crews's study of Hawthorne? Few, it turns out. Nevertheless, Crews understands why one needs to search for nurturing parents. He quotes Thomas Wolfe's statement that the "deepest search in life," the "thing that in one way or another was central to all living was man's search to find a father, not merely the father of his flesh, not merely the lost father of his youth, but the image of a strength and wisdom external to his need and superior to his hunger, to which the belief and power of his own life could be united" (61). One of the themes of Hawthorne's *The Marble Faun* is the search for a benevolent father figure, a search that, alas, rarely proves successful for the novelist.

Had Crews been more skeptical of psychoanalysis earlier in his career, he might have been less skeptical later in his career. The author of *The Sins of the Fathers* may not have regarded himself at the time as Freud's disciple, but he comes across as a true believer. Ending his study of Hawthorne with an epitaph from Freud, Crews must have later been struck by the disturbing ironies implicit in the title of his book. Crews uses Freud to help illuminate the sins of Hawthorne's fathers, but Crews's Freud soon becomes another version of the sinful father.

It is "incorrect to say that psychoanalysis remains wholly unverified," Crews wrote in an influential statement on "Literature and Psychology" published by the Modern Language Association in 1967. "Certain of its aspects *have* been tested by experiment, and have withstood as much scrutiny as experiment could cast on them." The unconscious has been corroborated by "jokes and errors, primitive institutions and ritual, myths, and of course literature itself." Crews concludes that for an "unverified science psychoanalysis has had a remarkably profound effect on such apparently unrelated disciplines as anthropology, sociology, and educational theory" ("Literature and Psychology," 76–7).

"Anaesthetic Criticism"

Crews's edited volume *Psychoanalysis and Literary Process* (1970) represents his last book sympathetic to Freudianism. The work has two purposes, he informs us in the preface: "to demonstrate the range and potential usefulness of psychoanalytic criticism and to assist readers who are disposed to practice it themselves" (v). The volume grew out of a graduate seminar in psychoanalytic criticism that Crews led at Berkeley in 1967. The five young scholars—all men—who attended the seminar included Albert D. Hutter (1941–2004), David Leverenz (1942–2017), Sheldon R. Brivic (1943), Richard L. Stein (1943), and Murray M. Schwartz (1942). All went on to have notable careers as college English professors and literary scholars, three of them (Hutter, Brivic, and Schwartz) in the area of psychoanalytic literary criticism. None of them repudiated psychoanalysis, as did Crews. Crews's lead essay, "Anaesthetic Criticism," reveals his view of the uses and misuses of psychoanalytic literary criticism. He singles out the influential Canadian literary critic Northrop Frye as representative of those who reject "extraliterary" approaches. Crews derides Frye for rejecting a central part of psychoanalytic theory. "Indeed, Frye dares to hope that even the idea of the Oedipus complex will someday be exposed as nothing more than a misplaced compliment to the power of the Oedipus story" (4).

Without anticipating that in a few years he will be one of these critics, Crews explains why scholars reject psychological approaches to literature. "This vision of literature as its own progenitor is very far from being a unique indulgence. It is, in fact, a common fantasy among writers, a wish that art could be self-fathered, self-nurturing, self-referential, purified of its actual origins in discontent; and it is no less common among critics" (4–5). Crews invokes an Oedipal interpretation here to explain how male critics like Frye reject their biological fathers to father themselves. Crews is not the first to use psychological theory to explain an antipsychological approach, but he is on shaky ground here, if only because of his unchallenged assumption that Freud's theory of the Oedipus complex is universal. Erik Erikson offers a more refined generalization when he observes in *Young Man Luther* that "there is always an implicit psychology behind the explicit antipsychology" (36), a statement that doesn't depend upon the universal truth of a particular theory. Crews is not yet finished with Frye, calling his major scholarly work, *Anatomy of Criticism*, a book of "professional etiquette," inculcating the "civility" that is "in practice anti-intellectual" (7). In Crews's mind, Frye embodies the worst in literary criticism, a "lawgiver" who ends *Anatomy of Criticism* by "providing an apology for more timid work, indeed, for the most routine academic drudgery" (5). Crews judges Northrop Frye guilty of "anesthetic criticism," defined as anything that reduces art to "some combination of moral content and abstract form and genre conventions." Anesthetic criticism requires "keeping caged the anxieties that the artist set free and then recaptured" (14).

Crews does not limit his attack to nonpsychoanalytic critics. He reserves his most vitriolic criticism for a fellow psychoanalytic literary critic, Norman N. Holland. Crews's comments about Holland are glaringly contradictory. In the preface to *Psychoanalysis and Literary Process*, Crews praises Holland's *The Dynamics of Literary Response* (1968) for its "unmatched clarity and rigor" (vi), but a few pages later admiration turns to condemnation.

> A criticism that cheerfully catalogs the unconscious tricks we play on ourselves and equates literary power with a judicious recipe of wishes and tactics, introjection and intellection, cannot avoid becoming a new version of anaesthesia—a version using Freud's terminology but lacking Freud's sympathy for the way great artists court unconscious engulfment in order to recreate the conditions of a human order. (19)

Crews's denigration of Holland must have been troubling for Murray Schwartz, Holland's colleague for many years at SUNY-Buffalo and coauthor of "The Delphi Seminar," first published in *College English* in 1975 and then expanded into a book in 2008.

For the first time in any of his writings, Crews admits the limitations of psychoanalysis. "Unfortunately, Freud's achievement is entangled in an embarrassingly careless scientific tradition. The slowness of psychoanalysis to purge itself of unsubstantial folklore and outmoded concepts cannot be denied" (17). There's nothing about Freud's character or integrity, however, that arouses Crews's ire: devaluation of Freud must wait until Crews's next book.

Crews ends "Anaesthetic Criticism" with perhaps the most autobiographically disclosing paragraph found anywhere in his books up to this time. Among the many possibilities for literary exchange, he suggests, one relationship is frequent enough to merit special attention:

> An author often places his reader in the role of parent and begs his absolution. By revealing what has been on his mind, mixing oblique confession with a reassertion of commitment to decency and reality and beauty, and by involving the reader in everything he discloses, the author claims the right to be accepted as he is. But since everyone remains filial on the deep level where literature is registered, the reader does not use the communication quite as it was meant; he welcomes the represented self-exculpation, not as applying to someone else, but as a subtle brief in his own defense. (23)

Crews does not discuss in his early writings one of Freud's most significant discoveries, transference and countertransference, yet he appears to be referring to these dynamics here, in an Oedipal framework. He refuses to elaborate on why he believes an author "begs" readers, who are surrogate parents, for "absolution," but the idea is consistent with his belief, expressed earlier in the essay, that Freud "discovered that human beings can neither freely accept nor freely deny the parental demand that sexual and aggressive drives be tamed" (12). In light of Crews's belief that critics like Northrop Frye reject psychological approaches to literature because of the fantasy that art can be self-fathered, can we conclude that Crews's ultimate rejection of Freud is, in reality, a wish to be free from the internalized father? To be self-fathering? In authoring *The Sins of the Fathers*, Crews appeared to be writing about two ambivalent father figures, Hawthorne's father and Freud. And possibly a third, the literary critic's own father.

Out of My System

Crews's next book, *Out of My System* (1975), is a collection of essays previously published in literary journals or, in the case of "Anaesthetic Criticism," in an earlier book. The title of the new volume is apt, for Crews castigates a wide variety of thinkers, including Herbert Marcuse, Wilhelm Reich, and Norman O. Brown for rejecting mainstream psychoanalysis in pursuit of their quixotic utopian agendas. By debunking these Freudian ideologues, Crews is getting them out of his system, casting them off, like a stubborn virus. Yet there is an unintended irony in the title, for in the larger trajectory of his career, Crews is only *beginning* to purge himself of Freudianism, a scourge that insidiously infects his thought, never completely out of his system.

Viewing his publications from the perspective of time, if only a few years, Crews admits in the preface his "[d]iscontent with my successive attempts to marry evidential circumspection and explanatory zeal." The resulting book is an "evolving document, an oblique case history of sorts." For a writer intimately familiar with Freud's case studies, Crews is remarkably vague in offering anything about his own life. Writing about himself in the third person, he notes wryly that "[p]urveyors of iconoclastic critical doctrines appear generally to be animated, not just by rational considerations, but by an intuitive anti-authoritarianism, a penchant for unearthing 'real' significance that the established sages have been too timid or prudish or servile to acknowledge" (x). Crews's next sentence is even more arresting. "Although this Oedipal fervor can easily get out of hand, in itself it seems no worse than many another motive that might be found to have influenced a scholar's work; it may even be a useful safeguard against pedantry" (x–xi), Crews's writing is never pedantic, though his statements are highly polemical and dichotomizing. He blames the Vietnam War for turning him into a "radical polemicist" (ix), yet this impulse may be seen in *The Sins of the Fathers*, written before Southeast Asia erupted into conflagration. He acknowledges, accurately, that all the essays in the present volume, "for better or worse, are internal dialogues between rebellion and caution" and then adds, also accurately, that his "vocation, it seems, is to be forever deciding that I would rather not be a fanatic of one sort or another" (xiv).

In light of these candid observations about his struggle between rebellion and caution, prometheanism and conformity, it's curious that Crews disparages Holland's theory of a "reader's identity theme," discussed in the last chapter, "Reductionism and Its Discontents." The tone of the chapter, Crews confesses in the headnotes, is jarring. "If my way of arguing, as usual, is somewhat negative, the purpose is affirmative: to renew appreciation of the criteria that enable rational, nonsectarian discourse about literature to occur" (165). But the tone of the chapter is more than "somewhat negative," and part of the reason, we suspect, is that the idea of a reader's identity theme remains threatening to Crews. He had denounced Holland's *The Dynamics of Literary Response* in "Anaesthetic Criticism," but he is openly hostile to Holland's *5 Readers Reading* (1975), a discussion of anonymous college students' responses to literature. We don't go to criticism to discover students' or critics' identity themes, Crews opines; rather, we go to criticism "because we hope to learn more about literature than we could have figured out for ourselves" (179). Crews dismisses the "subjectivism" that is both "in the air" and in the idea of a reader's identity theme, a subjectivism that reminds him, unpleasantly, of the ethos of encounter groups.

One might have expected Crews to be intrigued by the idea of a reader's identity theme. Reading is an interaction, Holland suggests, between the text that is "out there" and the reader's subjectivity. Readers shape meaning by their characteristic adaptive and defensive strategies. One cannot escape the subjectivity of interpretation, but the best interpretations are those that have the greatest explanatory power in accounting for the facts of a story. The knowledge that one's own identity theme involves, in part, a clash between rebellion and caution would be helpful to guard against Oedipal defiance, on the one hand, and unquestioning acceptance, on the other. Armed with such knowledge, one would be better able to avoid the extremes of idealization and devaluation. Yet Crews finds nothing of value in the concept of a reader's identity theme, nothing that might help him understand his own reading or misreading of Freud.

Crews rejects not only *5 Readers Reading* but also those scholars who support Holland. "As one of Holland's supporters remarks of the new attitude,

'This in-mixing of self and other makes interpretation a potentially private affair, but it also can lead to a more inclusive sharing of emotional as well as intellectual dynamics than is now available'" (181). A footnote identifies the Holland "supporter" as Murray Schwartz. It may seem trivial that Crews doesn't mention Schwartz by name in the text, relegating him to a mere footnote, but it's remarkable that Schwartz, one of Crews's own Berkeley graduate students and a contributor to *Psychoanalysis and Literary Process*, now becomes dismissed as an opposing scholar's ally. Crews admits in the preface to *Out of My System* that intellectual rebels sometimes end up embodying the authoritarianism they spurn, a pattern that is true in many of his own writings.

Murray Schwartz observes, in his 1979 review of *Out of My System*, that Crews "enacts the ambiguity of its title repeatedly, with Crews both subject and object of his own systematic ambivalence, first absorbed in a system (an encoded, configurational totalization of reality) and then aggressively separating from that other through the power of language" (43). Additionally, Schwartz points out Crews's characteristic style, portraying issues in dichotomous terms, as Freud did: "One is either layman or priest, pious or skeptical, rational or fanatic, contained or released, infantile or adult" (44). Schwartz remarks in his 2018 essay "Psychoanalysis in My Life: An Intellectual Memoir" that "Crews's later furious combat against Freud and psychoanalysis, an obsession that continues to this day and is impervious to dialogue, has always registered for me as a deep disappointment and betrayal. All objections to his caricatures came to be treated as so many curve balls to be swatted out of the park" (135).

Crews's growing doubts about the validity of psychoanalysis reverberate throughout "Reductionism and Its Discontents." He calls into question both the theory and practice of psychoanalysis. The "greater part of Freudian criticism is not just reductive, as it is bound to be, but reductionistic as well, and to a degree unmatched in any other school" (169). The only solution to reductionism, he argues, is "rational skepticism," a term that will become increasingly important in his writings. Crews is not yet ready in *Out of My System* to spurn Freud, however. The creator of psychoanalysis may have licensed a spirit of "dogmatically rebellious interpretation," but he was also modest and scrupulous, the embodiment of everything Crews continues to admire. "In his writings vast presumption—a wish to expose all hypocrisy, unify all knowledge, assume a godlike distance from deluded mankind—is pitted against empirical and mundane loyalties that make such ambitions look unrealizable" (xii). In a later essay in the volume, Crews refers to the "stoic Freud, who urged us to restrain our impulses but denied that we possess a native conscience; who made self-knowledge his ideal but characterized the mind as a self-deceiving organ; and who plunged us into the chthonian unconscious while steadfastly maintaining the humdrum secular norm of healthy functioning" (155). *Out of My System* is Crews's last book in which he worships the Faustian Freud, the bringer of dark knowledge.

Skeptical Engagements

The theme running throughout the essays in Crews's next book, *Skeptical Engagements* (1986), is the "fear of facing the world, including its works of literature, without an intellectual narcotic readily at hand" (x). Psychoanalysis has been reduced to an anodyne, capable of numbing but not ameliorating the pain of existence. Crews doesn't trace the fear that idealization will not be able to withstand the test of reality to its early developmental origins, when children invest omnipotent power in their parents and caretakers in order to feel safe, but one can infer his pain over the loss of a protective authority. Those he has previously admired have betrayed him and are now summarily rejected. Erik Erikson has been from the beginning "less a sober clinical researcher than a virtuoso, mingling sensitive observations with a blend of Freudian dogma, conventional sentiment, and engrossing self-dramatization" (16). Literary critics Crews formerly praised in *The Sins of the Fathers*, such as Leslie Fiedler, are reduced to cruel caricatures. "He is like a bag lady permanently camped on the doorstep of criticism, muttering imprecations at the insiders and keeping warm by waving enthusiastically to oblivious passers-by" (209).

Crews is no less critical of Heinz Kohut, the founder of self psychology. "Kohut's practice, to speak bluntly, is always to throw a bone to Freud while saving the choicest, most humanistic-looking morsels of theory for himself" (33). Some of Crews's explicit criticisms of Kohut are implicit self-criticisms, as when he castigates Kohut for doing everything possible to "minimize the extent of his departure from orthodoxy" (32), a statement that is true of Crews when he acknowledges that people like himself who fall under the "spell" of Freud find it hard to return to the "enigmatic, uncathartic world we actually inhabit" (72). In a footnote, Crews quotes Kohut's statement about Kafka's *Metamorphosis*—"Gregory Samsa experiences himself as nonhuman while his parents in the next room speak about him in the third person singular"—which Crews then ridicules: "Had they spoken about 'Gregory' in some other person or number, they might have been beyond even Dr. Kohut's help" (37–8, n.12).

It's true that Kohut's statement is not earth-shattering, but Crews's derision is startling.

Dispensing with Kohut in a few condescending paragraphs, Crews never discusses one of Kohut's most salient contributions to psychoanalytic theory, the idealizing transference, which he regarded as an early phase of psychic development that is later revived in therapy. "Since all bliss and power now reside in the idealized object," Kohut writes in *The Analysis of the Self* (1977), "the child feels empty and powerless when he is separated from it and he attempts, therefore, to maintain a continuous union with it" (37). Those who have been narcissistically injured may forever attempt to "achieve a union with the idealized object" (55). For Kohut, an essential part of the working-through process is the ego's loss of the narcissistically experienced object. Kohut urged analysts to be as empathic as possible when working with narcissistically injured patients. If analysts cannot be empathic, he warned, "they cannot observe and collect the data which they need; if they cannot step beyond empathy, they cannot set up hypotheses and theories, and thus, ultimately, cannot achieve explanations" (303).

Crews's difficulty is not his inability to devise explanatory or counter-explanatory systems but his failure to reach nuanced conclusions. He quotes Janet Malcolm's dismissive characterization of him as the "neo-Freudophobe Frederick Crews" (43), yet his characterizations of Freud in *Skeptical Engagements* are so shrill as to become unrecognizable. Crews admits that he "spent a decade inching his way from a pro-psychoanalytic stance to an opposite one" (89); he doesn't admit, however, that the opposite stance, based on virulent devaluation, may be as profoundly misleading as the earlier one, based on idealization. Crews appears to be stuck in what might be called a *deidealizing* transference. Paradoxically, Crews's desire not to be a "fanatic of one sort or other," to break his thralldom to Freud, has resulted in the opposite form of fanaticism, the inability to tolerate a more realistic vision of the creator of psychoanalysis. He approaches psychoanalysis with prosecutorial fervor or, to change metaphors, with puritanical zeal, searching for anything that strikes him as pseudoscience.

Hardly anyone is spared from Crews's withering contempt in *Skeptical Engagements*, even authors of books highly critical of Freud. Crews is sympathetic to Frank Sulloway's *Freud, Biologist of the Mind: Beyond the Psychoanalytic Legend* (1979), yet he cannot tolerate Sulloway's assertion that Freud's works represent a "major achievement, which certainly places Freud among the great creative scientific minds of all time" (99). Crews enlists Seymour Fisher and Roger P. Greenberg's 1977 book *The Scientific Credibility of Freud's*

Theories and Therapy for confirmation that Freud's case studies contradict his therapeutic claims, yet he rejects their conclusion, in response to his review of their book, that he is an "extremist" (39). For Crews, there is no truth or value in psychoanalysis, and he scolds those scholars who, no matter how critical of Freud they may be, fail to take his own all-or-nothing, take-it-or-leave-it approach.

Afterword to The Sins of the Fathers

To an anti-Freudian, *The Sins of the Fathers* was an obvious embarrassment, and Crews had to find a way to justify his approach to Hawthorne without endorsing the validity of psychoanalytic criticism. The book was reissued in 1989 with a thirteen-page afterword. "If much of *Sins* still feels right to me today, that is because Hawthorne-as-problem, not Freud-as-solution, usually remains in view" (276). It's odd to invoke Freud as the "solution" to literature instead of as a way to help illuminate literature. Crews doth protest too much in his efforts to excise psychoanalysis from *The Sins of the Fathers*; the act of self-mutilation fails, and we are left, fortunately, with the integrity of the original work intact.

The afterword is revealing not for Crews's struggle to justify the use of Freudian theory for its descriptive rather than explanatory power but for his terse confession about his "love affair with psychoanalysis" (278)—and his characteristic refusal to offer any personal reason for why he fell in and out of love, or why, as a rejecting or rejected lover, he turned against his former betrothed with such fury. No less curious is his reference to the academic community who kept wondering about the bad breakup. "My dramatically changed relation to *Sins* and to psychoanalysis has itself, I realize, become a topic of academic notice, provoking responses ranging from puzzlement to titillation to dismay. Such a recantation would seem to have few precedents outside the sphere of political and religious deconversion" (283). Crews's two major metaphors to describe his changed view of Freud—falling out of love and losing faith—both involve highly emotional states, yet he fails to elaborate. By referring to this titillating gossip, whatever it might have been, Crews draws renewed attention to it, piquing our interest, but then he retreats and gives only an intellectual reason, avoiding any discussion of the underlying personal reasons for why he was first smitten by psychoanalysis and then turned away from it in revulsion.

"Terminating Analysis": The Crews Interview

Adam Begley's article about Crews, "Terminating Analysis," which appeared in a 1994 issue of *Lingua Franca*, heightened the titillating gossip. Begley interviewed Crews two months before his retirement, while he was visiting the University of Toledo to give a lecture on Freud. The article opens with a student's assertion that after reading one of Crews's essays, she was struck by the similarities between Freud and Hitler, a comparison of which Nabokov would have approved. To Begley's mortification, Crews enthusiastically agreed with the remark. Begley characterizes Crews as "quiet, unassuming, the kind of guy you just have to call mild-mannered." The only evidence of Crews's passion, continues Begley, "is his deadly polemical vendetta: He really hates Freud" (24).

The interview has a melancholy, elegiac quality that cannot be explained entirely by Crews's impending retirement from teaching. He appears to be evaluating his life's work and, concluding that he has not been entirely successful in his profession, blaming the person responsible for his failure. "I feel I could have had a more productive career as an intellectual if I had never heard the word 'Freud'" (27). One recalls Marlon Brando's line in *On the Waterfront*: "I coulda been a contender." But Crews was no washed-up boxer turned longshoreman; he was an academic superstar who still had plenty of books in him, all attacking Freud. Begley offers a few details about his biographical subject, but he coyly precedes these revelations with a tantalizing warning: "Psychobiographers take note: Crews had a rocky relationship with his father, who wanted him to become a physicist or a mathematician. His father, says Crews, was 'extremely good at science'" (27–8).

According to Begley, Crews "wolfed down" Freud when he was a graduate student at Princeton in the mid-1950s. His fascination for Freud was reignited when he wrote *The Sins of the Fathers*. "Crews was more than just a convert. He soon began to preach the gospel himself" in his oversubscribed Berkeley graduate seminars on psychoanalytic literary criticism. In the mid-1960s, at the height of his interest in Freud, he considered becoming a lay analyst, but he could not afford to pay for a training analysis: $10,000 a year for five years (28). Crews abandoned the plan to become a psychoanalyst "with real regret"—and then slowly turned against his intellectual hero in the same way that he was drawn toward him: through reading.

Crews freely admits in the interview that he exhibits "the God That Failed syndrome" (29), though he doesn't acknowledge how this syndrome has affected his ability to see Freud accurately. Nor does he acknowledge, as Murray Schwartz points out in the article, that by attacking psychoanalysis, he seeks to discredit Freud, the looming father surrogate in his life. Given the fact that Crews has become an influential authority in literary criticism, intolerant of those who disagree with him, Begley asks an obvious question: Is Crews himself "now trapped in the role of the Freudian father, trying to kill off his sons?" (29). Begley doesn't answer the question, allowing others to engage in psychobiographical speculations. Without remarking on the biographical ironies, Begley quotes one of Crews's most provoking statements in *Skeptical Engagements*: "Though Freud loved to sermonize about courageously opposing the human penchant for self-deception, it is no exaggeration to say that his psychoanalytic career was both launched and maintained by systematic mendacity" (Begley 29; *Skeptical Engagements* 101). Part of the statement characterizes Crews: his literary career has been maintained by systematically opposing the mendacious Freud. There are other ironies in Begley's interview, including John Forrester's insight that Crews maintains a "highly idealized vision of what science does." Crews's Berkeley colleague Martin Jay agrees. "Virtually all science is methodologically inconsistent with its highest standards." To which Begley adds, "The gist of this agreement is that though Freud's methods fall short of the mark, so do almost everybody's; and valid results often follow from flawed procedures" (30).

The Memory Wars

Crews's next book, aptly named *The Memory Wars: Freud's Legacy in Dispute* (1995), contains two lengthy essays that were first published in the *New York Review of Books*: "The Unknown Freud" and "The Revenge of the Repressed." Crews is listed as the editor, but the title page contains the names of eighteen correspondents who agreed to have their critical letters to the *New York Review of Books* reprinted. Crews notes genially in his acknowledgments that the contributors knew that he would have the first word (in introducing them) and the last word (in responding to their critiques). "That is sportsmanship!" Other correspondents are represented only in summary, as Crews admits. "Understandably, they did not wish to contribute actively to a book whose main emphasis struck them as mistaken" (ix).

Crews thrives on controversy, and he has no problem responding to his correspondents' complaints that become grist for his mill. A provocateur, like Peter Swales, he is tone deaf to the dismay and outrage of some of the contributors. "I believe my findings have been taken out of context and misused by Crews," fumed J. Schimek, professor of clinical psychology at New York University and a training analyst. "To conclude from my arguments that Freud made up all the sexual material he got from his patients, and that his theories were dominated by 'dishonesty and cowardice,' is arbitrary, farfetched, and remote from my intent. I want hereby to dissociate myself completely from such indiscriminate and ill formed Freud bashing" (77). Herbert S. Peyser, a New York City psychiatrist, complained that "The Unknown Freud" has an "angry and ad hominem" tone that reminded him of his "younger days" when he encountered the "bitter criticisms of Marxism by former adherents, once devoted, now disillusioned and feeling betrayed. I cannot say that this is the origin of Professor Crews's point of view but the situation as it appears in a number of cases is similar" (86). The New York City analyst Mortimer Ostow could not resist punning on Crews's name. "It should not be surprising if psychoanalysts felt impelled to respond to Crews's missile attack on their profession and its founder" (97). Charlotte Krause Prozan, a San Francisco psychoanalyst and author of two books on feminist psychoanalytic psychotherapy, objected to the "snide, contemptuous tone" of "The Revenge of the Repressed."

> Those of us who actually practice the professions of psychoanalysis and psychotherapy are also deeply concerned about the issues of truth and justice in this field, but polarizing the topic by vindictive, bitter, and emotional attacks against those who disagree with you serves to shed no light on these vital questions, but only to polarize and alienate and thereby divert our search for wisdom. (235)

Crews could not have chosen a more psychologically revealing title than "The Revenge of the Repressed," for it conveys his lifelong need, since his late thirties, to deidealize and demonize the man whose ideas he once worshiped. One recalls Kohut's observations about narcissistic rage: "the need for revenge, for righting a wrong, for undoing a hurt by whatever means, and a deeply anchored, unrelenting compulsion in the pursuit of these aims, which gives no rest to those who have suffered a narcissistic injury" ("Thoughts on Narcissism and Narcissistic Rage," vol. 2, 637–8). The idea of "writing/righting wrong," first proposed by the literary critic Sandra M. Gilbert in her spousal loss memoir *Wrongful Death* (1995), can be seen throughout many authors' scholarship, and it can be healthy or not, depending on a number of factors, including whether one treats opponents respectfully or disrespectfully—or, worse, demonically.

In light of *The Sins of the Fathers*, in which Crews analyzes Hawthorne's ambivalent relationship to his Salem ancestors, it's ironic that he judges Freud guilty of fathering the satanic ritual abuse phenomenon, a movement that bedeviled psychotherapy for years. By the mid-1980s, Lawrence Wright reported in *Remembering Satan* (1994), the number of alleged satanic murders reached the tens of thousands, perhaps as high as fifty or sixty thousand people a year in the United States, a figure that far surpassed the total number of homicides a year (86). Crews tapped into this phenomenon. Not content merely to deidealize Freud, Crews now demonized him. Crews's conclusion that psychoanalysis is demonology is based partly on Freud's use of a line from Virgil's *Aeneid* for the epigraph to *The Interpretation of Dreams*: "If I cannot move heaven, I will raise hell." That Freud was using the sentence metaphorically, not literally, is irrelevant to Crews, who accuses Freud of beginning a witch hunt that led to the satanic abuse movement (219).

Crews categorically rejects the existence of transference, which he suggests in a footnote is merely a self-serving concept fabricated by Freud to retain power over patients. The "'analysis of the transference' tends to underrate the immediate source of the patient's irritability: the contemporary behavior of the therapist, an unequal partner in dialogue who deflects every legitimate complaint about his own needling manner onto the patient's enduring fixations" (14–15, n.9). Crews never concedes the possibility that understanding transference and countertransference can yield important insights. Nor does he respond to the statement made by the Columbia psychoanalyst David D. Olds that "*[w]hen used properly*, countertransference has become a valuable lens rather than a destructive nuisance" (93).

The Memory Wars contains useful critique of the excesses of the recovered memory movement, as Robert Michels, professor of Psychiatry at Cornell University Medical College, pointed out in his review, adapted from a debate with Crews sponsored by the *New York Review of Books* in 1995, and later published in the *Journal of the American Psychoanalytic Association*. Michels tries to find common ground with Crews, admitting to sharing with Crews (and with Peter Swales, to whom Crews dedicated *The Memory Wars*) a fascination with uncovering information that undermines our idealization of heroes. Michels then effectively rebuts Crews's criticisms. "The question in 1995 should not be whether Freud's observations supported his initial ideas, but rather whether a century of observations have confirmed or refuted them" (575). Responding to Crews's charge that clinical psychoanalytic research is contaminated by suggestion, Michels agrees but then adds, "suggestion is universal in all psychotherapeutic treatment, and, indeed, in almost all medical treatment" (575). Agreeing with Crews that Freud had flaws both as a person and as a researcher, Michels remarks that the value of psychoanalysis is no more dependent on Freud's personality "than the value of theories in physics is affected by revelations regarding Einstein's relationship with his wife, or the value of modern genetics [is] diminished by the discovery that Mendel fudged his data" (577). Michels criticizes Crews for reaching absolute judgments about clinical cases of recovered memories that went counter to jury decisions. "Neither Crews nor I were there, and I do not think we can decide without more evidence" (578). Michels concludes his review with praise for Crews. "There is no doubt that Crews is superb with words and with ideas. His book is fun to read, and those who know psychoanalysis well will enjoy it—they may be infuriated, but they will enjoy being infuriated." Michels then adds a noteworthy caveat. "However, it is not a book about psychoanalysis, although it has an interesting critique about some early psychoanalytic notions. It is not an unbiased book about Freud, although it is an entertaining antidote to other oppositely biased books about Freud" (579). It's true that Crews is a brilliant writer. His annihilating wit and polemical exaggeration are best seen in his two satires of academic life: *The Pooh Perplex* (1965) and *Postmodern Pooh* (2001). But it's doubtful whether the contributors to *The Memory Wars* enjoyed being eviscerated. Crews did not. In *Follies of the Wise* he refers to Michels's criticisms as "meretricious" (77).

Peter L. Rudnytsky's "Wrecking Crews," published in *American Imago* in 1999, highlights the greatest defect of *The Memory* Wars: "the proclivity to reduce complex issues to an either/or dichotomy in which one side is right and the other wrong." This outlook, Rudnytsky adds, "which precludes the possibility of genuine dialogue," is compounded by Crews's refusal "to interrogate himself, while impugning the character and motives of his opponents" (286).

Unauthorized Freud: Doubters Confront a Legend

These criticisms are even more strikingly true in Crews's next book. "There is no team of 'Freud bashers' at work here," he claims in the opening paragraph of the preface to his 1998 edited volume *Unauthorized Freud*. Crews promises to "restore the mythified 'discoverer of the unconscious' to human size" (ix), but, in fact, he reduces Freud to Lilliputian stature. Crews grants that his book "incurs the risks of overkill" (xi), which is, no doubt, his intention. "Multiple paths of inquiry must be broached, but they all lead inexorably to the wizard's empty palace" (xi). The volume's lurid title reveals his editorial decision to portray psychoanalysis in the worst possible light despite the fact that "some of the contributing scholars hold milder views" (ix).

Crews's only minor concession is that some features of classical psychoanalysis "do have a ring of initial truth about them." One cannot easily dismiss, he admits, the "proposal that 'defense mechanisms' such as projection, identification, and denial affect mental productions" (xxv). Even one of Crews's mentors, Adolf Grünbaum, author of *The Foundation of Psychoanalysis: A Philosophical Critique* (1984), affirms the "intuitive attractiveness" of these Freudian concepts, which make possible hermeneutic interpretation. Crews's complaint is that psychoanalysts can use these terms cynically to justify any interpretation. Consequently, there is no "empirical basis" for deciding if and when a reader or patient is engaging in projection, identification, or denial. Crews rejects the theory of defense mechanisms along with Freud's concept of "overdetermination," whereby one action or expression can carry a variety of meanings. "These were the tools not of a scientist but of an intellectual megalomaniac" (xxvii).

Paradoxically, Crews's main criticism of ego psychology, defense mechanisms, and, in his later writings, transference and countertransference is not that they are inherently reductionistic but that they add *too much complexity* to the interpretive process. But how can he have thought otherwise? Empiricism takes us only so far in deciphering a literary text or a human interaction. To have thought otherwise—that there is a master key unlocking human knowledge—is astonishing.

Follies of the Wise

Crews continues his assault on psychoanalysis in *Follies of the Wise* (2006), the title of which does not refer to Freud, who was wise only for a few of Crews's misguided years. He notes in passing that he was "seduced" by Freud "around the age of thirty-two" but "by thirty-seven I was over it" (84), a considerably shorter period of time than he reported in *Skeptical Engagements*, in which he admits that he was a Freudian "for a decade or so" (35). If we include the reference in his Forster book to Freud's "great discovery," Crews's love affair with psychoanalysis is closer to a decade-and-a-half.

Having confidently predicted in his earlier books the demise of psychoanalysis, Crews is forced to concede the "continuing resilience of the Freud legend, which tends to snap back into shape at every point that is not under immediate pressure" (31). Unrelenting in his own pressure, Crews's strategy is to praise books that find fault with Freud, such as *Father Knows Best: The Use and Abuse of Power in Freud's Case of Dora*, but then to find fault with the authors, Robin Tolmach Lakoff and James C. Coyne, for being "insufficiently skeptical toward Freud himself." Crews objects to their statement that there is "no clear reason to dispute any of Freud's interpretations of the material" (30). He takes the same approach to John Kerr's *A Most Dangerous Method: The Story of Jung, Freud, and Sabina Spielrein* (1993). He lauds the book but then points out that like Frank Sulloway, Kerr goes astray when he refers to Freud as a "systematic thinker of the highest rank" (39–40). Crews commends Sander L. Gilman for going farther than "any accused Freud basher toward reducing psychoanalysis to a manifestation of one madcap improviser's eccentricity" but then notes with dismay that "Gilman's startling indictment never causes him to reconsider his own Freudianism" (184).

After renewing his attack on Norman Holland, Crews then finds fault with those who criticized him at a symposium titled "Whose Freud" held at Yale in April 1998. Disagree with Crews and you can be sure to be pilloried in his next publication. In reporting an interaction with his Berkeley colleague Judith Butler, who had told him that he "might profit from cultivating greater philosophical sophistication on the one hand and less unsavory soulmates on the other," Crews accuses her of "indulging in a form of McCarthyism that has become routine in university life." He then adds, ominously, "If, instead of being comfortably pensioned, I were an untenured colleague of Professor Butler's, I might want to sing a more prudent tune; my very livelihood might hang in the balance" (79, 81). Crews doesn't imagine the opposite possibility, that if he were evaluating Butler's scholarship for a tenure case, he would judge her work insufficiently skeptical. Nor does he mention in *Follies of the Wise* that he had skewered Butler in *Postmodern Pooh*, mocking and decontextualizing her statement from *Gender Trouble* that there are "as many sexes as there are individuals" (59). Butler is not the only panelist at the "Whose Freud?" conference whom Crews associates with evil. He accuses the Berkeley philosophy professor Richard Wollheim of using the same kind of Freudian logic that "has resulted, over time, in everything from witch burnings through the Edsel to the Gulf of Tonkin Resolution" (86). Crews then compares the entire two-day Yale conference to a "'cruise to nowhere' on the Titanic" (87).

The volume *Whose Freud?: The Place of Psychoanalysis in Contemporary Culture*, coedited by Peter Brooks and Alex Woloch, contains discussions of the 1998 Yale conference, including Crews's original talk, "Unconscious Deeps and Empirical Shallows," as well as his critique of the entire conference.

Brooks notes ruefully that Crews's heated opposition to the other discussants would have evoked, had there been enough time, an endless number of equally heated counterresponses. "Such a back-and-forth discussion," which would resemble the angry letters published in the *New York Review of Books*, "would suit the content of Crews's position: the repeated dead ends of mutual recriminations that characterize this kind of exchange rhetorically demonstrate the incommensurability of psychoanalysis with discourse outside the discipline" (18).

Freud becomes in *Follies of the Wise* the embodiment of all evil, a hoaxster, con artist, and "male chauvinist par excellence" (122). Crews sardonically invests psychoanalysis with royal status, referring to it as the "queen of modern pseudosciences" (12) and the emperor's new clothes (31). No one else has "matched Freud's skills in self-glorification" (354). "Take my Freud—please! But do you really want him—the fanatical, self-inflated, ruthless, myopic, yet intricately devious Freud who has been unearthed by the independent scholarship of the past generation?" (73). Crews has spent half his life, more than forty years, trying to get his arch-nemesis out of his system, and in doing so, he has defined his identity as a Schadenfreudian. Indeed, Crews views Freud as a secular antichrist: the anti-Freud of all that is holy, empirical science. To extirpate the evil wrought by Freud and his followers, the sins of the fathers, requires a scholar who is also an exorcist. Crews continues to perform the role with unsurpassed puritanical fervor.

Freud: The Making of an Illusion

Crews chose a quote by Nietzsche for one of the two epigraphs of his 2017 Freud biography: "However far human beings may reach with their knowledge, however objective they may seem to themselves to be: in the end they carry away nothing but their own biography." The quote is apt: Freud's personal life indelibly shaped his life's work, the creation of psychoanalysis. But the inseparability of Freud's life and work was, in Crews's view, catastrophic, insofar as the thesis of his biography lies in two questions he raises in the preface: "How and why did a studious, ambitious, and philosophically reflective young man, trained in rigorous inductivism by distinguished researchers and eager to win their favor, lose perspective on his wild hunches, efface the record of his mistakes, and establish an international cult of personality?" (3). Tellingly, Crews does not turn his gaze inward to ponder how his *own* biography shaped his understanding or misunderstanding of Freud. Crews's other epigraph comes from George Constanza's jest in *Seinfeld*: "It's not a lie if *you* believe it." Crews never doubts that the entirety of Freud's work was based on a cruel deception.

In *Freud: The Making of an Illusion*, Crews reduces his biographical subject's complex motivation to a single cause: lust for fame. Crews ignores Freud's other motives, including intellectual curiosity, the desire for psychological knowledge, and the wish to alleviate suffering. Throughout the biography, Crews leaps to the worst possible conclusions to indict Freud for envious malice. An example is Freud's misguided use of cocaine to help his mentor, friend, and fellow physician Ernst Fleischl von Marxow break his addiction to morphine. Crews relies on the pioneering research of Albrecht Hirschmüller, who painstakingly reconstructed the circumstances of Freud's relationship to the pharmaceutical company Parke, Davis, which sold a form of cocaine inferior to that of its rival, Merck. Crews criticizes Freud for endorsing the quality of the cocaine sold by Parke, Davis, censures Freud for authoring a "scatterbrained" essay published under a pseudonym, and indicts Freud for stooping to "trickery and self-promotion" (125). Elsewhere, Crews accuses Freud of committing a "masquerade" in advocating cocaine (111) and perpetrating a "grave breach of medical ethics" (113). These are serious allegations, but if one looks at Hirschmüller's article from which Crews draws his evidence, one sees a strikingly different judgment of Freud's cocaine experience:

> Indeed, the cocaine papers demonstrate that Freud was a scientist with curiosity and intuition, who took his own observations so seriously that he could not rest until he had found explanations for them. They show that Freud was a man who was used to relying more upon his own experience than upon the scientific literature he read—and who was often justified in doing so. They show Freud as a young doctor, eager to advance quickly by his scientific work, and consequently in danger of jumping too quickly to conclusions, rather than grounding his theories through more reserved and patient scientific work. Freud's works on cocaine also show that he used the drug without prejudice, and took the risk of ignoring critical and cautious warnings. (Hirschmüller 77)

Crews concludes his discussion of this fraught chapter in Freud's life by observing that above the iconic couch in Freud's cluttered office was a photograph of Fleischl. "It is unimaginable," writes Crews, "that the combative, perennially self-justifying Freud would have kept that image staring over him for decades if its principal meaning to him were accusatory. With the healing of time, he must have settled into thinking of Fleischl with unalloyed affection and gratitude"

(139). Crews thus assumes that he is a mind reader and that the two-dimensional Freud he created was incapable of feeling grief, guilt, and regret along with more positive emotions.

Crews never misses an opportunity to pathologize Freud's feelings. He quotes a letter Freud wrote to Martha in which he confesses being awed in the presence of Charcot, to which Crews responds: "He seemed to feel, bizarrely, that what he craved was already the property of another" (194). A more empathic biographer would be less judgmental. Crews then quotes another letter to Martha in which Freud complains about ill health. Crews's response? "Appalled by such mewling, the levelheaded Martha reminded her betrothed that he was privileged to have been given this free time for self-development in a foreign capital" (194–5). Unless we read carefully, we may be seduced into believing that this was Martha's condemnation rather than Crews's. Nor is it likely that Martha would agree with Crews's characterization of her "milquetoast husband" (196). In another letter to Martha, Freud conveys astonishment that he can communicate with a Frenchman, an admission Crews regards as "unseemly gloating" (203). In another letter to Martha, Freud remarks that he is "no genius" and "not even very gifted," a statement that Crews labels as a "maudlin confession" (208). Another biographer would have pointed out the striking irony of Freud's words. Employing "heads I win, tails you lose" logic, Crews accepts at face value Freud's many self-reproaches but rejects as meretricious Freud's self-assurances.

Crews's contempt for Freud parallels his contempt for many of Freud's patients, including Anna von Lieben ("Frau Cäcilie M."). "Lieben was a spoiled, willful, histrionic tyrant whose self-absorption and self-pity were underwritten by her wealth," Crews disdainfully asserts. "She was more in need of something constructive to do than she was of therapy, which only provided a stage for her long-running theatrics" (288). Everything about Lieben strikes Crews as repellent, including the idea that she *deserved* therapeutic relief. Let her suffer, Crews appears to be saying, the wealthy bring on their own problems, and they don't merit help. The most Crews is willing to say about the legitimacy of her illness was that "Anna's model of neurosogenesis through disgust and self-reproach had a measure of verisimilitude in her rarefied milieu" (283), a sentence devoid of compassion. Following the notoriously unreliable footsteps of Peter Swales, Crews condemns Freud for his interest in Lieben: "the benefit to his wallet," Crews sneers, "was secondary to decisive intellectual stimulation" (281), implying that it was prurience, or perhaps boredom, that motivated Freud. Lieben's stated reason for terminating therapy, Freud wrote to Minna Bernays, was because of her suspicion that he didn't treat her "out of friendship, but only for money" (291). Crews judges the monetary motive reprehensible, but others will find it understandable that the often impecunious Freud struggled to make a living. To describe Lieben's morphine addiction, Crews uses as a subchapter title "The Cabinet of Dr. Freud," an allusion to the 1920 German silent film horror "The Cabinet of Dr. Caligari," about a crazed physician who is a murderer.

The master of invidious innuendo, Crews casts Freud as obsessed with sex, but when Freud ethically refuses to respond to a patient's sexual advances, Crews gives him no credit. He tells us that Freud was "encouraging unfulfilled women to put him into the role of a surrogate lover" (274), a comment that recalls a similar statement by Peter Swales, whom Crews quotes repeatedly, always in full agreement. To emphasize the sexualizing of their relationship, Crews remarks that Freud and Lieben were "caught up in an iatrogenic tango whose dips and bends grew more extreme" (288). Crews observes that Fanny Moser ("Emmy von N."), according to earlier scholars, "nearly always seems to have had lovers and erotic relationships, sometimes with doctors whom she consulted at the spas, or who lived in her house as her personal doctors" (296). Instead of praising Freud for not succumbing to a sexual boundary violation, Crews merely refers to him as the "straight-backed Dr. Freud" (296)—an odd way of describing a physician's integrity.

Crews can't help himself in sullying Freud. "Although Freud massaged 'her whole body' twice a day, with emphasis on the abdominal area where she reported gastric pains and 'ovarian neuralgia,' and though he also hypnotized her twice daily, probing for intimate revelations, only superficial ones were granted" (296–7). Unlike some of Freud's contemporaries, such as Hippolyte Bernheim, who was guilty of sexually touching his patients, Freud was not; instead, Crews uses a damning metaphor to describe Freud's clinical strategy. "Dropping any pretense of investigative neutrality, he began implementing his pressure technique in a prosecutorial manner. With Freud's hand on her brow, each patient was given to understand that if she were serious about getting well, it would not be a permissible option to withhold details of her sexual history" (306). Similarly, in treating Ilona Weiss ("Elisabeth von R."), Freud did not touch the "large hysterogenic zone on her right thigh," but, opines Crews, "sex was on his mind, and we can picture him bearing down on Ilona for the particulars of that daily scene" (309).

Throughout the discussion of Bertha Pappenheim, the patient called "Anna O." in *Studies on Hysteria*, Crews fluctuates between two hypotheses, dissimulation and organic disease, to explain her condition. Though he insists that the story is complex and requires patience, he does everything possible to devalue the patient along with Breuer and Freud. As an example, Crews remarks that Pappenheim convinced Breuer that "simply by inquiring into the reason for a 'hysterical' symptom, he might free her from its grip." Crews then asks, parenthetically, "But how genuine was a disability that could be suspended for the purpose of answering a question?" (342). Another example: "At that time she was just inventing fairy tales and reciting them to a captive audience of one" (346). And a third example:

> Bertha had made herself sick when being neglected, insulted, and undervalued. Now, however, she found that a tender-minded physician could be induced to play her game instead of her own. Her symptoms, whatever their source, became the stakes of that game, to be paid out in improved health only when Breuer allowed himself to be governed by her. But that was a recipe not for cure but for dragging out the coyness ad infinitum. (347)

As the chapter progresses, so does Crews's scorn, as when he says, "During some thousand hours with Pappenheim, Breuer had humored her whims and tried not to be bored by her made-up tales, petty complaints, and banal day-by-day reminiscences" (353). One cannot find a biographer more insensitive to mental health issues than Crews.

"It would be hard to overstate Freud's hubris" (402), Crews warns, albeit no one can accuse him of failing to try. Although he accuses Freud of being an "all-or-nothing proponent of revealed truths" (498), this is precisely Crews's own strategy. He never concedes that Freud created anything of genuine medical, psychological, or literary value. The reason Freud writes about his patients' physical complaints, Crews tells us, is to endear himself to "science-envying littérateurs" (283), which is to say, many of Crews's own readers. He casts a negative spin on some of Freud's most celebrated statements, as when he admits in *Studies on Hysteria* that "it still strikes me myself as strange that the case histories I write should read like short stories and that, as one might say, they lack the serious stamp of science" (*SE*, vol. 2, 160). Crews's response? "This passage exemplifies a Freudian specialty that we might call *the self-effacing boast*, or a demure gesture that casts the author in a better light than ever" (382).

To be fair to Crews, he is often correct about the rigidity of psychoanalytic thinking. My late coauthor Paul Mosher observed in our Crews-discussion group that he had to suppress his doubts about libido theory when he was in training to become an analyst. The idea was "so sacrosanct that my raising the issue could have resulted in my ejection from the institute had I not backed down and shut up" (Berman, "Paul Mosher: Coauthor and Friend" 97).

The title of the final chapter in Crews's biography, "Imposing His Will," contains an unexpected irony: Crews seeks to impose his own will of Freud on us. In the first paragraph, he calls Freud, without much sarcasm, a "closet Antichrist" (641), and he then proceeds, as he does throughout the biography, to demonize Freud. As a "critic of mores," Crews remarks, Freud was spurred to offer liberal counsel "not by concern for the miseducation and torment of millions but by frustration within his marriage" (642). As usual, Crews reduces the complexity of human motivation to a single cause. And again, as usual, Crews attributes to Freud only the most sinister motivation. Reading Crews's biography is, finally, a disturbing experience, not only because it portrays Freud as monomaniacally obsessed with fame, unscrupulous enough to do anything to achieve it, but also because it demonstrates how a once-superb literary scholar, the author of a groundbreaking study of Nathaniel Hawthorne, has gone off the tracks. *Freud: The Making of an Illusion* is a cautionary tale of what happens when one chooses to see only the dark side of a person's life. Freud stated ruefully in "On the History of the Psycho-Analytic Movement" that psychoanalysis "brings out the worst in everyone" (*SE*, vol. 14, 39), an insight that Crews must have feared was true of his own life.

Conclusion

Neither Freud Idolaters nor Schadenfreudians: Contemporary Psychoanalysts

What do Freud idolaters and Schadenfreudians have in common? To begin with, most are true believers and true disbelievers. With the conspicuous exception of Frederick Crews and, to a lesser extent, D. H. Lawrence and Thomas Szasz, their attitudes toward Freud did not change much over time. The Freud idolaters were either disciples or devotees, committing much if not most of their writings to spreading the good word about their master, even if they had reservations about psychoanalysis, as did Trilling and Bloom. The Schadenfreudians were more likely to engage in binary thinking, inclined to practice the hermeneutics of suspicion, obsessed with unmasking the great unmasker. Reveling in the belief that Freud was a fraud, the Schadenfreudians saw nothing of value in either the creator or the creation. Freud's confession that he always needed an intimate friend and a hated enemy is strikingly true of the Schadenfreudians, who saw him as the embodiment of evil. "He who fights with monsters should be careful lest he thereby become a monster," Nietzsche cautioned. "And if thou gaze long into an abyss, the abyss will gaze into thee."

Psychoanalysis was for the Trillings a family affair. Lionel, Diana, and James Trilling had strikingly different experiences in psychoanalysis, which lasted many years for each of them. Lionel Trilling admired Freud partly because of the analyst's acceptance of the inevitability of suffering. The "tragic Freud" compelled the literary critic's attention. Psychoanalysis enabled Diana Trilling to become a prominent published writer, but her experience with several psychoanalysts was unsatisfactory; her increasing interest in feminism coincided with her decreasing interest in psychoanalysis. James Trilling rejected Freud because of the failure of psychoanalysis to mitigate his own suffering. It may be impossible to separate the son's rejection of Freud from his rejection of his father. It is not a surprise that one's experiences in psychoanalysis shape one's attitude toward Freud; but it is a surprise to learn about the startlingly different attitudes toward Freud in the same family. One can only imagine for the Trillings having two Freudians and one Schadenfreudian in the same family. Paraphrasing the opening of *Anna Karenina*, one can say that the Trillings' unhappy family was unhappy in its own way toward Freud.

Harold Bloom celebrated the agonistic Freud, which is how Bloom came across himself for most of his career. Bloom was simultaneously a Freudian and a Schadenfreudian, lionizing the creator but gleefully maligning the creation. Radically revising Freudian theory, Bloom extolled repression, not sublimation, as the source of great poetry. Bloom did not believe in the talking cure, except when it involved classroom teaching, but he never lost faith in the reading and writing cure, at which he excelled. The work of mourning becomes increasingly evident in Bloom's late elegiac writings, where the ghosts of the dead reappear. Contrary to Freud's injunction in "Mourning and Melancholia" that the griever must withdraw libidinal attachment from the lost love object lest mourning become pathological, Bloom holds the dead in loving memory, suggesting a theory of bereavement based on continuing bonds with the deceased.

Trilling and Bloom revered Freud the writer but not Freud the psychoanalyst. No such distinction or compartmentalization existed for Kurt Eissler, who tirelessly defended the man and his work. Perceiving Schadenfreudians everywhere, Eissler became one too, unleashing a torrent of vituperative attacks against those who did not think kindly about the master. The man who denounced revisions to Freudian theory as the poison of eclecticism, and who did everything he could to preserve the purity of psychoanalysis, remained a loyalist to the end, a guardian of the faith.

No one was more of a Freudenfreudian than Peter Gay, who protected the creator of psychoanalysis against his own self-criticisms. Provoked by the wild accusations of Peter Swales, who never missed an opportunity to demonize Freud, Gay was measured in his defense of the creator of psychoanalysis. Gay was not, like Eissler, a defender of all things Freudian, but his faith in both the man and his work never wavered. If I am correct that his case study of an engineering professor was a disguised account of himself, Gay used his experience in psychoanalysis to help him solve a personal dilemma.

Briefly a Freudian and then a Schadenfreudian, D. H. Lawrence did not understand either Freud or psychoanalysis, but his creative misunderstanding engendered two fascinating books, *Psychoanalysis and the Unconscious* and *Fantasia of the Unconscious*. Since its publication, *Sons and Lovers* has provoked intense psychoanalytic scrutiny, critics showing its indebtedness to Freud, but the influence is reciprocal: the novel helped shape evolving psychoanalytic theory, especially in pre-Oedipal developments: the child's early relationship with the mother. Lawrence's depiction of the smother-mother in *Sons and Lovers* and *Women in Love* anticipated John Bowlby's attachment theory and Margaret Mahler's theory of separation-individuation.

Never a Freudian, Vladimir Nabokov, the world's most infamous Schadenfreudian novelist, rendered the Viennese witch doctor into his hated doppelganger. No one took more gleeful pleasure than Nabokov in skewering psychoanalysis. It's unlikely that anything new will be discovered about Nabokov's biography that explains his lifelong detestation of psychoanalysis, yet, as with Lawrence, Nabokov could not have penned his greatest novel, *Lolita*, without Freud. Nabokov mocked Freud's writings on the Oedipus complex, but *Lolita* illuminates Freud's insights on rescue fantasies and the family romance.

Freud became, for Thomas Szasz, a base rhetorician, but Szasz's own rhetoric became increasingly shrill, polarizing, and polemical. Like Nabokov, he demonized the mental health profession, regarding it as the harbinger of the therapeutic state. Mental illness did not exist in Szasz's world; rather, he reduced those who could not function, psychologically, to malingers, impersonating socially acceptable roles of illness. Szasz never wrote about his former wife or her suicide in "An Autobiographical Sketch," or in any of his other voluminous writings, but the event heightened his opposition to suicide prevention, enabling him to deny the dark emotions associated with suicide, especially anger and guilt. Szasz's pleasure in turning the tables on his critics, shaming the shamers, as he did with Kay Redfield Jamison, contains an element of Schadenfreude.

For Frederick Crews, falling out of love with Freud is a more intriguing story than falling in love with him. The trajectory of Crews's career demonstrates his transformation of Freud from an all-good figure in the literary critic's early writings to an all-bad figure in his later writings. Unable to get Freud out of his system, Crews's writings on Freud betray a deidealizing transference relationship in which all references to authority are reduced to the sins of the fathers. Despite his best efforts to slay the ghost of Freud, he remains disillusioned that the exorcism has failed, but one can imagine him drawing consolation from St. Thomas Aquinas's observation in *Summa Theologiae*: "The blessed in the Kingdom of heaven will see the punishments of the damned, so that their bliss will lie that much greater."

It's always risky to explain or reduce a person's criticisms of another person to a psychological defense mechanism, but for the Schadenfreudians, we can see what Melanie Klein called "projective identification," an unconscious fantasy in which an individual's unacceptable aspects of the self are split off and then projected upon and attributed to another person, with whom the individual then identifies. Klein originally used the term, which is similar to what Anna Freud called "identification with the aggressor," to describe how an infant projects aggressive impulses onto the mother, so that the mother becomes, in effect, the persecutor, but projective identification can be used by adults who, unable to tolerate aggression or imperfection, project it onto others. The Schadenfreudians saw Freud as a persecutory figure, destroying everything good and noble about human nature.

Psychoanalytic Credos

The Freud idolaters and Schadenfreudians often refer to psychoanalysis, though none offer a present-day perspective, one that is radically different from half a century ago. What are the beliefs and aims of contemporary psychoanalysts? How do they see themselves and their profession? How have older analysts changed their theoretical thinking and psychoanalytic practice? How do younger analysts view their life work? Who are the most influential psychoanalysts, past and present? Where is the profession headed? In short, how has psychoanalysis, the "impossible profession," changed since the passing of the "golden age" of psychoanalysis? Responses to these crucial questions appear in *Psychoanalytic Credos: Personal and Professional Journeys of Psychoanalysts* (2022), edited by Jill Salberg, a clinical associate professor, consultant, and supervisor at the NYU Postdoctoral Program in Psychotherapy and Psychoanalysis. Contemporary analysts' credos are markedly different from the psychoanalytic belief systems of the eight Freudenfreudians and Schadenfreudians I have discussed.

Years ago, Salberg began assigning her students articles focusing on psychoanalysts' personal credos. She credits the idea to Emmanuel Ghent's article "Credo: The Dialectics of One-Person and Two-Person Psychologies" (1989). The exercise worked so well that Salberg conceived of the present volume, comprising reprints of noteworthy articles and newly commissioned essays. Salberg wanted to include a broad theoretical spectrum of views that may be called the American counterpart to the British "middle school" or "independent tradition," with most analysts identifying themselves as relational, object relational, contemporary Freudian, or Kleinian/Bionian—and a few who defy any affiliation. The contributors include both psychoanalytic superstars and rising stars. Twenty-seven essays appear spanning five decades: 1960s (Sheldon Bach and Haydée Faimberg); 1970s (Ricardo Bernardi, Christopher Bollas, Stephen Mitchell, Jay Greenberg, Nancy McWilliams, and Michael Parsons);

1980s (Lewis Aron, Jessica Benjamin, Steven Cooper, Adrienne Harris, Thomas Ogden, Donna Orange, Jill Salberg, and Joyce Slochower); 1990s (Mary Brady, Ken Corbett, Elizabeth Corpt, Dianne Elise, Bruce Reis, Stephen Seligman, and Melanie Suchet); and 2000s (Stephen Hartman, Ilana Laor, Avgi Saketopoulou, and Chana Ullman). Most of the analysts were born in the United States, where they practice, but some are from Uruguay (Bernardi), the United Kingdom (the American-born Bollas and Michael Parsons), France (Faimberg), Israel (Laor and Ullman), and Greece (Saketopoulou). Together, these essays offer both retrospective and prospective views of psychoanalysis.

Without exception, the contributors to *Psychoanalytic Credos* imply that they love their work, which for them is a passion, a mission, a calling. "I cannot imagine what else I could be doing with my time that would be more gratifying," Sheldon Bach observes (13). Unlike Harold Bloom, who predicted the demise of psychoanalysis, and Kurt Eissler, who lamented that psychoanalysis had lost its popularity and prestige, most of the analysts are optimistic about the future despite the many challenges facing their profession. One could not guess, based on the essays in this volume, that psychoanalysis is on the decline.

Many speak about the importance of active, careful listening, or, as Faimberg says, "listening to listening" (21). The notion of listening to listening may recall Bloom's belief that Shakespeare invented the concept of self-overhearing, particularly hearing the shattering reality of others. Faimberg's expression inspired Nancy Chodorow, who unfortunately does not have an essay in *Psychoanalytic Credos*, to distinguish between "listening for" and "listening to." In a 2005 interview conducted by Paul Elovitz and Bob Lentz and published in the psychohistorical journal *Clio's Psyche*, Chodorow divides analysts into two groups. "Those who 'listen for' are more theory-driven—I'm thinking of the Kleinians, the Kohutians, the Lacanians, the close-process ego psychologists. As you read them or hear them present, there's often the sense that they know, are even looking for, what they're going to find. Their theory guides what they hear." By contrast, Chodorow continues, "there are those who 'listen to,' who, although they have theory in mind, seem to range more freely across theories and to focus with a more open ear and mind on the particularity of the particular patient, and perhaps that the patient at different times can be best understood by different theories" (142). Most contributors to *Psychoanalytic Credos* would probably define themselves as "listening to" analysts, as Chodorow defines herself.

Contrary to Lawrence's and Nabokov's conviction that psychoanalysis is a monolithic force, the contributors to *Psychoanalytic Credos* believe in the importance of pluralism, searching for common ground, a middle road. In

Bernardi's words, "Pluralism allows us to recognize that there are different ideal models of 'true psychoanalysis'" (34). Creating a wide umbrella for a multiplicity of psychoanalytic theories and approaches becomes a goal of contemporary analysts wary of the schisms and divisions that have bedeviled psychoanalysis from its beginnings. Eissler's notion of psychoanalytic purity would be regarded with bemused skepticism. Psychoanalytic unity appears to be an impossible goal: All of the contributors would agree that psychoanalysis will grow stronger, not weaker, if there is an active, honest discussion of differences and uncertainties. No one wishes to return to the ideological wars. Tellingly, sometimes the middle road is a dangerous path, as Greenberg remarks: "Now, I have come to see that middle-road solutions simply add one more voice to the cacophony—and that the middle road is as radical as any of the extremes" (69).

Creating a wide interdisciplinary umbrella reminds us that psychoanalysis is not only a form of therapy, aimed at relieving suffering, but also a hermeneutics, a search for meaning. Insofar as psychoanalysis involves interpretation, it becomes a key hermeneutic activity, one that involves both the analysand's and analyst's subjectivity. Jürgen Habermas and Paul Ricoeur are the major psychoanalytic hermeneutic theorists. Ricoeur's 1970 book *Freud and Philosophy* focuses on the hermeneutics of suspicion, which the Schadenfreudians have embraced. Elyn R. Saks, a law professor with a long-standing interest in psychoanalysis, notes in her 1999 book *Interpreting Interpretation* that the "history of hermeneutics in general and of hermeneutic psychoanalysis in particular is vast and sprawling" (2, n.2), but it's clear that truth claims of any human (as opposed to natural) science are inherently difficult to validate. Donald P. Spence's 1984 book *Narrative Truth and Historical Truth* raises the vexing challenge of authenticating a patient's story.

There are no Freudian "true believers" in the volume, no Freud idolaters, no one who thinks that the founder of psychoanalysis discovered immutable universal truths, as Lionel Trilling, Kurt Eissler, and Peter Gay maintain. Nor are there any Schadenfreudians, analysts like Thomas Szasz who believed that Freud was a base rhetorician. Contemporary analysts seek *a* truth, not *the* truth. None is a psychoanalytic fundamentalist. Freud remains a towering figure, but more often than not the analysts in this volume challenge Freudian thinking, debating and entering into dialogue with him. "If Freud were alive today," Bach remarks, "he would be writing very differently than he wrote in 1939" (11). Freud insisted that the Oedipus complex was psychological bedrock, but few contemporary analysts share this view. Benjamin criticizes the "patriarchal bias" of the Oedipus complex (96). There are many more references in the volume to "mother" than to "father," suggesting not only a greater emphasis on pre-Oedipal issues but also the importance of feminist thinking. Analysts no longer mention "penis envy"; there is not a single entry to it in the index. Nor does the index contain other classical Freudian concepts, such as "castration fear" and the "death drive." A few analysts refer to libido theory, but this no longer appears to be a central psychoanalytic concept. Surprisingly, given the volume's emphasis on identity, there is only one reference to Erik Erikson, who devoted his career to studying identity formation.

Eissler regarded *any* revision of classical Freudian theory as the "poison of eclecticism," but some analysts openly, and proudly, confess to "heresies." Ogden, for example, does not believe in Freud's "fundamental rule," arguing that patients have the "right to privacy" and therefore should not be instructed to say everything that comes to mind. Seligman questions both the dual-instinct model, with its insistence on human destructiveness, and the idea of infantile sexuality. These heresies would have resulted in banishment and excommunication a century ago, but now they are a part of a healthy ongoing debate.

A paradigm shift in psychoanalysis occurred with the work of Stephen Mitchell (1946–2000), whose 1983 book *Object Relations in Psychoanalytic Theory*, written with Jay Greenberg, has become a classic, initiating relational analysis. After Freud, Winnicott, and Lacan, Mitchell is the most cited author in the volume, followed by Bion, Ogden, Fairbairn, and Ferenczi. In 1990, Mitchell established *Psychoanalytic Dialogues: A Journal of Relational Perspectives*, which published many of the reprinted essays in the volume. Mitchell supported the creation of the Division of Psychoanalysis (Division 39) of the American Psychological Association. His essay "My Psychoanalytic Journey," originally published in *Psychoanalytic Inquiry* in 2004, is one of the most significant in the volume, showing how he and Greenberg intended the word *relational* as a "bridge between interpersonal relations and internal object relations" (55). Curiously, Greenberg's "An Autobiographical Fragment," published in the same issue of *Psychoanalytic Inquiry*, makes only a brief mention of his disagreements with Mitchell. "Because of personal preferences, Steve gravitated to the thinking of theorists of what we called the *relational model*; similarly, my history led me to respect authors working within the tradition of Freudian drive theory" (65). Aron offers additional information about the split between Mitchell and Greenberg. "Steve pushed to be the revolutionary. And I was too conflicted about being a revolutionary because I have too much of a conservative side. And this was true of Jay Greenberg also. It's why Jay and Steve split" (91).

Neither the Freud idolaters nor the Freud bashers engaged with the feminist thought of their age, but this is one of the goals of Jessica Benjamin. She is one of the major analysts of the 1980s, and her 1988 book *The Bonds of Love* has become, like *Object Relations in Psychoanalytic Theory*, another classic. Embracing the "both/and of intrapsychic and intersubjective" became one of her goals (98). Another Benjamin insight was the analyst's acknowledgment of vulnerability, or as Michael Parsons puts it, analysts' willingness to step out of their comfort zone. Reading *The Bonds of Love* had a powerful impact on Melanie Suchet, enabling her to understand the "master-slave dynamic, the appeal of domination and submission, and the deep search for recognition" (202). In her 2018 book *Beyond Doer and Done To*, Benjamin affirms the need for social healing, which includes the transformative power of "witnessing, suffering, and admitting the truth of injustice or injury on a broader scale" (102).

The French psychoanalytic and philosophical tradition may be seen in Dianne Elise's essay "Analytic Eroticism," in which she regards Julia Kristeva's concept of maternal eroticism as the theoretical and developmental counterpart to Freud's view of infantile sexuality. "Joining maternal eroticism and infantile sexuality, we can now theorize the potential space of the mother-infant erotic matrix" (177). Christopher Bollas points out that Lacan's categories of the Symbolic, Imaginary, and Real gave him a new way of viewing his analysands. "Before this I had not seen what I could now see" (46). Elizabeth A. Corpt refers to the French phenomenological philosopher Maurice Merleau-Ponty's essay *Cezanne's Doubt* as resonating with her own experience of becoming a psychoanalyst.

A key insight in *Psychoanalytic Credos* is the importance of the patient–analyst relationship, which is probably the most accurate predictor of therapeutic success. "My analyst believed in me long before I could believe in myself," Donna Orange admits, "and taught me that a basic kindness was fully compatible with an analytic process" (129). Most contributors follow the unspoken tradition of not naming their training analysts or supervisors, but they place great value on those who were supportive and complain bitterly of those who were not. One of Nancy McWilliams's "pet peeves" was born when supervisors praised students for achieving positive results with a patient but then added the caustic comment, "'it was not really analysis,' as if adherence to a particular analytic technique is more important than therapy outcome" (73).

None of the contributors refers to the "Dodo Bird" effect, limned in Saul Rosenzweig's provocative 1936 article, "Some Implicit Common Factors in Diverse Methods of Psychotherapy"; its colorful subtitle, "At Last the Dodo Bird Said, Everybody Has Won and All Must Have Prizes," refers to Lewis Carroll's 1865 novel *Alice's Adventures in Wonderland*. Rosenzweig's article showed that all forms of psychotherapy can be equally beneficial under certain conditions. As

Bruce Wampold and Zac Imel observe in *The Great Psychotherapy Debate* (2015), common factors—"hope, expectation, relationship with the therapist, belief, and corrective experience" (33)—are far more important than a particular theoretical approach. The Dodo Bird effect remains highly controversial, partly because of the ambiguity of "effective treatment," which, as some therapists maintain, must involve deep psychological change, while others believe it connotes little more than symptomatic relief. Some researchers argue that certain treatments produce better outcomes for psychological problems, such as anxiety disorders, but as Wampold and Imel assert, the Dodo Bird effect "has survived many tests and must be considered 'true' until such time as sufficient evidence for its rejection is produced" (156). The Hungarian-born British psychoanalyst Peter Fonagy reaches the same conclusion in a 2015 study: "Any apparent superiority of long-term psychodynamic therapies is attributable to the prolonged contact between patient and therapist" (145). Or as the existential psychiatrist Irvin D. Yalom states in his 2005 novel *The Schopenhauer Cure*, "*It's not ideas, nor vision, nor tools that truly matter in therapy*. If you debrief patients at the end of therapy about the process, what do they remember? *Never* the ideas—it's always the relationship. They rarely remember an important insight their therapist offered but generally fondly recall their personal relationship with the therapist" (62–3). Would the Trillings' attitude toward psychoanalysis have been different, we can only wonder, if their analysts were aware of the Dodo Bird Effect? It's possible that Lionel Trilling had read Rosenzweig's article; the two knew each other, and we recall that the former wrote to the latter in 1944 rejecting Edmund Wilson's wound-and-bow theory of artistic creation.

A striking difference between older and younger analysts is the latters' emphasis on race, class, and gender. Writing her essay enabled Elizabeth Corpt to express her "outrage, disappointment, and utter puzzlement" regarding the traumatizing silence of psychoanalysis on the topic of social class (171). Having grown up near Johannesburg, South Africa, Melanie Suchet was horrified to realize that she was implicated in the Apartheid system that she abhorred. One cannot analyze the depression of an African patient, Suchet points out, without exploring the impact of that system. Stephen Hartman bemoans conservative analysts who deny the reality of gender dysphoria. Bloom pilloried the "School of Resentment," which included approaches to literature based on race, class, and gender, but such discussions, psychoanalytic or not, can have a transforming impact on our understanding of the past and present.

As a literature professor, I was struck by how many of the contributors cite novels, poems, and plays not primarily to confirm psychoanalytic theory, as

Freud did, but to deepen understanding of their patients' lives as well as their own. Avgi Saketopoulou was thirteen when she read *The Words to Say It*, Marie Cardinal's largely autobiographical 1976 novel about her Algerian childhood, her conflicted relationship with her mother, her mental illness, and her decision to enter a psychoanalysis that lasted seven years. Reading the story, Saketopoulou fell in love with psychoanalysis and made the fateful decision to become an analyst. Two of the contributors, Christopher Bollas and Thomas Ogden, have written several novels apiece—and Ogden teaches creative writing. Ogden's main teachers have been Freud, Klein, Fairbairn, Winnicott, Bion, Loewald, and Searles, yet he learned as much about psychoanalysis from poets, novelists, and playwrights. Faimberg cites John Keats's idea of "negative capability"—"When man is capable of being in uncertainties, Mysteries, doubts, without any irritable reaching after fact and reason" (Keats 261)—to understand the listening position. And Bruce Reis quotes a long passage from a short story by the Canadian Nobel laureate Alice Munro (2015) to suggest how the reader, like an analyst, approaches a story. In Munro's words, "A story is not like a road to follow, I said, it's more like a house. You go inside and stay there for awhile, wandering back and forth and settling where you like and discovering how the room and corridors relate to each other, how the world outside is altered by being viewed from these windows" (quoted in Salberg 186). Adam Phillips declares in *Promises, Promises* (2001) that literature is "probably a better preparation for the practice of psychoanalysis than the reading of anything else" (xvi). Freud believed, in Harold Bloom's view, that poetry was a discipline parallel to psychoanalysis, but Phillips, one of the United Kingdom's leading psychoanalysts and literary critics, offers a more radical claim at the end of *Promises, Promises*: "For me—for all sorts of reasons—there has always been only one category, *literature*, of which psychoanalysis became a part" (364).

There has long been a productive cross-fertilization between psychoanalysis and academic disciplines, as Adam Phillips's writings demonstrate. This cross-fertilization may be seen in Nancy Chodorow's writings. In *The Psychoanalytic Ear and the Sociological Eye* (2020), Chodorow proposes a new interdisciplinary academic department, "Individuology," to study human complexity. If such a department existed, *Psychoanalytic Credos* would be recommended or required reading. One can imagine that, in a "history of psychoanalysis" course taught in the Department of Individuology, selected writings of Trilling, Bloom, Eissler, Gay, Lawrence, Nabokov, Szasz, and Crews would be studied. Fifty years ago, few analysts would have dared to express publicly their doubts, uncertainties, and heresies. "There lives more faith in honest doubt," Tennyson wrote in *In*

Memoriam, "Believe me, than in half the creeds." Salberg could have chosen these lines as the epigraph to *Psychoanalytic Credos*. We have entered an age in which honest doubt, rather than defensive rigidity and dogma, will inspire new psychoanalytic thinking, producing a generation of clinicians, theorists, and literary scholars who will recognize Freud's profound contributions without worshiping or demonizing him. Regardless of whether the twenty-first century is the Age of Schadenfreude, we would then be able to look at Freud's limitations without malicious joy.

Works Cited

Almond, Richard. "Thoughts on the Future of Psychoanalysis." *The American Psychoanalyst* 54 (2020): 10–13.

Altman, Sig. *The Comic Image of the Jew: Explorations of a Pop Culture Phenomenon.* Rutherford, NJ: Fairleigh Dickinson University Press, 1971.

American Psychiatric Association. *Diagnostic and Statistical Manual of Mental Disorders: DSM-III.* New York: American Psychiatric Association, 1968.

Andreasen, Nancy. *The Creating Brain: The Neuroscience of Genius.* New York: Dana Press, 2005.

Bayley, John. *Iris and Her Friends: A Memoir of Memory and Desire.* New York: Norton, 2000.

Begley, Adam. "Terminating Analysis." *Lingua Franca* 4 (1994): 24–30.

Benjamin, Jessica. *Beyond Doer and Done to: Recognition Theory, Intersubjectivity, and the Third.* London and New York: Routledge, 2019.

Benjamin, Jessica. *The Bonds of Love: Psychoanalysis, Feminism, and the Problem of Domination.* New York: Pantheon, 1988.

Berger, G. M. "Idealization and Its Discontents: A Reconsideration of the Functions and Limits of a Psychic Phenomenon." *Journal of the American Academy of Psychoanalysis* 21 (1993): 45–61.

Berman, Jeffrey. *Dying in Character: Memoirs on the End of Life.* Amherst, MA: University of Massachusetts Press, 2012.

Berman, Jeffrey. *Mad Muse: The Mental Illness Memoir in a Writer's Life and Work.* Bingley: Emerald, 2019.

Berman, Jeffrey. *Narcissism and the Novel.* New York: New York University Press, 1990.

Berman, Jeffrey. *Norman N. Holland: The Dean of American Psychoanalytic Literary Critics.* New York: Bloomsbury Academic, 2021.

Berman, Jeffrey. "Paul Mosher: Coauthor and Friend." In *Paul Mosher: Psychoanalytic Citizen and Visionary*, edited by Judith S. Schachter, 89–100. New York: International Psychoanalytic Books, 2022.

Berman, Jeffrey. *Psychoanalytic Memoirs.* London: Bloomsbury Academic, 2023.

Berman, Jeffrey. "Review of *Lost Subjects, Contested Objects: Toward a Psychoanalytic Inquiry of Learning*," by Deborah P. Britzman. *JPCS: Journal for the Psychoanalysis of Culture & Society* 3 (1998): 180–2.

Berman, Jeffrey. *Risky Writing: Self-Disclosure and Self-Transformation in the Classroom.* Amherst: University of Massachusetts Press, 2001.

Berman, Jeffrey. *The Talking Cure: Literary Representations of Psychoanalysis*. New York: New York University Press, 1985.

Berman, Jeffrey and Paul W. Mosher. *Off the Tracks: Cautionary Tales About the Derailing of Mental Health Care*. 2 vols. New York: International Psychoanalytic Books, 2019.

Berman, Jeffrey and Paul W. Mosher. "Review of *A Psychoanalyst in the Classroom: On the Human Condition in Education*," by Deborah P. Britzman. *Journal of the American Psychoanalytic Association* 64 (2016): 835–9.

Bloom, Harold. *Agon: Towards a Theory of Revisionism*. New York: Oxford University Press, 1982.

Bloom, Harold. *The American Religion: The Emergence of the Post-Christian Nation*. New York: Simon & Schuster, 1992.

Bloom, Harold. *The Anatomy of Influence*. New Haven, CT: Yale University Press, 2011.

Bloom, Harold. *The Anxiety of Influence: A Theory of Poetry*. New York: Oxford University Press, 1973; 2nd edn, 1997.

Bloom, Harold. *Blake's Apocalypse: A Study in Poetic Argument*. Garden City, NY: Doubleday, 1963.

Bloom, Harold. *The Book of J.*, translated from the Hebrew by David Rosenberg. Interpreted by Harold Bloom. New York: Grove Weidenfeld, 1990.

Bloom, Harold. *The Bright Book of Life: Novels to Read and Reread*. New York: Knopf, 2020.

Bloom, Harold. *The Daemon Knows: Literary Greatness and the American Sublime*. New York: Spiegel & Grau, 2015.

Bloom, Harold. *Fallen Angels*. New Haven, CT: Yale University Press, 2007.

Bloom, Harold, editor. *Falstaff*. New York: Chelsea House, 1992.

Bloom, Harold. *Genius: A Mosaic of One Hundred Exemplary Creative Minds*. New York: Warner, 2002.

Bloom, Harold. *How to Read and Why*. New York: Scribner, 2000.

Bloom, Harold. *Jesus and Yahweh: The Names Divine*. New York: Riverhead Books, 2005.

Bloom, Harold. *Kabbalah and Criticism*. New York: Seabury Press, 1975.

Bloom, Harold. *A Map of Misreading*. New York: Oxford University Press, 1975.

Bloom, Harold. *Omens of Millennium: The Gnosis of Angels, Dreams, and Resurrection*. New York: Riverhead Books, 1996.

Bloom, Harold. *Poetry and Repression: Revisionism from Blake to Stevens*. New Haven, CT: Yale University Press, 1976.

Bloom, Harold. *Possessed by Memory: The Inward Light of Criticism*. New York: Knopf, 2019.

Bloom, Harold. *The Ringers in the Tower: Studies in Romantic Tradition*. Chicago: University of Chicago Press, 1971.

Bloom, Harold. *Ruin the Sacred Truths: Poetry and Belief from the Bible to the Present*. Cambridge, MA: Harvard University Press, 1989.

Bloom Harold. *Shakespeare: The Invention of the Human*. New York: Riverhead Books, 1998.

Bloom, Harold. *Shelley's Mythmaking*. New Haven, CT: Yale University Press, 1959.

Bloom, Harold. *Take Arms Against a Sea of Troubles: The Power of the Reader's Mind Over a Universe of Death*. New Haven, CT: Yale University Press, 2020.

Bloom, Harold. *The Visionary Company*. Ithaca, NY: Cornell University Press, 1961.

Bloom, Harold. *Wallace Stevens: The Poems of Our Climate*. Ithaca, NY: Cornell University Press, 1977.

Bloom, Harold. *The Western Canon: The Books and Schools of the Ages*. New York: Harcourt Brace, 1994.

Bloom, Harold. *Where Shall Wisdom Be Found?* New York: Riverhead Books, 2004.

Bloom, Harold. *Yeats*. New York: Oxford University Press, 1970.

Bollas, Christopher. *The Shadow of the Object: Psychoanalysis of the Unthought Known*. New York: Columbia University Press, 1987.

Boxer, Sarah. "Kurt Eissler, 90, Director of Sigmund Freud Archives." *New York Times*, February 20, 1999.

Boyd, Brian. *Stalking Nabokov: Selected Essays*. New York: Columbia University Press, 2011.

Boyd, Brian. *Vladimir Nabokov: The American Years*. Princeton, NJ: Princeton University Press, 1991.

Boyers, Robert. *Lionel Trilling: Negative Capability and the Wisdom of Avoidance*. Columbia, MO: University of Missouri Press, 1977.

Boynton, Robert S. "Peter Swales, Malcolm's Uncalled Witness: A Profile of Peter Swales." *New York Observer*, May 24, 1993.

Bracher, Mark. *The Writing Cure: Psychoanalysis, Composition, and the Aims of Education*. Carbondale, IL: Southern Illinois University Press, 1999.

Bradley, Arthur. "The Impossibility of Reading: Bloom and the 'Yale School' of Criticism." In *Reading, Writing, and the Influence of Harold Bloom*, edited by Alan Rawes and Jonathan Shears, 259–82. Manchester: Manchester University Press, 2010.

Breger, Louis. *Freud: Darkness in the Midst of Vision*. New York: John Wiley & Sons, 2000.

Breuer, Josef and Sigmund Freud. *Studies on Hysteria*. 1893–1895. In *The Standard Edition of the Complete Psychological Works of Sigmund Freud*, translated and edited by James Strachey. Vol. 2. London: The Hogarth Press, 1955.

Britzman, Deborah P. *Lost Subjects, Contested Objects: Toward a Psychoanalytic Inquiry of Learning*. Albany: State University of New York Press, 1998.

Britzman, Deborah P. *A Psychoanalyst in the Classroom: On the Human Condition in Education*. Albany: State University of New York Press, 2015.

Brooks, Peter and Alex Woloch, editors. *Whose Freud? The Place of Psychoanalysis in Contemporary Culture*. New Haven, CT: Yale University Press, 2000.

Buckley, F. H. "Schadenfreude and Laughter." In *Schadenfreude: Understanding Pleasure at the Misfortune of Others*, edited by Wilco W. van Dijk and Jaap W. Ouwerkerk, 219–26. Cambridge: Cambridge University Press, 2014.

Burrow, Trigant. *A Search for Man's Sanity: The Selected Letters of Trigant Burrow*. Foreword by Herbert Read. New York: Oxford University Press, 1958.

Burrow, Trigant. *The Social Basis of Consciousness: A Study in Organic Psychology Based upon a Synthetic and Societal Concept of the Neuroses*. New York: Harcourt, Brace & Company, 1927.

Chace, William M. *Lionel Trilling: Criticism and Politics*. Stanford, CA: Stanford University Press, 1980.

Chambers, Jessie ["E.T."]. *D.H. Lawrence: A Personal Record*. London: Jonathan Cape, 1935; 2nd edn. Barnes and Noble, 1965.

Chambliss, Catherine and Amy C. Hartl, editors. *Empathy Rules: Depression, Schadenfreude and Freudenfreude Research on Depression Risk Factors and Treatment*. New York: Nova Science Publishers, 2016.

Chodorow, Nancy J. *The Psychoanalytic Ear and the Sociological Eye: Toward an American Independent Tradition*. London: Routledge, 2020.

Clifton, Gladys M. "Humbert Freud? and the Limits of Artistic License." In *Nabokov's Fifth Arc*, edited by J. E. Rivers and Charles Nicol, 153–70. Austin, TX: University of Texas Press, 1982.

Colt, George Howe. *The Enigma of Suicide*. New York: Touchstone, 1992.

Cowan, James C. *D.H. Lawrence: Self and Sexuality*. Columbus, OH: Ohio State University Press, 2002.

Cowan, James C. *D.H. Lawrence and the Trembling Balance*. University Park, PA: Pennsylvania State University Press, 1990.

Crews, Frederick. "Afterword" to *The Sins of the Fathers*. 2nd edn. Berkeley: University of California Press, 1989.

Crews, Frederick. "Anaesthetic Criticism." In *Psychoanalysis and Literary Process*, edited by Frederick Crews, 1–24. Cambridge, MA: Winthrop, 1970.

Crews, Frederick. *The Critics Bear It Away: American Fiction and the Academy*. New York: Random House, 1992.

Crews, Frederick. *E.M. Forster: The Perils of Humanism*. Princeton: Princeton University Press, 1962.

Crews, Frederick. *Follies of the Wise: Dissenting Essays*. New York: Shoemaker Hoard, 2006.

Crews, Frederick. *Freud: The Making of an Illusion*. New York: Metropolitan Books, 2017.

Crews, Frederick. "Literature and Psychology." In *Relations of Literary Study: Essays on Interdisciplinary Contributions*, edited by James Thorpe, 73–87. New York: Modern Language Association, 1967.

Crews, Frederick, et al., editors. *The Memory Wars: Freud's Legacy in Dispute*. New York: New York Review Book, 1995.

Crews, Frederick. *Out of My System: Psychoanalysis, Ideology, and Critical Method*. New York: Oxford University Press, 1975.

Crews, Frederick. *The Pooh Perplex: A Freshman Casebook*. New York: Dutton, 1965.

Crews, Frederick. *Postmodern Pooh*. New York: North Point Press, 2001.

Crews, Frederick. *The Sins of the Fathers: Hawthorne's Psychological Themes*. London: Oxford University Press, 1966; rpt. 1970.

Crews, Frederick. *Skeptical Engagements*. New York: Oxford University Press, 1986.

Crews, Frederick. *The Tragedy of Manners: Moral Drama in the Later Novels of Henry James*. New Haven, CT: Yale University Press, 1957.

Crews, Frederick, editor. *Unauthorized Freud: Doubters Confront a Legend*. New York: Viking, 1998.

Curle, Richard. *The Last Twelve Years of Joseph Conrad*. Garden City, NY: Doubleday, 1928.

Decker, Hannah S. *Freud, Dora, and Vienna 1900*. New York: Free Press, 1992.

De la Durantaye, Leland. "Vladimir Nabokov and Sigmund Freud, or a Particular Problem." *American Imago* 62 (2005): 59–73.

De La Rochefoucauld, François. http://.www.quotationspage.com/quotes/François_de_LaRochefoucauld. Accessed September 20, 2023.

DeSalvo, Louise. *Writing as a Way of Healing: How Telling Our Stories Transforms Our Lives*. New York: HarperOne, 1999.

Diamond, Eliezer. "But Is It Funny? Identifying Humor, Satire, and Parody in Rabbinic Literature." In *Jews and Humor: Studies in Jewish Civilization*, vol. 22, edited by Leonard J. Greenspan, 33–54. West Lafayette, IN: Purdue University Press, 2009.

Diment, Galya. "Sudden Sunburst: Evidence that Vladimir Nabokov Suffered from a Mild Form of Epilepsy." *Times Literary Supplement*, August 5, 2016.

Eissler, Kurt R. *Discourse on Hamlet and HAMLET: A Psychoanalytic Inquiry*. New York: International Universities Press, 1971.

Eissler, Kurt R. *Freud as an Expert Witness: The Discussion of War Neuroses Between Freud and Wagner-Jauregg*, translated from the German by Christine Trollope. Madison, CT: International Universities Press, 1986.

Eissler, Kurt R. *Freud and the Seduction Theory: A Brief Love Affair*. Madison, CT: International Universities Press, 2001.

Eissler, Kurt R. *Goethe: A Psychoanalytic Study, 1775–1786*. 2 vols. Detroit, MI: Wayne State University Press, 1963.

Eissler, Kurt R. *Leonardo da Vinci: Psychoanalytic Notes on the Enigma*. New York: International Universities Press, 1961.

Eissler, Kurt R. *Medical Orthodoxy and the Future of Psychoanalysis*. New York: International Universities Press, 1965.

Eissler, Kurt R. *The Psychiatrist and the Dying Patient*. New York: International Universities Press, 1955.

Eissler, Kurt R. *Talent and Genius: The Fictitious Case of Tausk Contra Freud*. New York: Quadrangle, 1971.

Eissler, Kurt R. *Three Instances of Injustice*. Madison, CT: International Universities Press, 1993.

Eissler, Kurt R. *Victor Tausk's Suicide*, with Comments by Prof. Dr. Marius Tausk. New York: International Universities Press, 1983.

Ellenberger, Henri F. *The Discovery of the Unconscious: The History and Evolution of Dynamic Psychiatry*. New York: Basic Books, 1970.

Elovitz, Paul and Bob Lentz. "Nancy J. Chodorow: Psychoanalyst and Gender Theorist." *Clio's Psyche* 11 (2005): 113, 134–43.

Erikson, Erik H. "The Nature of Clinical Evidence." *Daedalus* 87 (1958): 68–87.

Erikson, Erik H. *Young Man Luther*. New York: Norton, 1958.

Fenichel, Otto. *The Psychoanalytic Theory of Neurosis*. New York: Norton, 1945.

Field, Andrew. *Nabokov: His Life in Art*. Boston: Little, Brown, 1967.

Field, Andrew. *Nabokov: His Life in Part*. New York: Viking, 1977.

Field, Joanna [Marion Milner]. *A Life of One's Own*. London: Chatto & Windus, 1936; rpt. Los Angeles: J.P. Tarcher, 1981.

Fitzgerald, F. Scott. *The Crack-Up*. New York: New Directions, 1945.

Fonagy, Peter. "The Effectiveness of Psychodynamic Psychotherapies: An Update." *World Psychiatry* 14 (2015): 137–50.

Forster, E. M. *Aspects of the Novel*. London: Edward Arnold, 1927.

Fowler, Douglas. *Reading Nabokov*. Ithaca, NY: Cornell University Press, 1974.

Fraga, Juli. "Shared Joy Acts Like Social Glue." *New York Times*, December 6, 2022.

Frances, Allen. "The Myth and Reality of Mental Illness." In *Thomas Szasz: An Appraisal of His Legacy*, edited by C. V. Haldipur, J. L. Knoll, and E. Luft, 169–76. Oxford: Oxford University Press, 2019.

Frank, Arthur W. *The Wounded Storyteller: Body, Illness, and Ethics*. Chicago: University of Chicago Press, 1995.

Freud, Anna. *The Ego and the Mechanisms of Defense*. New York: International Universities Press, 1937; rev. 1976.

Freud, Sigmund. *Analysis Terminable and Interminable*. 1937. *The Standard Edition of the Complete Psychological Works of Sigmund Freud*, translated and edited by James Strachey. Vol. 23. London: The Hogarth Press, 1964.

Freud, Sigmund. *Beyond the Pleasure Principle*. 1920. *The Standard Edition of the Complete Psychological Works of Sigmund Freud*, translated and edited by James Strachey. Vol. 18. London: The Hogarth Press, 1955.

Freud, Sigmund. *Civilization and Its Discontents*. 1930. *The Standard Edition of the Complete Psychological Works of Sigmund Freud*, translated and edited by James Strachey. Vol. 21. London: The Hogarth Press, 1961.

Freud, Sigmund. *'Civilized' Sexual Morality and Modern Nervous Illness*. 1908. *The Standard Edition of the Complete Psychological Works of Sigmund Freud*, translated and edited by James Strachey. Vol. 9. London: The Hogarth Press, 1959.

Freud, Sigmund. *A Comment on Anti-Semitism*. 1938. *The Standard Edition of the Complete Psychological Works of Sigmund Freud*, translated and edited by James Strachey. Vol. 23. London: The Hogarth Press, 1964.

Freud, Sigmund. *Creative Writers and Day-Dreaming*. 1908. *The Standard Edition of the Complete Psychological Works of Sigmund Freud*, translated and edited by James Strachey. Vol. 9. London: The Hogarth Press, 1959.

Freud, Sigmund. *Delusions and Dreams in Jensen's Gradiva*. 1907. *The Standard Edition of the Complete Psychological Works of Sigmund Freud*, translated and edited by James Strachey. Vol. 9. London: The Hogarth Press, 1959.

Freud, Sigmund. *A Difficulty in the Path of Psycho-Analysis*. 1917. *The Standard Edition of the Complete Psychological Works of Sigmund Freud*, translated and edited by James Strachey. Vol. 17. London: The Hogarth Press, 1955.

Freud, Sigmund. *Dostoevsky and Parricide*. 1928. *The Standard Edition of the Complete Psychological Works of Sigmund Freud*, translated and edited by James Strachey. Vol. 21. London: The Hogarth Press, 1961.

Freud, Sigmund. *The Dynamics of Transference*. 1912. *The Standard Edition of the Complete Psychological Works of Sigmund Freud*, translated and edited by James Strachey. Vol. 12. London: The Hogarth Press, 1958.

Freud, Sigmund. *Family Romances*. 1909. *The Standard Edition of the Complete Psychological Works of Sigmund Freud*, translated and edited by James Strachey. Vol. 9. London: The Hogarth Press, 1959.

Freud, Sigmund. Foreword to *David Eder: Memoirs of a Modern Pioneer*, edited by J. B. Hobman. London: Victor Gollancz, 1945.

Freud, Sigmund. *Fragment of an Analysis of a Case of Hysteria*. 1905. *The Standard Edition of the Complete Psychological Works of Sigmund Freud*, translated and edited by James Strachey. Vol. 7. London: The Hogarth Press, 1953.

Freud, Sigmund. *From the History of an Infantile Neurosis*. 1918. *The Standard Edition of the Complete Psychological Works of Sigmund Freud*, translated and edited by James Strachey. Vol. 17. London: The Hogarth Press, 1955.

Freud, Sigmund. *The Future of an Illusion. The Standard Edition of the Complete Psychological Works of Sigmund Freud*. Translated and edited by James Strachey. Vol. 21. London: The Hogarth Press, 1961.

Freud, Sigmund. *The Interpretation of Dreams*. 1900. *The Standard Edition of the Complete Psychological Works of Sigmund Freud*, translated and edited by James Strachey. Vol. 4. London: The Hogarth Press, 1953.

Freud, Sigmund. *Introductory Lectures on Psycho-Analysis*. 1916–1917. *The Standard Edition of the Complete Psychological Works of Sigmund Freud*, translated and edited by James Strachey. Vol. 15. London: The Hogarth Press, 1961.

Freud, Sigmund. *Jokes and Their Relation to the Unconscious*. 1905. *The Standard Edition of the Complete Psychological Works of Sigmund Freud*, translated and edited by James Strachey. Vol. 8. London: The Hogarth Press, 1960.

Freud, Sigmund. *The Letters of Sigmund Freud*, edited by Ernst L. Freud, translated by Tania Stern and James Stern. New York: Basic Books, 1975.

Freud, Sigmund. *Leonardo da Vinci and a Memory of His Childhood*. 1910. *The Standard Edition of the Complete Psychological Works of Sigmund Freud*, translated and edited by James Strachey. Vol. 11. London: The Hogarth Press, 1957.

Freud, Sigmund. *Mourning and Melancholia*. 1917. *The Standard Edition of the Complete Psychological Works of Sigmund Freud*, translated and edited by James Strachey. Vol. 14. London: The Hogarth Press, 1957.

Freud, Sigmund. *New Introductory Lectures on Psycho-Analysis*. 1933. *The Standard Edition of the Complete Psychological Works of Sigmund Freud*, translated and edited by James Strachey. Vol. 22. London: The Hogarth Press, 1964.

Freud, Sigmund. *On the History of the Psycho-Analytic Movement*. 1914. *The Standard Edition of the Complete Psychological Works of Sigmund Freud*, translated and edited by James Strachey. Vol. 14. London: The Hogarth Press, 1957.

Freud, Sigmund. *On Narcissism: An Introduction*. 1914. *The Standard Edition of the Complete Psychological Works of Sigmund Freud*, translated and edited by James Strachey. Vol. 14. London: The Hogarth Press, 1957.

Freud, Sigmund. *On the Universal Tendency to Debasement in the Sphere of Love*. 1912. *The Standard Edition of the Complete Psychological Works of Sigmund Freud*, translated and edited by James Strachey. Vol. 11. London: The Hogarth Press, 1957.

Freud, Sigmund. *Psychopathic Characters on the Stage*. 1942. *The Standard Edition of the Complete Psychological Works of Sigmund Freud*, translated and edited by James Strachey. Vol. 7. London: The Hogarth Press, 1953.

Freud, Sigmund. *The Psychopathology of Everyday Life*. 1901. *The Standard Edition of the Complete Psychological Works of Sigmund Freud*, translated and edited by James Strachey. Vol. 6. London: The Hogarth Press, 1960.

Freud, Sigmund. *The Question of Lay Analysis*. 1926. *The Standard Edition of the Complete Psychological Works of Sigmund Freud*, translated and edited by James Strachey. Vol. 20. London: The Hogarth Press, 1959.

Freud, Sigmund. *A Religious Experience*. 1928. *The Standard Edition of the Complete Psychological Works of Sigmund Freud*, translated and edited by James Strachey. Vol. 21. London: The Hogarth Press, 1961.

Freud, Sigmund. *Screen Memories*. 1899. *The Standard Edition of the Complete Psychological Works of Sigmund Freud*, translated and edited by James Strachey. Vol. 3. London: The Hogarth Press, 1962.

Freud, Sigmund. *A Short Account of Psycho-Analysis*. 1924. *The Standard Edition of the Complete Psychological Works of Sigmund Freud*, translated and edited by James Strachey. Vol. 19. London: The Hogarth Press, 1961.

Freud, Sigmund. *A Special Type of Choice of Object Made by Men*. 1910. *The Standard Edition of the Complete Psychological Works of Sigmund Freud*, translated and edited by James Strachey. Vol. 11. London: The Hogarth Press, 1957.

Freud, Sigmund. *The 'Uncanny.'* 1919. *The Standard Edition of the Complete Psychological Works of Sigmund Freud*, translated and edited by James Strachey. Vol. 17. London: The Hogarth Press, 1955.

Fromm, Erich. *The Forgotten Language: An Introduction to the Understanding of Dreams, Fairy Tales, and Myths*. New York: Rinehart, 1951.

Frosch, Thomas R. "Parody and Authenticity in *Lolita*." In *Nabokov's Fifth Arc*, edited by J. E. Rivers and Charles Nicol, 188–94. Austin, TX: University of Texas Press, 1982.

Gay, Peter. *Freud for Historians*. Oxford: Oxford University Press, 1985.

Gay, Peter. *Freud, Jews and Other Germans: Masters and Victims in Modernist Culture*. Oxford: Oxford University Press, 1978.

Gay, Peter. *Freud: A Life for Our Time*. New York: Norton, 1988.

Gay, Peter. *The Freud Reader*. New York: Norton, 1989.

Gay, Peter. *A Godless Jew: Freud, Atheism, and the Making of Psychoanalysis*. New Haven, CT: Yale University Press, 1987.

Gay, Peter. *My German Question: Growing Up in Nazi Berlin*. New Haven, CT: Yale University Press, 1998.

Gay, Peter. *Reading Freud: Explorations & Entertainments*. New Haven, CT: Yale University Press, 1990.

Gay, Ruth. *Unfinished People: Eastern European Jews Encounter America*. New York: Norton, 1996.

Genzlinger, Neil. "Peter Swales, Who Startled Freud Scholarship, Dies at 73." *New York Times*, April 21, 2022.

Ghent, Emmanuel. "Credo: The Dialectics of One-Person and Two-Person Psychologies." *Contemporary Psychoanalysis* 25 (1989): 169–211.

Gilbert, Sandra M. *Wrongful Death: A Memoir*. New York: Norton, 1995.

Gilman, Sander L. *Difference and Pathology: Stereotypes of Sexuality, Race, and Madness*. Ithaca: Cornell University Press, 1985.

Gilman, Sander L. *Freud, Race, and Gender*. Princeton, NJ: Princeton University Press, 1993.

Gilman, Sander L. *Jewish Self-Hatred: Anti-Semitism and the Hidden Language of the Jews*. Baltimore, MD: Johns Hopkins University Press, 1986.

Gilman, Sander L. "Review of Gay's *A Godless Jew* and *Freud: A Life*." *The Jewish Quarterly Review* 79 (1989): 251–3.

Gordan, David J. *D.H. Lawrence as a Literary Critic*. New Haven, CT: Yale University Press, 1966.

Green, Geoffrey. *Freud and Nabokov*. Lincoln: University of Nebraska Press, 1988.

Greenberg, Jay and Stephen A. Mitchell. *Object Relations in Psychoanalytic Theory*. Cambridge, MA: Harvard University Press, 1983.

Greene, Graham. *Ways of Escape*. New York: Simon and Schuster, 1980.

Grimes, William. "Peter Gay, Historian Who Explored Social History of Ideas, Dies at 91." *New York Times*, May 12, 2015.

Grunbaum, Adolf. *The Foundations of Psychoanalysis: A Philosophical Critique*. Berkeley: University of California Press, 1984.

Guttman, Samuel A., Randall L. Jones, and Stephen M. Parrish, editors. *The Concordance to the Standard Edition of the Compete Psychological Works of Sigmund Freud*. Boston, MA: G.K. Hall, 1980.

Haldipur, C. V., James L. Knoll IV, and Eric v.d. Luft, editors. *Thomas Szasz: An Appraisal of His Legacy*. Oxford: Oxford University Press, 2019.

Hale, Nathan G., editor. *James Jackson Putnam and Psychoanalysis: Letters Between Putnam and Sigmund Freud, Ernest Jones, William James, Sandor Ferenczi, and Morton Prince, 1877–1917*. Cambridge, MA: Harvard University Press, 1971.

Harris, Judith. *The Poetry of Loss: Romantic and Contemporary Elegies*. London: Routledge, 2023.

Hartman, Geoffrey. *A Scholar's Tale: Intellectual Journey of a Displaced Child of Europe*. New York: Fordham University Press, 2007.

H.D. *Tribute to Freud*. Foreword by Norman Holmes Pearson. Introduction by Kenneth Fields. Boston: David R. Godine, 1974.

Henke, Suzette A. *Shattered Subjects: Trauma and Testimony in Women's Life-Writing*. New York: Palgrave Macmillan, 1998.

Hiatt, L. R. "Nabokov's *Lolita*: A Freudian Cryptic Crossword." *American Imago* 24 (1967): 360–70.

Hirschmüller, Albrecht. "Freud's Studies on Cocaine." In *The Pre-Psychoanalytic Writings of Sigmund Freud*, edited by Gertrudis Van de Vijver and Filip Geerardyn, 70–7. London: Karnac, 2002.

Hoffman, Frederick J. *Freudianism and the Literary Mind*. 2nd edn. Baton Rouge: Louisiana State University Press, 1957.

Holland, Norman N. *The Dynamics of Literary Response*. New York: Oxford University Press, 1968; rpt. New York: Norton, 1975. rpt. New York: Morningside-Columbia University Press, 1989.

Holland, Norman N. *Psychoanalysis and Shakespeare*. New York: McGraw-Hill, 1966; rpt. New York: Octagon Books, 1976.

Holland, Norman N. *The Shakespearean Imagination*. New York: Macmillan, 1964; rpt. Bloomington, IN: Midland-Indiana University Press, 1968.

Holland, Norman N. "Tickled Rats and Human Laughter." *Neuro-Psychoanalysis* 9 (2007): 41–57.

Holland, Norman N. *5 Readers Reading*. New Haven, CT: Yale University Press, 1975.

Holland, Norman N. and Murray M. Schwartz. "The Delphi Seminar." *College English* 36 (1975): 789–800. Expanded into *Know Thyself: Delphi Seminars*. Gainesville, FL: PsyArt Foundation, 2008.

Hubbard, L. Ron. *Handbook for Preclears*. Los Angeles: Bridge Publications, 1989.

Hyde, G. M. *Vladimir Nabokov: America's Russian Novelist*. London: Marion Boyars, 1977.

Jamison, Kay Redfield. *Night Falls Fast: Understanding Suicide*. New York: Knopf, 1999.

Jamison, Kay Redfield. *Robert Lowell: Setting the River on Fire*. New York: Knopf, 2017.

Jamison, Kay Redfield. *Touched with Fire: Manic-Depressive Illness and the Artistic Temperament*. New York: Simon & Schuster, 1993; rpt. Free Press, 1994.

Jamison, Kay Redfield. *An Unquiet Mind: A Memoir of Moods and Madness*. New York: Knopf, 1995.

Jones, Ernest. *Hamlet and Oedipus*. New York: Norton, 1949.

Jones, Ernest. *The Life and Work of Sigmund Freud*. 3 vols. New York: Basic Books, 1953–1957.

Jordan, Judith V., Alexandra G. Kaplan, Jean Baker Miller, Irene P. Stiver, and Janet L. Surrey. *Women's Growth in Connection: Writings from the Stone Center*. New York: Guilford Press, 1991.

Kardiner, Abram. *My Analysis with Freud: Reminiscences*. New York: Norton, 1977.

Karlinsky, Simon, editor. *The Nabokov-Wilson Letters*. New York: Harper and Row, 1979.

Kaufmann, Walter. *The Faith of a Heretic*. Garden City, NY: Doubleday, 1961.

Keats, John. *Selected Poems and Letters*. Cambridge, MA: Riverside Press, 1959.

Kerr, John. *A Most Dangerous Method: The Story of Jung, Freud, and Sabina Spielrein*. New York: Knopf, 1993.

Kirsch, Adam. *Why Trilling Matters*. New Haven, CT: Yale University Press, 2011.

Knoll, James L. IV. "Suicide Prohibition: Shame, Blame, or Social Aim?" In *Thomas Szasz: An Appraisal of His Legacy*, edited by C. V. Haldipur, J. L. Knoll, and E. Luft, 104–23. Oxford: Oxford University Press, 2019.

Kohut, Heinz. *The Analysis of the Self: A Systematic Approach to the Psychoanalytic Treatment of Narcissistic Personality Disorders*. New York: International Universities Press, 1977.

Kohut, Heinz. "Thoughts on Narcissism and Narcissistic Rage." In *The Search for the Self: Selected Writings, 1950–1978*, edited by Paul H. Ornstein, 4 vols. New York: International Universities Press, 1978.

Krüll, Marianne. *Freud and His Father*. New York: Norton, 1986.

Krupnick, Mark. *Lionel Trilling and the Fate of Cultural Criticism*. Evanston, IL: Northwestern University Press, 1986.

Kuttner, Alfred Booth. "A Freudian Appreciation." *The Psychoanalytic Review* 3 (1916): 293–317.

Kwon, Teckyoung. *Nabokov's Mimicry of Freud: Art as Science*. Lanham, MD: Lexington Books, 2017.

Laing, R. D. *The Divided Self: An Existential Study in Sanity and Madness*. London: Tavistock, 1960.

Lask, Thomas. "Lionel Trilling, 70, Critic, Teacher and Writer, Dies." *New York Times*, November 7, 1975.

Lawrence, D. H. *Lady Chatterley's Lover*. New York: Grove Press, 1928.

Lawrence, D. H. *The Letters of D.H. Lawrence*. Vol I, edited by James T. Boulton; vol. II, edited by George J. Zytaruk and James T. Boulton; vol. III, edited by James T. Boulton and Andrew Robertson; vol. IV, edited by Warren Roberts, James T. Boulton, and Elizabeth Mansfield; vol. V, edited by James T. Boulton and Lindeth Vasey; vol. VI, edited by James T. Boulton and Margaret Boulton, with Gerald Lacy; vol. VII, edited by Keith Sagar and James T. Boulton; vol. VIII, edited and compiled by James T. Boulton. Cambridge: Cambridge University Press, 1979–2001.

Lawrence, D. H. *Phoenix: The Posthumous Papers of D.H. Lawrence*, edited and with an Introduction by Edward D. McDonald. New York: Viking Compass Edition, 1972.

Lawrence, D. H. *Phoenix II: Uncollected, Unpublished, and Other Prose Works by D.H. Lawrence*, Collected and Edited with an Introduction and Notes by Warren Roberts and Harry T. Moore. New York: Viking Compass Edition, 1970.

Lawrence, D. H. "Pornography and Obscenity." In *Phoenix*, 170–87.

Lawrence, D. H. "Prologue to *Women in Love*." In *Phoenix II*, 92–108.

Lawrence, D. H. *Psychoanalysis of the Unconscious and Fantasia of the Unconscious*. Introduction by Philip Rieff. New York: Viking, 1960.

Lawrence, D. H. "Review of The Social Basis of Consciousness, by Trigant Burrow." In *Phoenix*, 377–82.

Lawrence, D. H. "Sex versus Loveliness." In *Phoenix II*, 527–31.

Lawrence, D. H. *Sons and Lovers: Text, Background, and Criticism*, edited by Julian Moynahan. New York: Viking, 1968.

Lawrence, D. H. *Studies in Classic American Literature*. New York: Viking, 1969.

Lawrence, D. H. *Women in Love*. New York: Viking, 1982.

Lawrence, Frieda. *"Not I, But the Wind . . ."* New York: Viking, 1934.

Lehrman, Philip R. "Freud's Contributions to Science." *Harofé Haivri* 1 (1940): 161–76.

Lepore, Stephen J. and Joshua M. Smyth, editors. *The Writing Cure: How Expressive Writing Promotes Health and Emotional Well-Being*. Washington, DC: American Psychological Association, 2002.

Lesser, Simon O. *Fiction and the Unconscious*. Preface by Ernest Jones. New York: Vintage, 1957.

Lewitzka, U., C. Sauer, M. Bauer, and W. Felber. "Are National Suicide Prevention Programs Effective? A Comparison of 4 Verum and 4 Control Countries Over 30 Years." *BMC Psychiatry* 19 (2019). https://doi.org/10.1186/s12888-019-2147-y.

Lieberman, E. James and Robert Kramer, editors. *The Letters of Sigmund Freud & Otto Rank: Inside Psychoanalysis*. Letters Translated by Gregory C. Richter. Baltimore, MD: Johns Hopkins University Press, 2012.

Lieberman, Jeffrey A. *Shrinks: The Untold Story of Psychiatry*. With Ogi Ogas. New York: Little, Brown and Company, 2015.

Loftus, Elizabeth. "Remembering Dangerously." *Skeptical Inquirer* 19 (1995). http://www.csicop.org/si/show/rememboring_dangerously.

Loftus, Elizabeth and Katherine Ketcham. *The Myth of Repressed Memory: False Memories and Allegations of Sexual Abuse*. New York: St. Martin's Press, 1994.

MacFarquhar, Larissa. "The Prophet of Decline: Harold Bloom's Influential Anxieties." *The New Yorker*, September 22, 2002. https://www.newyorker.com/magazine/2009/09/30/the-prophet-of-decline. Accessed October 8, 2021.

Makari, George. *Revolution in Mind: The Creation of Psychoanalysis*. New York: Harper Perennial, 2008.

Malcolm, Janet. *In the Freud Archives*. New York: Knopf, 1984.

Maltby, Kate. "Harold Bloom, an Irreplaceable Genius of Criticism." *The Jewish Chronicle*, October 24, 2019. https://www.thejc.com/culture/books/an-irreplaceable-genius-of-criticism. Accessed November 5, 2021.

Masson, Jeffrey Moussaieff, translator and editor. *The Complete Letters of Sigmund Freud to Wilhelm Fliess, 1887–1904*. Cambridge, MA: Belknap Press of Harvard University Press, 1985.

McGuire, William, editor. *The Freud/Jung Letters: The Correspondence Between Sigmund Freud and C.G. Jung*, translated by Ralph Manheim and R. F. C. Hull. Princeton, NJ: Princeton University Press, 1974.

Menand, Louis. "Regrets Only: Lionel Trilling and His Discontents." *The New Yorker*, September 22, 2008. https://www.newyorker.com/magazine/2008-09/regrets-only-louis-menand.

Meng, Heinrich and Ernst L. Freud, editors. *Psychoanalysis and Faith: The Letters of Sigmund Freud & Oskar Pfister*, translated by Eric Mosbacher. New York: Basic Books, 1963.

Michels, Robert. "Review of *The Memory Wars*." *Journal of the American Psychoanalytic Association* 44 (1996): 573–8.

Miller, Alice. *Thou Shalt Not Be Aware: Society's Betrayal of the Child*. New York: Farrar, Straus, Giroux, 1984.

Miller, Jean Baker and Irene Pierce Stiver. *The Healing Connection: How Women Form Relationships in Therapy and Life*. Boston: Beacon Press, 1997.

Moore, Harry T. *The Priest of Love: A Life of D.H. Lawrence*. New York: Farrar, Strauss & Giroux, 1974.

Moore, Michael S. "Some Myths About 'Mental Illness.'" In *Thomas Szasz: Primary Values and Contentions*, edited by Richard E. Vatz and Lee S. Weinberg, 181–92. Buffalo, NY: Prometheus Books, 1983.

Nabokov, Vladimir. *Ada or Ardor: A Family Chronicle*. New York: McGraw-Hill, 1969.

Nabokov, Vladimir. *The Annotated Lolita*, edited, with Preface, Introduction, and Notes by Alfred Appel, Jr. New York: McGraw-Hill, 1970.

Nabokov, Vladimir. *Bend Sinister*, 1947; rpt. New York: McGraw-Hill, 1974.

Nabokov, Vladimir. *The Defense*, 1930. English translation by Nabokov and Michael Scammell. New York: Putnam, 1966.

Nabokov, Vladimir. *Despair*, 1965; rpt. New York: Vintage, 1989.

Nabokov, Vladimir. *The Eye*. 1938. New York: Phaedra, 1965.

Nabokov, Vladimir. *Glory*, 1932. English translation by Dimitri Nabokov and Vladimir Nabokov. New York: McGraw-Hill, 1971.

Nabokov, Vladimir. *King, Queen, Knave*, 1928. English translation by Dimitri Nabokov and Vladimir Nabokov. New York: McGraw-Hill, 1968.

Nabokov, Vladimir. *Lectures on Literature*, edited by Fredson Bowers. New York: Harcourt Brace Jovanovich, 1980.

Nabokov, Vladimir. *Pale Fire*. New York: Putnam, 1962.

Nabokov, Vladimir. *Pnin*. New York: Doubleday, 1962.

Nabokov, Vladimir. *The Portable Nabokov*, 3rd edn, edited by Page Stegner. New York: Viking, 1973.

Nabokov, Vladimir. *The Real Life of Sebastian Knight*, 1941. New York: New Directions, 1959.

Nabokov, Vladimir. *A Russian Beauty and Other Stories*. New York: McGraw-Hill, 1973.

Nabokov, Vladimir. *Speak, Memory: An Autobiography Revisited*. Rev. edn. New York: Putnam, 1966.

Nabokov, Vladimir. *Strong Opinions*. New York: McGraw-Hill, 1973.

Nabokov, Vladimir. *Think, Write, Speak: Uncollected Essays, Reviews, Interviews, and Letters to the Editor*, edited by Brian Boyd and Anastasia Tolstoy. New York: Knopf, 2019.

Nabokov, Vladimir. *The Waltz Invention*, 1938. New York: Phaedra, 1966.

Nehls, Edward, editor. *D.H. Lawrence: A Composite Biography*. 3 vols. Madison WI: University of Wisconsin Press, 1957–1959.

Nietzsche, Friedrich. *Basic Writings of Nietzsche*, translated and edited, with commentaries, by Walter Kaufmann. New York: Modern Library, 1968.

Obholzer, Karin. *The Wolf-Man: Conversations with Freud's Patient—Sixty Years Later*, translated by Michael Shaw. London: Routledge & Kegan Paul, 1982.

O'Hara, Daniel T. *Lionel Trilling: The Work of Liberation*. Madison, WI: University of Wisconsin Press, 1988.

Oring, Elliott. *The Jokes of Sigmund Freud: A Study in Humor and Jewish Identity*. Philadelphia: University of Pennsylvania Press, 1984.

Pennebaker, James. *Opening Up: The Healing Power of Expressing Emotions*. New York: Guilford Press, 1990.

Pfister, Oskar. *The Psychoanalytic Method*, translated by Charles Rockwell Payne. New York: Moffat, Yard and Company, 1919.

Phillips, Adam. *Becoming Freud: The Making of a Psychoanalyst*. New Haven, CT: Yale University Press, 2014.

Phillips, Adam. *Equals*. New York: Basic Books, 2002.

Phillips, Adam. *Monogamy*. New York: Random House, 1996.

Phillips, Adam. *On Balance*. New York: Farrar, Straus and Giroux, 2010.

Phillips, Adam. *Promises, Promises: Essays on Psychoanalysis and Literature*. New York: Basic Books, 2001.

Phillips, Adam. *Winnicott*. Cambridge, MA: Harvard University Press, 1988.

Phillips, Adam and Barbara Taylor. *On Kindness*. New York: Farrar, Strauss and Giroux, 2009.

Phillips, Elizabeth. "The Hocus-Pocus of *Lolita*." *Literature and Psychology* 10 (1960): 97–101.

Phillips, William, editor. *Partisan Review: The 50th Anniversary Edition*. New York: Stern & Day, 1985.

Pines, Malcolm. "Trigant Burrow." *Encyclopedia. Com*. https://www.encyclopedia.com/psychology/dictionaries-thesauruses-pictures-and-press-releases/burrow-trigant-1875-1950.

Pitzer, Andrea. *The Secret History of Vladimir Nabokov*. New York: Pegasus, 2013.
Polansky, Steve. "A Family Romance: Northrop Frye and Harold Bloom: A Study of Critical Influence." *Boundary* 29 (1981): 227–46.
Portmann, John. *When Bad Things Happen to Other People*. New York: Routledge, 2000.
Rambeau, James R. "Nabokov's Critical Strategy." In *Nabokov's Fifth Arc*, edited by J. E. Rivers and Charles Nicol, 22–32. Austin, TX: University of Texas Press, 1982.
Rancour-Laferriere, Daniel, editor. *Self-Analysis in Literary Study: Exploring Hidden Agendas*. New York: New York University Press, 1994.
Rank, Otto. *The Double*, translated and edited by Harry Tucker, Jr. New York: Meridian, 1979.
Rank, Otto. *The Myth of the Birth of the Hero and Other Writings*, 1909. New York: Vintage, 1959.
Rice, Emanuel. *Freud and Moses: The Long Journey Home*. Albany: State University of New York Press, 1990.
Ricoeur, Paul. *Freud and Philosophy: An Essay on Interpretation*, translated by Denis Savage. New Haven, CT: Yale University Press, 1970.
Riviere, Joan. "A Character Trait of Freud's." *International Journal of Psychoanalysis* 100 (2019): 637–9.
Roazen, Paul. *Brother Animal: The Story of Freud and Tausk*. New York: Knopf, 1969.
Robins, Natalie. *The Untold Journey: The Life of Diana Trilling*. New York: Columbia University Press, 2017.
Robitscher, James. *The Powers of Psychiatry*. Boston: Houghton Mifflin, 1980.
Rorty, Richard. *Contingency, Irony, and Solidarity*. Cambridge: Cambridge University Press, 1989.
Rosenzweig, Saul. "Some Implicit Common Factors in Diverse Methods of Psychotherapy: 'At Last the Dodo Bird Said, Everybody Has Won and All Must Have Prizes.'" *American Journal of Orthopsychiatry* 6 (1936): 412–15.
Roth, Phyllis A. "Toward the Man Behind the Mystification." In *Nabokov's Fifth Arc*, edited by J. E. Rivers and Charles Nicol, 43–59. Austin, TX: University of Texas Press, 1982.
Ruderman, Judith. *D. H. Lawrence and the Devouring Mother: The Search for a Patriarchal Ideal of Leadership*. Durham, NC: Duke University Press, 1984.
Rudnytsky, Peter L. "Wrecking Crews." *American Imago* 56 (1999): 285–98.
Said, Edward. *On Late Style: Music and Literature Against the Grain*. Foreword by Marian C. Said. Introduction by Michael Wood. New York: Pantheon, 2006.
Saks, Elyn R. *Interpreting Interpretation: The Limits of Hermeneutic Psychoanalysis*. New Haven, CT: Yale University Press, 1999.
Salberg, Jill, editor. *Psychoanalytic Credos: Personal and Professional Journeys of Psychoanalysts*. London: Routledge, 2022.
Schaler, Jeffrey A. "Kaddish for Thomas Szasz." The Thomas S. Szasz, M.D. Cybercenter for Liberty and Responsibility. http://www.szasz.com.

Schaler, Jeffrey A., editor. *Szasz Under Fire: The Psychiatric Abolitionist Faces His Critics*. Chicago: Open Court, 2004.

Schapiro, Barbara Ann. *D.H. Lawrence and the Paradoxes of Psychic Life*. Albany: State University of New York Press, 1999.

Schapiro, Barbara Ann. *Literature and the Relational Self*. New York: New York University Press, 1993.

Schiff, Stacy. *Véra (Mrs. Vladimir Nabokov)*. New York: Modern Library, 1999.

Schoenfeld, C. G. "An Analysis of the Views of Thomas Szasz." In *Thomas Szasz: Primary Values and Contentions*, edited by Richard E. Vatz and Lee S. Weinberg, 199–206. Buffalo, NY: Prometheus Books, 1983.

Schopenhauer, Arthur. *On the Basis of Morality*, translated by E. F. J. Payne. Indianapolis, IN: Bobbs Merrill, 1965.

Schur, Max. *Freud: Living and Dying*. New York: International Universities Press, 1972.

Schwartz, Murray M. "Psychoanalysis in My Life: An Intellectual Memoir." *American Imago* 75 (2018): 125–52.

Schwartz, Murray M. "Review of *Out of My System*: Psychoanalysis, Ideology, and Critical Method." *The Psychohistory Review* 7 (1979): 43–5.

Seelye, Katharine Q. "Janet Malcolm, Provocative Journalist with a Piercing Eye, Dies at 86." *New York Times*, June 17, 2021.

Shamay-Tsoory, S. G., D. Ahronberg-Kirschenbaum, and N. Bauminger-Zviely. "There Is No Joy Like Malicious Joy: Schadenfreude in Young Children." *PLOS One*, July 2, 2014. https://doi.org/10.1371/journal.pone0100233.

Shechner, Mark. "Psychoanalysis and Liberalism: The Case of Lionel Trilling." *Salmagundi* 41 (1978): 3–32.

Slater, Lauren. *Lying: A Metaphorical Memoir*. New York: Random House, 2000, rpt. Penguin, 2001.

Smith, Dinitia. "Harold Boom, Critic Who Championed Western Canon, Dies at 89." *New York Times*, October 14, 2019.

Smith, Richard H. *The Joy of Pain: Schadenfreude and the Dark Side of Human Nature*. Oxford: Oxford University Press, 2013.

Smith, Tiffany Watt. *Schadenfreude: The Joy of Another's Misfortune*. New York: Little, Brown Spark, 2018.

Spence, Donald R. *Narrative Truth and Historical Truth: Meaning and Interpretation in Psychoanalysis*. New York: Norton, 1984.

Spilka, Mark. "For Mark Schorer with Combative Love: The *Sons and Lovers* Manuscript." In *D.H. Lawrence: A Centenary Consideration*, edited by Peter Balbert and Phillip L. Marcus, 29–44. Ithaca, NY: Cornell University Press, 1985.

Sprengnether, Madelon. *Mourning Freud*. New York: Bloomsbury Academic, 2018.

Stegner, Page. *Escape Into Aesthetics*. New York: Dial Press, 1966.

Steiner, George. *Errata: An Examined Life*. New Haven, CT: Yale University Press, 1998.

Stekel, Wilhelm. *The Autobiography of Wilhelm Stekel: The Life Story of a Pioneer Psychoanalyst*, edited by Emil A. Gutheil, introduction by Hilda Stekel. New York: Liveright, 1950.

Styron, William. *Darkness Visible: A Memoir of Madness*. New York: Random House, 1990.

Swales, Peter J. "A Fascination with Witches." *The Sciences* 22 (1982): 21–5.

Swales, Peter J. "Freud, His Teacher and the Birth of Psychoanalysis." In *Freud: Appraisals and Reappraisals*, edited by Paul E. Stepansky, vol. 1, 2–82. Hillsdale, NJ: The Analytic Press, 1986.

Swales, Peter J. "Freud, Katharina, and the First 'Wild' Analysis." In *Freud: Appraisals and Reappraisals*, edited by Paul E. Stepansky, vol. 3, 81–164. Hillsdale, NJ: The Analytic Press, 1988.

Swales, Peter J. "Freud, Minna Bernays and the Conquest of Rome: New Light on the Origins of Psychoanalysis." *New American Review* 1 (1982): 1–23.

Swift, Jonathan. *The Poems of Jonathan Swift*, edited by Harold Williams. Vol. 2. Oxford: Oxford University Press, 1937.

Syracuse Post-Standard. "Obituary of Thomas Szasz." September 12, 2012.

Szasz, Thomas. "An Autobiographical Sketch." In *Szasz Under Fire: The Psychiatric Abolitionist Faces His Critics*, edited by Jeffrey A. Schaler, 1–20. Chicago: Open Court, 2004.

Szasz, Thomas. *Coercion as Cure: A Critical History of Psychiatry*. New Brunswick, NJ: Transaction Publishers, 2007.

Szasz, Thomas. *Cruel Compassion: Psychiatric Control of Society's Unwanted*. New York: John Wiley & Sons, 1994.

Szasz, Thomas. *The Ethics of Psychoanalysis: The Theory and Method of Autonomous Psychotherapy*. New York: Basic Books, 1965.

Szasz, Thomas. *Faith in Freedom: Libertarian Principles and Psychiatric Practices*. New Brunswick, NJ: Transaction Publishers, 2004.

Szasz, Thomas. *Fatal Freedom: The Ethics and Politics of Suicide*. Westport, CT: Praeger, 1999.

Szasz, Thomas. *Heresies*. Garden City, NY: Anchor, 1976.

Szasz, Thomas. *Karl Kraus and the Soul-Doctors: A Pioneer Critic and His Criticism of Psychiatry and Psychoanalysis*. Baton Rouge, LA: Louisiana State University Press, 1976; reprinted as *Anti-Freud: Karl Kraus's Criticism of Psychoanalysis and Psychiatry*. Syracuse, NY: Syracuse University Press, 1990.

Szasz, Thomas. *Law, Liberty, and Psychiatry: An Inquiry into the Social Uses of Psychiatry*. Syracuse: Syracuse University Press, 1963.

Szasz, Thomas. *Liberation by Oppression: A Comparative Study of Slavery and Psychiatry*. New Brunswick, NJ: Transaction Publishers, 2002.

Szasz, Thomas. *The Medicalization of Everyday Life: Selected Essays*. Syracuse, NY: Syracuse University Press, 2007.

Szasz, Thomas. *"My Madness Saved Me": The Madness and Marriage of Virginia Woolf.* New Brunswick, NJ: Transaction Publishers, 2006.

Szasz, Thomas. *The Myth of Mental Illness: Foundations of a Theory of Personal Conduct.* New York: Harper & Row, 1961; updated with a new preface and additional material, 2010.

Szasz, Thomas. *Pain and Pleasure: A Study of Bodily Feelings.* New York: Basic Books, 1957; 2nd Expanded Edition. Syracuse, NY: Syracuse University Press, 1988.

Szasz, Thomas. *Pharmacracy: Medicine and Politics in America.* Westport, CT: Praeger, 2001.

Szasz, Thomas. *Psychiatric Justice.* New York: Macmillan, 1965.

Szasz, Thomas. *Psychiatric Slavery: When Confinement and Coercion Masquerade as Cure.* Syracuse, NY: Syracuse University Press, 1977.

Szasz, Thomas. *Psychiatry: The Science of Lies.* Syracuse, NY: Syracuse University Press, 2008.

Szasz, Thomas. *Schizophrenia: The Sacred Symbol of Psychiatry.* Syracuse, NY: Syracuse University Press, 1976.

Szasz, Thomas. *The Second Sin.* Garden City, NY: Anchor, 1973.

Szasz, Thomas. *Suicide Prohibition: The Shame of Medicine.* Syracuse, NY: Syracuse University Press, 2011.

Szasz, Thomas. *The Therapeutic State: Psychiatry in the Mirror of Current Events.* Buffalo, NY: Prometheus, 1984.

Szasz, Thomas. *Words to the Wise: A Medical-Philosophical Dictionary.* New Brunswick, NJ: Transaction Publishers, 2004.

Tausk, Marius. "Victor Tausk as Seen by His Son." *American Imago* 30 (1973): 323–35.

Torrey, E. Fuller. *Freudian Fraud: The Malignant Effect of Freud's Theory on American Thought and Culture.* New York: HarperCollins, 1992.

Trilling, Diana. *The Beginning of the Journey: The Marriage of Diana and Lionel Trilling.* New York: Harcourt Brace & Company, 1993.

Trilling, Diana. *Claremont Essays.* New York: Harcourt, Brace & World, 1964.

Trilling, James. "My Father and the Weak-Eyed Devils." *The American Scholar* 68 (1999): 17–41; "The Reader Replies." *The American Scholar* 68 (1999): 149–58.

Trilling, Lionel. *Beyond Culture: Essays on Literature and Learning.* New York: Viking Press, 1965.

Trilling, Lionel. *E.M. Forster.* Norfolk, CT: New Directions, 1943.

Trilling, Lionel. *The Experience of Literature: A Reader with Commentaries.* New York: Holt, Rinehart and Winston, 1967.

Trilling, Lionel. *Freud and the Crisis of Our Culture.* Boston, MA: Beacon Press, 1955.

Trilling, Lionel. *A Gathering of Fugitives.* Boston, MA: Beacon Press, 1956; London: Secker & Warburg, 1957.

Trilling, Lionel. *The Journey Abandoned: The Unfinished Novel*, edited and with an introduction by Geraldine Murphy. New York: Columbia University Press, 2008.

Trilling, Lionel. *The Last Decade: Essays and Reviews, 1965–75*, edited by Diana Trilling. New York: Harcourt Brace Jovanovich, 1979.

Trilling, Lionel. *The Liberal Imagination: Essays on Literature and Society*. New York: Viking Press, 1950; rpt. Anchor Books, 1953.

Trilling, Lionel. *Life in Culture: Selected Letters of Lionel Trilling*, edited by Adam Kirsch. New York: Farrar, Straus and Giroux, 2018.

Trilling, Lionel. *Matthew Arnold*. New York: Columbia University Press, 1939.

Trilling, Lionel. *The Middle of the Journey*, with a new Introduction by the Author. New York: Scribner's, 1947; rpt. 1975.

Trilling, Lionel. *Of This Time, of That Place and Other Stories*. New York: Harcourt Brace Jovanovich, 1979.

Trilling, Lionel. *The Opposing Self: Nine Essays in Criticism*. New York: Viking Press, 1955; rpt. 1968.

Trilling, Lionel. *Sincerity and Authenticity*. Cambridge, MA: Harvard University Press, 1972.

Trilling, Lionel. *Speaking of Literature and Society*, edited by Diana Trilling. New York: Harcourt Brace Jovanovich, 1980.

Valenstein, Elliot S. *Blaming the Brain: The Truth About Drugs and Mental Health*. New York: The Free Press, 1998.

Van Dijk, Wilco W., Guido M. Koningsbruggen, Jaap W. Ouwerkerk, and Yoka M. Wesseling. "Self-Esteem, Self-Affirmation, and Schadenfreude." *Emotion* 11 (2011): 1445–9.

Van Dijk, Wilco W. and Jaap W. Ouwerkerk. *Schadenfreude: Understanding Pleasure at the Misfortune of Others*. Cambridge: Cambridge University Press, 2014.

Vatz, Richard E. and Lee S. Weinberg, editors. *Thomas Szasz: Primary Values and Contentions*. Buffalo, NY: Prometheus Books, 1983.

Wampold, Bruce E. and Zac E. Imel. *The Great Psychotherapy Debate: The Evidence for What Makes Psychotherapy Work*. 2nd edn. New York and London: Routledge, 2015.

Wang, Shensheng, Scott O. Lilienfeld, and Philippe Rochat. "Schadenfreude Deconstructed and Reconstructed: A Tripartite Motivational Model." *New Ideas in Psychology* 52 (2019): 1–11. https://www.sciencedirect.com/science/article/abs/pii/S073218X183.

Webster, Brenda. *The Last Good Freudian*. New York: Holmes & Meier, 2000.

Webster, Richard. *Why Freud Was Wrong: Sin, Science and Psychoanalysis*. New York: HarperCollins, 1995.

Weiss, Daniel. *Oedipus in Nottingham*. Seattle, WA: University of Washington Press, 1962.

Williams, William Carlos. *The Autobiography of William Carlos Williams*. New York: Random House, 1951.

Wilson, Edmund. *The Wound and the Bow: Seven Studies in Literature*. New York: Oxford University Press, 1947; rpt. 1965.

Wilson, Edward O. *Consilience: The Unity of Knowledge*. New York: Knopf, 1998.

Winnicott, D. W. "Transitional Objects and Transitional Phenomena. A Study of the First Not-Me Possession." *International Journal of Psycho-Analysis* 34 (1953): 89–97.

The Wolf-Man. *The Wolf-Man by the Wolf-Man*, edited, with notes, an introduction, and chapters by Muriel Gardiner. New York: Basic Books, 1971.

Wollheim, Richard. "In Freud We Trust: Review of *Freudian Fraud*." *New York Times*, June 28, 1992.

Wood, James. "Misreading Harold Bloom." *The New Yorker*, October 16, 2019. https:/www.newyorker.com/culture/postscript/misreading-harold-bloom. Accessed November 17, 2019.

Worthen, John. *D.H. Lawrence: The Life of an Outsider*. New York: Counterpoint, 2005.

Wright, Elizabeth. *Psychoanalytic Criticism: Theory in Practice*. London: Routledge, 2002.

Wright, Lawrence. *Remembering Satan: A Case of Recovered Memory and the Shattering of the American Family*. New York: Knopf, 1994.

Yalom, Irvin D. *The Schopenhauer Cure*. New York: HarperCollins, 2005.

Yeats, William Butler. *The Autobiography of William Butler Yeats*. New York: Macmillan, 1938.

Yorke, Clifford. "Kurt Eissler Obituary." *Guardian*, March 22, 1999.

Young-Bruehl, Elisabeth. *Anna Freud: A Biography*. New York: Summit, 1988.

Young-Bruehl, Elisabeth. *Subject to Biography: Psychoanalysis, Feminism, and Writing Women's Lives*. Cambridge, MA: Harvard University Press, 1998.

Zeligs, Meyer A. *Friendship and Fratricide: An Analysis of Whittaker Chambers and Alger Hiss*. New York: Viking, 1967.

Index

Printed in the USA
CPSIA information can be obtained
at www.ICGtesting.com
CBHW052142031224
18175CB00086B/124